*'Thrive is different, once I'd understood the concept and ideas of this program it was a light-bulb moment - my path to getting rid of the anxiety was suddenly very clear and very simple. I just wish I'd found Thrive sooner!'*

*'A friend of mine cured themself of depression using the insights and techniques within this book, and recommended it to me. Three weeks after buying it and using it, my emetophobia is completely gone!!! I mean COMPLETELY gone! For the first time in twenty years I feel alive and happy.'*

*'After suffering from depression for 12 years this method has finally made me realise that I create my negative thoughts but that I can change them which in turn has improved my life for the better!'*

*'After spending the last 25 years being overweight and generally dysfunctional, I was introduced to the system this book describes. Quite simply it helped me to regain control and direction in my life. I'm happy, in control and enjoying my life, now I really have one. Oh and I've lost 5 stone using the techniques described by Rob Kelly.'*

*'In just three weeks my anxiety and depression have reduced by about 90%, and I'm confident they will be gone completely in another few weeks. Who would have thought a book could be so powerful?'*

*'All I can say is that after understanding the technique in this book I totally rid myself of my life-long fear of flying.'*

*'This is a fantastic book. For years I used to say "I just want to be happy" but didn't know how to be; reading this book and changing how I think about things that happen in my life has changed my whole life.'*

*'This book is superb. As I life coach and psychotherapist I have recommended many books to my patients over the years, but none have been received so well as this one. It's now the only book I recommend.'*

*'As a psychology graduate I have spent 3 years reading tedious scientific journals to understand people, however I have learnt so much more about how people think, their thought processes and motivation in this single book.'*

*'I have so many dreams, goals and ambitions that I used to think could maybe happen, but deep down I never really believed it. But now, I truly feel that the sky's the limit...and even further than that!'*

*'To make significant and lasting changes, you need to understand yourself and your limiting beliefs. This is the real advantage of this book, it doesn't just give you the tools to improve your life, it teaches you how and why they work.'*

*'This book has helped me stop, not just cope with, my social anxiety and low self-esteem. Life is great and I know that I can keep it this way'*

*'I was a very heavy drinker, and I was ruining my life - and the lives of those around me - with alcohol... ...I have achieved more by myself, using this book, than I ever did in therapy, on drugs, or at 'AA' meetings. My kids use this book, my wife uses the book, my friends use this book.'*

*'If you think your drinking is out of control, or you just can't stop stuffing your face, or maybe you want to stop smoking or all of the above, but you've tried and failed so many times that you feel there is no way out - then this book will make you laugh out loud with relief.'*

*'We purchased this book to help my 16-year old daughter to cope with the exam stress she was experiencing during her final year at secondary school whilst taking her GCSEs. She is now approaching the exams in a much more relaxed and positive state of mind and feels if she sets her mind to it she will achieve her goals.'*

*'I have read LOTS and LOTS of self-help books all promising various things but largely failing to deliver. This is so much more than a self-help book. As far as I'm concerned it's a manual for life. I've only read through it once (quickly - I couldn't put it down!) and I already feel different - less anxious, more optimistic, and I know my worth. I feel excited for the first time in ages. Goodness knows what will happen when I read through it again slowly and do all the exercises! Well, actually, I think I do know what will happen. Watch out world! This time last year I was in bits with severe depression and anxiety. Reading this book made realise how I got myself into that situation, and how to stop it from happening again. Don't hesitate to buy this wonderful book.'*

*'I have had Rob's book for a little over nine months, and I have haven't had a drink (or smoked!) since about a week after buying it. I haven't had a drink, I haven't needed a drink, and I haven't wanted a drink.'*

*'Knowledge is power, Thrive empowers you, and YOUR life can be fixed, by you.'*

*'In the last 5 years I can't remember a time when I had a happy feeling; but during reading the book and upon completing it and implementing the techniques described I have felt what it is like to be happy again and have started to gain control of my life.'*

*'Our whole way of thinking has been completely re-trained, making us realise the reality in events and experiences, other than letting our negative inner voices take over. We have gained complete clarity and perspective allowing us to continuously feel happy, relaxed and confident. This will last a life time!'*

*'This book will change your life; or, to be more precise, this book will teach you how you can change your life. It doesn't matter what problem or symptom you have, you probably feel that you have no control to change it, it's something that you're stuck with and can't be changed. One of the most important things you'll learn is that you do have the power to take control of your thoughts, emotions and behaviour. Thinking is so important, it can be liberating or limiting. Your life is controlled by the way you think. If you think and believe that you can't achieve something, you won't. The only person that's stopping you having the life you want, is you. It's easy to get into a very negative and limiting way of thinking, creating all sorts of problems. But the good news is, this can be easily changed and you can take control of your thinking, using the techniques in this book.'*

The above extracts from testimonials can be found on Amazon, and on www.thriveprogramme.org

# Thrive

**Rob Kelly**

Illustrations and research by Charlotte Allen
Research assistant Roisin Kelly

Published by Rob Kelly Publishing
Cambridge, England



www.thriveprogramme.org
www.facebook.com/thriveprogramme
@thriveprogramme

ISBN 978-0-9565166-1-9

9 780956 516619

## About the Author

I have never met anyone like Rob Kelly as he conforms to no stereotype! He touches people's lives both professionally and personally on a daily basis with such warmth and generosity. Regardless of what is happening in his own life I would defy anyone to remain unsmiling within moments of meeting him, although he is far from being a 'people-pleaser'! With his clients he has the tremendous ability to keep the atmosphere light whilst enabling them to confront their deepest issues. He is not afraid to challenge anyone if it means it will help them in the long run: I do not know of another therapist that puts so much into their clients getting better.

Personally, Rob leads a full and varied life: he plays football for his village team and flies four different types of aircraft (one to international competition standard). He loves music (performing and listening), off-road motorcycling, snowboarding, scuba diving, reading, socialising, martial arts, and the list goes on, in many of which he includes his two children to whom he is a fantastic father.

Rob is a highly experienced and excellent therapist; he remains a great inspiration to me in my own practice: to this day I continue to seek out his pearls of wisdom and greatly enjoy his training seminars. I have known Rob for many years but it wasn't before quite some time that I inadvertently discovered that he had been through greater hardship in his life than most. If asked, he might describe his childhood as 'challenging' where others would use the word 'abusive'. Subsequently propelled into his teens with a great deal of anxiety and negligible self-esteem he was soon faced with a serious neurological disease that required a series of operations to the brain and spinal cord, which left him with problems in his neck, upper limbs and hands. Until recently, one of his favourite endeavours was playing the guitar and singing in a band, however his muscular problem took a turn for the worse rendering his left arm pretty useless. When asked about how he felt about not being able to play the guitar anymore his response, with a beaming smile, was 'I play the keyboard now - one handed'. Many of his friends and colleagues will be stunned to read this part of Rob's bio because he simply wouldn't have mentioned it. Rob never blames his past, other people or his illness for anything: he truly does 'walk the talk', living and breathing all that he teaches.

It was not surprising when Rob entitled his training programme 'Thrive', because that is exactly what he does.

Dr. Anna Forbes BMedSci(Hons), MBBS, DHP, MDCH, DipSIM
Integrative Medical Doctor in Mental Health

# Contents



Throughout this book clients' names and identifying details have been altered to preserve confidentiality, unless they have given permission for these to be included in the book.

# Hello and Welcome to The Thrive Programme!

First of all, I'd like to thank you for buying this book, the official manual of The Thrive Programme.

This book is all about learning to THRIVE, learning the skills, insights and techniques you need to have a happy, positive and exciting life – one in which you really flourish. It teaches you that you have a choice...

At the moment you possibly don't think you have many choices and believe you're stuck with your current symptoms, worries, illness, lack of success, or just your life in general. Like most people, you probably feel as though you are powerless to change your situation. There is plenty of research that shows this is exactly what the majority of people who are phobic, anxious, stressed or ill believe (for example, Abrahamsson *et al.*, 2002; Edwards *et al.*, 2007; Walters and Charles, 1997; and Seaman and Lewis, 1995).

I am very pleased to say, however, that although you, and millions of other people like you, believe this, you are wrong in your assumptions. You actually DO have the power to change your situation and to thrive: you have just never been shown how to do so. I'm going to help you to gain the necessary insights and skills over the course of this book. You don't need to believe me (sigh of relief), you don't need to have faith in what I'm saying, you just need to carefully read what I've written, do the exercises, and practise the techniques I'm offering you. You have absolutely nothing to lose whatsoever.

One of the stumbling blocks in making changes in our lives is that it can be frightening, but this usually only occurs when we are asked to take a big leap of faith, make a bold move, or attempt to achieve a big goal. I'm not going to ask you to do any of these things. We are going to build your self-esteem, your self-belief, your sense of control and a whole load of other psychological resources: slowly and safely. By the time you have finished studying The Thrive Programme, you will have developed all the insights and skills that you need to stop existing and start thriving in life.

## What is THRIVING?

There are stories in the news every week about people who have bounced back from serious problems, illnesses or issues in their lives, or people who have overcome huge obstacles and are now living the life they want. The media paints a picture of these people as being special or unique in some way... as if they have a magical one-in-a-million brain that has the power to do amazing things. We look at these people and read their stories and think: 'wouldn't it be amazing if I could be like that'.
Well now you can!

I'll say that again: now you can.

The 'magical' and amazing qualities these people seem to have, are just normal everyday skills, insights and techniques that anyone can learn. These are what The Thrive Programme teaches.

A plant or animal is said to be thriving when it is growing, developing and being as successful as it can be within its environment. When a person is thriving, it's because they have psychological skills, resources and attitude to flourish in every area of their lives. They know how to maintain a psychologically and physically healthy lifestyle. Thriving individuals have the self-insight and resources to overcome or avoid developing symptoms such as anxieties, phobias or depression, and the robustness to fight more serious problems and illnesses.

Thriving is about flourishing in life, regardless of where you are, what you are doing, what your past experiences were like, your relationships, how much money you have, or what job you have. It's about fine-tuning your mind and body, to get the very best from them.

Thriving is not about achieving perfection; it is having the resilience to bounce back from hurdles and adversity. It is being able to face difficulties and setbacks head on, knowing that you have the skills and resources to cope with them. Thriving is making the most out of your life - embracing challenges, learning new things and enjoying life.

## What is The Thrive Programme?

The Thrive Programme is a unique psychological training programme that will teach you everything you need to know in order to get yourself thriving! It is really the culmination of over twenty five years of studying people: what makes them happy, what makes them sad, what makes them sick, what makes them healthy? Why do some people keep getting colds, whilst others never get them? Why do some people get so depressed that they kill themselves, whilst others, despite sometimes terrible hardships, are resilient and face the pressures and stresses of life with a spring in their step and a smile on their face? The Thrive Programme was created based on unique insights gained during my twenty five years clinical experience as a forensic hypnotist – looking back into people's pasts in order to find out how they created their problems and symptoms in life.

Here's the thing: I can't change your life for you, and I can't make you better. I'd love to be able to say that I could but I can't. Sorry. I don't have any magical skills, I can't unlock your brain for you, and I can't show you the secrets that will provide you with eternal youth.

My point is that any change comes from YOU, not me. What this programme will do is teach you the self-insights and the skills that you need in order to thrive.

Just about every symptom and condition I have treated over the last twenty years was created, maintained or exacerbated by the client's limiting belief systems and unhelpful thinking styles. Only by changing those things will you learn to thrive. Think about it just for a second: as a kid you were taught how to brush your teeth, tie your shoelaces, cross the street, spell, read and write. Your parents taught (most of) you: good manners, how to eat your dinner properly, how to behave in public (unless you're a politician!). **But who taught you how to take control of your beliefs, thinking, feelings and imagination?**

What I'm getting at here is: it's not your fault. It's not your fault that you are faced with challenges at the moment. You were never shown the link between things like your belief systems, thoughts, how you perceive events, your imagination, your happiness, your success, your immune system and your health. You will soon, however, have the power and techniques to change all of this!

You don't need to undergo years of psychotherapy to understand how your mind 'works'. (In any case, all you would do is begin to understand how you became who you are now. This book is about your present and future, not your past.) You just need to spend a little time really gaining insights into your limiting belief systems, your negative thoughts, your strong emotions and your symptoms. Through The Thrive Programme, I will guide you to recognise, understand and alter these, quickly and easily.

### How does The Thrive Programme work?

Perhaps you are thinking that The Thrive Programme sounds too good to be true? Perhaps you've tried lots of self-help books or psychological therapies before, to no avail? Perhaps you don't understand how The Thrive Programme is any different to these other interventions?
Many self-help and 'change your life' type books contain good advice on how to make significant changes in your life. The vast majority of people who read these books will not, however, actually change their lives. They will devour the book, revelling in its promises of a bright future but spend, at most, a few

days of half-heartedly attempting to put into practice the offered techniques, then go back to their old ways (strangely, they will still tell everyone how fantastic and life-changing the book was for them!!). Yes, every author of a self-help or 'modern psychological techniques' type book can quote the names of a few people who have REALLY changed their lives after reading their book, but when you think that often these books have sold millions of copies... The same is often true for many psychological therapies or interventions.

So why do many books and training programmes often fail to deliver what they promise? Because, for the most part, they are ONLY offering you the *techniques* for change. Techniques alone don't really do very much. They are great for temporarily helping you to control a habit, fear or other symptom, but the overall positive effects tend to be small, and short-lived (Rosen, 1987). Books and interventions that only tell you what to do are overlooking 95% of the battle. The really important bit, the understanding behind WHY the techniques work, is almost never explained. If it is explained, it's usually shrouded in mystery, or some 'strange magical belief', for some reason. This is not empowering, it is disempowering, and I shall explain why later.

The Thrive Programme comes from a very different direction. 95% or more of what you really need to do, in order to make changes in your life, whether these changes involve building confidence, fighting illness, curing yourself of depression, stopping smoking or getting control of a phobia, is about really understanding your psychological make-up.

***I'm just going to say this again: 95% of what you need to do in order to change your life is to really understand yourself. To understand your psychological make-up, what makes you 'tick'. When you understand exactly how YOUR mind works, then, and ONLY then, can you set about changing it with relative ease.***

Here are the main reasons why this book will help EVERY reader to make significant changes in their life:

- When you genuinely understand how your mind works (the interaction between your beliefs, your thinking, your emotions and your experiences), you feel much more in control and empowered.

- Once you really understand how most of your problems, stresses, symptoms and ill health are either caused or made worse BY your beliefs and thinking, you feel FANTASTIC because if YOU are influencing these problems, then YOU can change them!

- Once you BELIEVE that you can achieve change, you will put in massive, determined effort to do so. Indeed research has suggested that the more you can perceive or imagine the benefits of your hard effort, the more hard effort you will put in (e.g. Eiser *et al.*, 1985). The techniques I will show you are very easy to put into practice.

Let me give you an example: I've recently completed a 14-month research survey into my smoking cessation method, which is based on the insights and techniques within this book. By focusing almost entirely on changing the belief system of the smoker (to that of a non-smoker), and getting them to believe that stopping smoking is going to be easy, we achieved a 92.5% success rate. Because the smokers believed it was going to be easy, they put in 100% effort. It wasn't that it WAS effortless; it was just easy because they really believed they could overcome their habit, and consequently put loads of effort in. People will stop smoking when they put in 100% effort to stop, and they will put in 100% effort once they BELIEVE they can stop. The same can be said for every symptom/anxiety/illness that has a cognitive component to it.

Earlier, I said that you don't need to believe what I have written, nor do you have to have faith in me. In fact, it would be MUCH better if you didn't do either of these things. I'm going to train you to believe in YOU, not me. I want you to read what I have written, study all the evidence and research I have provided and then make up your own mind. In order to make this as easy as possible, I have also included lots of the research that I have studied that corroborate my conclusions. If you are not used to reading surveys, research papers or academic journals (and believe me, I wasn't before I started work on this book), you probably aren't used to seeing things like this: (Eiser *et al.*, 1985). It's a reference - usually for a study or piece of research already undertaken, that's already in print, and has almost always been reviewed by other researchers and psychologists. It's EVIDENCE. If you turned to the back of this book now, you'll find the reference section. If you go to Eiser *et al.* (1985), you'll find all the information you need to know in order to find the original piece of research yourself. Easier still, I have put links to all these research papers in the resources section of The Thrive Programme website (www.thriveprogramme.org). As I mentioned earlier, many books and programmes written or designed to help people to change their lives are based on little or no scientific evidence whatsoever. In fact, many go completely the other way and are based on magical or pseudo-spiritual dogma - this isn't, it's based on REAL EVIDENCE.

What I am going to share with you in this book could never have been discovered by academics locked away in a university department, market researchers, newspaper columnists, or 'pop psychologists'. It is the product of spending around 30,000 hours (twenty five years) face to face with clients. So this book isn't based upon my observations of ten or twelve people, or some research I stumbled across (though I have, wherever possible, included relevant research) or the hundreds of self-help books I have read over the years. It is based on real insights – that I have gained from the clients I have worked with – into the way we think, feel, and process experiences.

This is REAL psychology, based upon REAL learning from REAL people that will, if you choose to apply it, change your life completely and permanently. None of the information in this book is speculation, guesswork, supposition, fantasy or magical belief. It's not mumbo jumbo or magic and I won't make you join a cult to benefit from it!

I'm not fond of 'psycho-babble'. I believe that, on the whole, it is unnecessary to use psychological or scientific language, especially when we are in the business of 'de-cloaking' and 'de-mystifying' how the mind works. This book is aimed at (fairly) normal people, like yourself. So, as far as possible, I have used 'plain English' throughout.

Who can help themselves with this book? Anyone. Anyone with something in their life they would like to change or improve: from simple things like phobias and fears, to huge life-changing illnesses like cancer or clinical depression. Maybe you want to free yourself from stress, aid recovery from an operation, get rid of social anxiety, defeat your depression, get into a good relationship or just 'thrive'? Whatever your aims, this book represents the very best way of taking back control of your life, and achieving the changes you desire.

## How can you use this book in the most effective manner?

Before we get started, you want to understand how to complete The Thrive Programme in the most effective way. This section is **important**, so please don't skip through it!

In order to gain the necessary insights, skills and resources to permanently change your life and learn to thrive, you need to work through the programme in a specific way. Don't view the process as ***reading*** the book but, instead, think about ***studying*** it and viewing it as an active process. You want to really engage with the programme and think about how you can squeeze every little bit of information out of the book! Don't rush through the programme. Take your time to fully understand everything you are reading. Make notes in the margins. Highlight sections that are important to you. Complete all the exercises.

Throughout the book there are exercises and **ACTION**s. The exercises are there to help you reinforce your learning and gain more self-insight, and the **ACTION**s are what you need to do in order to make changes. **You must complete all of the exercises and ACTIONs - even if you think they don't apply to you.**

Additionally, there are recap sections at the end of each chapter. Please pay attention to these, as they are there to help you ensure that you have understood the chapter. If you don't follow anything within a recap section then please go back and revise the chapter!

The best way to work through The Thrive Programme is to set aside some time every day to complete the programme. Each day, recap what you have learnt so far, study a bit more of the book, and complete the exercises.

Working through this book is like completing a jigsaw puzzle. The chapters will be providing you with a build-up of information; you will be gaining and fitting together the component parts of the puzzle. Yet, it is only when you have **all** the pieces will you be able to see the complete picture. You won't know everything you need in order to thrive until you reach the end of the book. Even after finishing the book, you will need to continue to implement the exercises and actions for 4 to 6 weeks, so that your new helpful beliefs, thinking styles and behaviours become habitual.

So, most of this book is focused upon helping you gain this self-knowledge and to enable you to start building and practising the skills and resources that you will need to conquer your symptoms, build resilience and thrive. Right at the end of the book, there is an overall 'Thriving Action Plan', where you will then be asked to combine all of your new resources and put them into practice, until they become ingrained.

### Remember: this book is not about overcoming symptoms, it's about thriving

This book isn't just (or even mostly) about overcoming your symptoms or issues. It's about learning to thrive. Lots of people have a strong desire for control (more about this later) and are very focused upon their symptom or problem, so their main goal is to control or avoid these. Trying to avoid symptoms is inherently negative. It can also mean that people tend to focus excessively upon finding the techniques that will help them resolve their problems, to the detriment of actually gaining the psychological insights and skills that will enable them to thrive.

So, whilst you work through The Thrive Programme, you don't want your aim to be overcoming your symptoms or problems, you want to focus upon learning to thrive. Rather than zooming in on anything that you believe will help you to avoid your symptoms, you want to think about building your psychological skills and resources generally. This will enable you to not only overcome your issues more easily but to improve many other areas of your life.

## Additional support whilst working through the book

Many people successfully work through The Thrive Programme and make huge improvements to their lives solely using this book. Some people, however, find additional support really helpful. Although this book contains everything that you need to know in order to thrive, people can sometimes find it difficult to apply all of the insights to themselves. Others may have some questions or concerns regarding particular parts of the programme. Different explanations, metaphors and examples can act as 'light bulb' moments for one person but not another. When writing the book it would have been impossible to contain every single relevant analogy and I didn't want to end up with a book that was so large nobody would read it!

So, there are many other resources where you can access additional help whilst working your way through the programme. There is a great deal of online support available via the Facebook page (https://www.facebook.com/thriveprogramme) and website (www.thriveprogramme.org), including videos and downloads. You can also ask me questions via Twitter, Facebook or email.

My licensed Thrive Consultants can, also, offer you more extensive personalised support, whether this is by guiding you through the full programme over 6 to 8 sessions (in face-to face sessions or via Skype) or by helping you to just tweak your understanding in a single session. All Thrive Consultants offer a free initial consultation, so that you can discuss your specific goals with them and ensure that you feel comfortable and safe working with them. If you want to contact a Thrive Consultant, please make sure that you check the list of licensed Thrive Consultants on the website. Only these listed individuals are up to date in their training. The programme is being continuously updated and improved and, consequently, training and mentoring is on going for all Consultants to ensure that they can deliver the programme in the most effective way possible.

## Feedback

Feedback is really important. As I have just mentioned, The Thrive Programme is regularly developed and improved. So I would love to hear from you about your experience of working through the book. You **do not**, however, want to start out by viewing the book itself through perfectionist glasses, with the aim of evaluating the programme! Rather than trying to spot spelling errors or evaluating the book, you want to be thinking about how you can use the book's contents to help you. Many people with psychological symptoms are doubtful that anything could enable them to overcome their issues, which is understandable, especially if they have already tried many treatments to no avail! They, therefore, tend to view any book, programme, or treatment through critical eyes. But you have already bought this book so don't waste your time suspiciously wondering whether it will help you. Instead make the most of the knowledge contained within these pages! Someone who works through the book with the mindset of 'how can I get the most out of this programme?' will gain much more from it than someone who is constantly analysing and assessing the spelling, grammar and contents of the book! If, once you have completed the book and used it to thrive, you would then like to re-read and evaluate the programme through more critical eyes, then feel free. I'd be glad to receive any feedback.

## Are you ready?

Before we go past this introduction, you have to ask yourself a question: Are you ready?

No, this isn't some super sales-type 'build 'em up before they read the book' question, it's a genuine question: Are you ready?

I ask, because change does take effort. You WILL be challenged reading this book. There will be bits you disagree with, bits you don't like, and bits might even really piss you off. These things usually occur when our belief systems are being challenged in some way, and they are expected. A lot of the work you will be asked to do involves changing the way you think, and changing the way you perceive events and experiences in your life. You may need to question ideas that you have held for a very long time, and some people can find this quite challenging. This book will guide and support you in making changes (and as I mentioned earlier, there is further support available) but learning to thrive will take real effort and commitment on your behalf.

If you have made the decision that you are ready to take responsibility and take control of your life, then you need to sign on the dotted line below the declaration. Yes, I know it seems a little over the top, but research suggests that by signing, you are making a real commitment towards helping yourself (e.g. Williams *et al.*, 2005; Neale, 1991). By signing here you are telling yourself that you really mean business, and that you are prepared to face up to any challenges along the way.

*This book is all about giving you choice - choosing to sign the following declaration is the first step in learning how to Thrive.*

## Declaration

I intend to change my life, and I accept that this will take time and effort. I am fully prepared to challenge my thinking and belief systems, even though this may mean leaving my comfort zone from time to time. I will complete all the exercises in this book with vigour, and will treat myself with compassion and kindness throughout the whole process.

*Signed*........Lida........

*Dated*........10/4/22........

**Congratulations**, you've taken the first step.

If you didn't sign on the dotted line though, ask yourself why?

Did it seem silly?
Did it seem that I was getting you to jump through hoops for no reason?
Did you think it couldn't possibly make any difference whether you signed or not?
Did you think it wasn't worth ruining the book by writing on it?
Did you not want to – in order to avoiding feeling a failure just in case you didn't manage to change your life?

My promise to you:

I promise you, that if you do everything I suggest within this book, you WILL feel incredibly empowered and you WILL build up your self-esteem, enabling you to then make really significant changes in your life.

Go to our website: www.thriveprogramme.org and read or watch some of the testimonials from other people who have used this book to change their lives. This will help to give you some kind of idea of just how powerful the knowledge contained within it is, when you apply it properly.

If you miss sections out though, or think that some of the exercises don't apply to you, then I still promise that this book will help you, but it probably won't change your life. Still, better than reading 'Hello!' or doing the crossword.

Humour me, please. There is no 'padding' in this book. There are no 'interesting asides' to fill up the page, or make it more fluffy. Everything in this book is in there, because it is really, REALLY important. If you are committed to changing your life, turn back a page and sign the declaration - you can thank me later.

## Online TQ Thrive Assessments

There are a number of online assessments for you to complete, all put together in one big quiz. You need to complete this quiz now before you start the programme, and again at the end once you've finished. These assessments are REALLY important as they form the backbone of the programme. You will be able to measure and VISIBLY SEE your success as you progress through the programme and beyond. The quiz will measure all of the individual psychological components that together form your 'Thrive Quotient' (TQ) - your 'thriveability' if you like - the skills and resources you have/you need in order to thrive. You need to take the quiz now, so find somewhere nice and quiet where you can focus for 15-20 minutes. Within five minutes of completing the quiz, you'll be emailed a very informative twelve-page report, which you'll need to keep referring back to as you make your way through the programme.

Please now, before you go any further, register on the support website and take the appropriate quiz: www.thrivesupport.org/manuals

(The assessments used to be contained within the manuals, but we were able to create much more detailed and helpful versions online. Having them online also helps us to collate the data and conduct various bits or research which in turn helps us to improve the programme) If, for some reason you cannot get access the quiz, please email us here: quiz@thriveprogramme.org

# Chapter

# 1

# A question of belief

# The importance of your belief systems

It is our underlying **'belief systems'** that drive the way we think, feel and behave. But what actually are 'belief systems'? They are sets of personal viewpoints, which provide us with fundamental principles and 'rules' by which we view or base EVERYTHING we think, do, say, or believe. They are created out of a need to organise and store life experiences in a way that makes sense to us. In other words, they help us to understand the world. We are constantly inundated with new information and to process this information more easily, we compare it to stuff we already know. This previously stored and grouped information is what creates our belief systems. All our different experiences are fitted together so that we can create an understandable representation of our world. We all have hundreds of different belief systems that have been built up from our many lifetime events.

Let's look at the processes by which a belief system is formed:

1. There is a need to see something in a certain way, so you adopt (buy into) a belief and you believe it to be true.
2. You then view life experiences through the rose-tinted (or maybe 'shit-tinted' depending on the positivity or negativity of the belief) spectacles of your belief system. You anticipate events to happen in line with your belief system.
3. This means that you are far more likely to see events and experiences that confirm your belief system than ones that challenge or negate it (in psycho-babble, this is known as 'confirmation bias').
4. Your belief is 'proven' to be correct, it becomes reinforced, and grows stronger.

Shit-tinted Spectacles

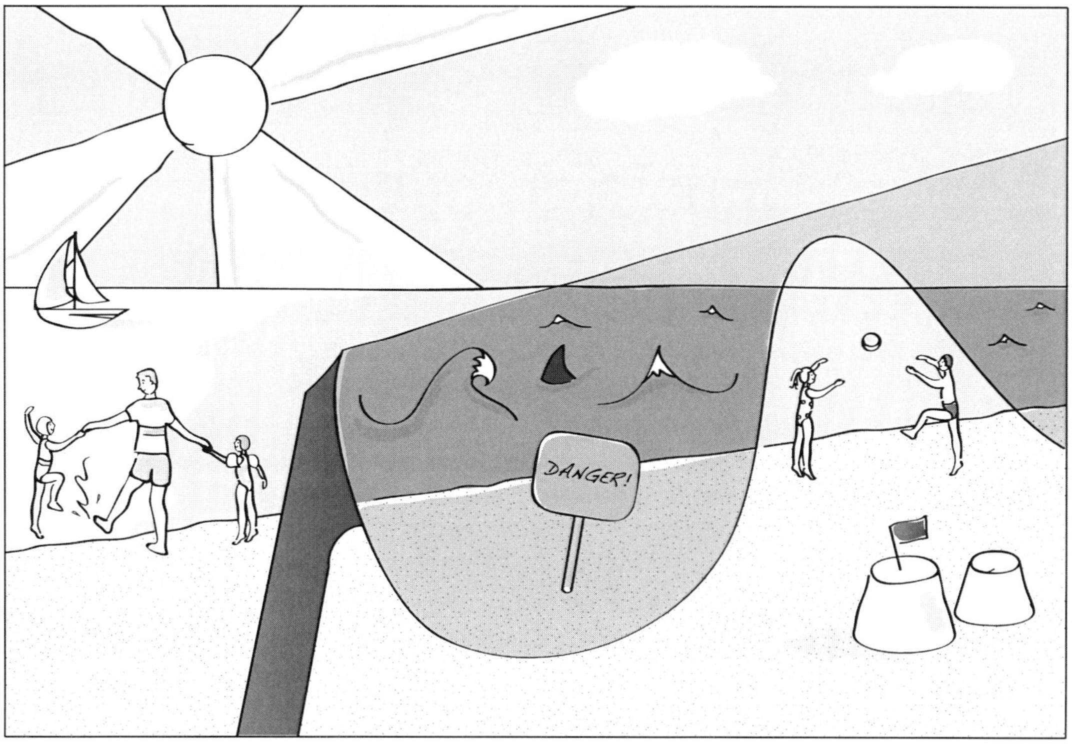


A good example of a belief system, and the one that I will use throughout this book, is that of 'nicotine addiction'. We all know someone who smokes, we all know someone who used to smoke (and may well go back to it one day!) and we all know someone who doesn't smoke. Now, I have the special process, which I mentioned earlier, that I take smokers through in order to get them to stop, and this process is a much shorter version of what I am teaching you in this book. In fact, it was helping over 6000 smokers to stop, most of them in just one hour (not the SAME hour though, obviously) really gave me a lot of insight into belief systems. 'The Rob Kelly Method', as it has come to be called (see www.stopsmokingeasily.com), basically helps the smoker to identify their genuine belief system about smoking. I then guide them to challenge their beliefs, and they become a non-smoker. Now that's clearly an over-simplified version, but that is basically what happens.

So, back to our smoker's belief that he is addicted to nicotine. Is this just a free-formed insignificant little belief that he has picked up along the way, like his belief that 'you shouldn't go outside if your hair is wet as you might catch a chill'?

No it isn't.

This is a very firm and robust belief that he has and he would argue the validity of it, were you to give him the opportunity. This chap NEEDS his belief, because it makes him feel better about himself. Why?

Well, the media, and the various medical professions around the world make us believe, rightly or wrongly, that smoking is very bad for us, could kill us, could give us cancer, will shorten our lives, will clog our arteries, will make us smell, will cost us thousands and thousands of pounds over our lifetime, makes us ingest thousands of potent and dangerous chemicals. Therefore, smoking is a stupid habit.

If smoking is a stupid habit, then it is stupid to smoke. If it's stupid to smoke, then anyone who smokes is stupid. Would you like to think of yourself, and have others think of you, as stupid? Well, don't worry, if you did smoke it wouldn't be your fault, it's because you're addicted, it's not your fault and you can breathe a big sigh of relief. The belief that our smoker holds, that he is addicted to smoking, spares him from having to think of himself as stupid, and his ego remains intact.

'Why not let him keep his belief system?' I hear you cry.
'What harm is it causing you?' you shout.

You're correct. It's not causing me any harm, but IT IS causing him a great deal. One of the most important factors in whether a person can achieve a goal, regardless of what that goal is, is how POWERFUL they feel in relation to achieving their goal, and how much CONTROL they feel they have over it. It's like a double-edged sword:

Believing you are addicted to smoking is great, if you want to maintain your smoking habit with little effect on your self-esteem (I'm not stupid, I'm addicted) but trying to get over an addiction, is much, MUCH harder than simply 'changing a little habit'. In my experience the single biggest reason why smokers find it so hard to quit (until they meet me, obviously) - and this is evidenced by the millions and millions of pounds (£118,000,000 in 2007-2008) that the NHS spend every year doling out nicotine dependency advice and drugs - is because they BELIEVE it is going to be really hard, because they BELIEVE they are addicted (Eiser *et al.*, 1985).

The same double-edged sword can be applied to any limiting belief system - the system works hard to keep you in it, but fights you when you want to leave it.

It will be useful later, when changing limiting beliefs, for you to think of a belief system as an impenetrable brick wall, a defence mechanism protecting you from outside influences that would otherwise challenge your view of your experiences in life. In this analogy, each brick in the wall is a significant experience that has helped to form the belief system, and the strength of the cement holding the bricks together relates to how much NEED (more about this later) you have to maintain it.

Carrying on with my 'nicotine addiction' analogy… someone who has been smoking, say, 40 a day for 40 years, may firmly believe that he is addicted to it. He may have a huge brick wall (a huge belief system about why he smokes) where every brick is an experience when he really needed a cigarette, or felt terrible cravings when he couldn't smoke, or tried to quit but couldn't. There may be millions of bricks in this wall, because he has had millions of significant experiences related to wanting or needing a cigarette. These experiences, the bricks in the wall, are the 'evidence' for the belief system, these are the 'facts' that the smoker thinks of when needing to reaffirm his belief. Every time he thinks about smoking, wants to smoke, has 'cravings' etc., he is adding yet more bricks to his belief system wall.

The cement holding this huge structure together is his NEED to see his smoking habit as an ADDICTION. This NEED is what drove the creation of his belief system in the first place…

Now, some smokers are not particularly socially phobic (feeling judged and scrutinised by others, more about this later), and therefore find it easier to integrate into their psyche the fact that they are a (fairly) sane person who just has a stupid habit that might kill them. They can cope with these two apparently opposing situations (they are sane, and yet they are possibly killing themselves) without suffering too much conflict. They probably don't care too much if other people do think they are stupid to smoke. As a result they don't need to (unconsciously) build up an elaborate belief system in order to protect themselves from people thinking they are 'stupid, and have no willpower'.

Ex-smokers, who believed that smoking was *just a habit*, tended to stop smoking easily without any side effects or cravings. Those smokers who (need to) believe that smoking is an addiction tend to find it very difficult to stop, and suffer 'cravings' and 'withdrawal symptoms'.

Many of our basic belief systems are created during childhood, as we learn about the world around us. All our experiences are processed and grouped together, creating belief systems about ourselves and other people. As we go through life, more and more experiences - bricks in the wall - are added into our belief systems, strengthening and reinforcing them.

An example of this occurring for a particular set of beliefs could be:

1. A young girl believes that there is a God.
2. She expects the world to be a certain way based on her belief: 'God will help me'.
3. Her prayers to God will help her Granny to recover from pneumonia.
4. Granny recovers.

5. This experience is processed, interpreted and stored by the girl, fitting it in to her belief system.
6. Reinforcement occurs: 'Praying helped me to communicate with God and he saved my Granny'.

Many belief systems are very useful and empowering for us. These days, most children brought up in the western world are taught that they have the right to be happy, the right to medical care, the right to social care, the right to be treated nicely - you get the picture.

A 'limiting belief system', is a set of personal beliefs that can have an incredibly negative or damaging effect on your life. In other words a limiting belief is ANY belief (or thought) that DOESN'T help you to achieve the life you really want. Limiting beliefs can cause you to suffer, for example, relationship problems, ill health, phobias, fears and anxieties, and even mental and physical illnesses.

Below is an example of a limiting belief system. This one is based on low self-confidence self-esteem:

1. 'I'm not academic - I'm bound to do badly in my exams'.
2. I expect failure to happen.
3. I imagine feeling nervous and that the exam will be really hard.
4. The exam does go badly. Due to the expectation and built up anxiety, I 'forget' things I know how to answer.
5. I process, interpret and store the experience, fitting it in to the belief system.
6. I believe 'I was right to think I'd do badly, I'm not very bright'.

A belief system is a firm, fixed, unshakeable brick wall of a belief. It isn't usually something that can change significantly from day to day. One of the difficulties when challenging our belief systems is that we often don't have very much perspective with which to view them, since we see everything through our 'belief system-tinted spectacles'.

We don't know that we are wearing these 'belief system-tinted spectacles' though, so we believe that our (distorted) perception is genuine. An obvious example of distorted thinking can be witnessed in an anorexia sufferer who believes she is fat. She can stand on the scales, read the size label in her clothes, and even have her doctor standing out in front of her telling her she is going to die because she is so thin, but she believes she is fat. She is lacking perspective because she is only seeking out 'evidence' that supports the belief she wants to maintain, the one where she is fat. So, whilst lying down, if she can pinch the tiniest bit of her flesh, this is her evidence that she is disgusting and fat. She is overlooking all the *overwhelming evidence to the contrary*.

'Jane' was a qualified therapist in the organisation that I run and, whilst having a Thrive Programme session with her one day, I got the sense that she was feeling a little bit judged by me, so I asked her if she was. She said something along the lines of, 'I know you don't really rate me as a therapist.' I was shocked, because I had always thought she was a great therapist, and a lovely person too! I probed her on why she thought this, and she remembered a joke I had made to her two years earlier at one of our conferences. She had commented on something she had done in her life that she thought was a bit mad, and I said that she must be a bit 'radio rental', which, of course, is cockney rhyming slang for 'mental'. Now, over the years I must have told Jane at least 100 times that I really respect her as a therapist, I thought she had great insight, I thought she was great with clients, etc. but she overlooked the hundreds of very positive comments, and focused on the one perceived negative remark. She WANTED to hear the negative comment, because it struck a chord with what she believed about herself, it fitted in with her belief system.

Some people still believe the earth is flat (www.theflatearthsociety.org), others that you can dowse for water (or other minerals) using a twig from a tree (www.dowsers.com), and I've even got a friend (until she reads this book!) who believes she can divine the sex of an unborn baby by dangling a pendulum over the expectant mother's womb. All of these people are, most probably, overlooking *overwhelming evidence* that very strongly suggests their beliefs are totally wrong. Now, if a person's beliefs in dowsing, divining or the earth being flat are not causing them any harm at all, then fine, why not? It takes all sorts. If, however, that person is suffering in some way, they may need to challenge these beliefs in order to do so.

### The balloon metaphor

"A belief is nothing more than a thought we keep on thinking"

The statement seems simplistic, but actually it's very accurate. A belief IS just a thought we keep on thinking. If the belief is an unhelpful one, we will continue to suffer its consequences as long as we believe it.

Imagine, if you would, a balloon (just a normal balloon, the sort you would have had – hopefully – at your birthday parties when you were a kid). Remember that within a couple of days of your party, the balloons would all go down? I was always a bit disappointed when the balloons went down. Sometimes I'd undo the knot or string, and blow some more air back into them to keep them going a bit longer.

An important and/or emotional belief system is just like one of those balloons... leave it alone and it will go down after a short while, it won't be important anymore. Think of a belief in ghosts for a minute: there are millions of people who believe in them, millions of people who believe they've actually seen one. You rarely come across a person who believes they've seen more than one, or many of them? Anyway, imagine you are a non-believer and you awake in the night to see a strange figure at the end of your bed. It's frightening, and you are convinced you've seen a ghost. Now, if you just go about your life normally for the next couple of weeks and don't think or talk about it too much, your belief will probably 'deflate like a balloon' and you'll soon be laughing about the whole thing and thinking it was ridiculous.

But what if you did think about it a lot? What if you told your family and friends about it? What if you Googled 'real ghosts' and visited 'ghost forums' on the Internet? If you did all these things, it would be hard for your belief to simply 'deflate like a balloon'. In fact what you'd be doing is untying the knot every day, and blowing more and more air into your belief/balloon... and hey presto your belief is getting bigger and bigger, stronger and stronger... as the days and weeks go by you become more and more confident in your belief that you actually saw a ghost, and your 'confirmation bias' just gets stronger and stronger. The more you believe, the less you question. At first, you were quite unsure of what happened: 'maybe I shouldn't have a beer before bedtime', 'maybe I was just over tired', 'maybe I was just dreaming' and 'c'mon I know ghosts don't exist'. But now, you stop asking those – very sensible – questions, because the more faith you have in your belief the less you question. Soon, you are utterly convinced you saw a ghost.

The only reason you are confident you saw a ghost is because you continued to blow air into your 'belief balloon'. If you just left it the hell alone, it would have deflated and shriveled up like a dried prune.

The same thing can be said of any strong belief system. Take a phobia for example. Imagine that you experience a bumpy aeroplane flight. If you leave the balloon alone after your flight though and let it deflate, you won't have a strong belief/phobia about flying by the next time you are due to fly. If you go the other way though, and react with anxiety and stress, feverishly blowing air into your 'flying is terrifying and dangerous' balloon, then don't be surprised if you start to create a strong negative belief about flying. Perhaps you tell everyone about your 'awful flight' and how 'the plane dropped thousands of feet in the turbulence'... If you keep on creating thoughts about flying and reacting in a powerless and emotional way... you are going to turn a slightly bumpy flight into a full blown phobia.

## How do you experience the world?

Whatever room or space you are in right now, what's it like? How would you describe it? At this very moment I am in my consulting room in Cambridge, UK. It's a fairly big (about 4m x 3m) room in a doctor's surgery. There are certificates and diplomas on the walls, as well as interesting pictures, and a few really thick, expensive looking psychology books with bright yellow post-it notes sticking out with 'I agree!' and 'spot on!' scribbled on them. You COULD describe it as a cross between a doctor's consulting room, and a nice, relaxed living room. I say 'could', because everyone would describe it differently, everyone would 'see' and 'feel' it differently.

Some people would describe the room as 'big', others, 'small'. Some people might say 'warm and cosy', others, 'cold and uncomfortable'. Some people would describe it as 'light and airy', others, 'dark and claustrophobic'. How is this possible? Surely the room is the same room for everyone? It is, but we all see things differently, based upon our belief systems, our expectations, and our different thinking styles - these things come together to create our 'perception'. In other words, we are not actually experiencing 'reality', but reality as filtered by our beliefs systems and thinking styles (our rose or shit-tinted spectacles). We believe that what we are experiencing is REAL, but it is not.

**We are not experiencing reality, but reality filtered through our beliefs systems and thinking styles.**

I am looking out of my window at a beautiful, exciting and energising spring day here in Cambridge, and yet my first client of the day is suffering from something labelled (incredibly unhelpfully, in my opinion) 'Seasonal Affective Disorder', SAD. How can this be? Are we not experiencing the same day? In the pots outside my window, the flowers are starting to bloom, leaves are starting to appear on the beech tree in our car park, squirrels have come out of hiding and are playing 'chicken' with the cars as they turn and park in our car park (one of them not very successfully by the look of things). There is definitely a sense of Spring in the air: Cambridge is starting to wake up after the winter freeze and you cannot fail to sense it, unless you 'suffer from a debilitating illness' called 'SAD' like Peter, my first client of the day.

Peter doesn't see the flowers. Actually, that's not true. He DOES see the flowers, but he doesn't 'process' them. The same thing goes for the leaves on the tree, the squirrels in the car park, and the exciting spring weather. He 'sees' all these things, but the message either doesn't reach his brain, or isn't processed into knowledge. Instead, what Peter sees is grey, cold, uninviting, depressive blandness, and this makes him feel depressed, lethargic, irritable and anxious. (I say 'makes him feel', but it doesn't actually 'make him' feel anything. He makes himself feel these things but he just doesn't know it.) The huge difference between what I see and experience, and what Peter sees and experiences, is all down to how we interpret what we see. I am going to have a great day today; Peter, I'm sorry to say, will probably have a shit one.

I could have fifty people in my consulting room (at a squeeze), and they would all have a different experience of being there, and they would all have a different experience of the day, because they would all be VIEWING these things from their own perspective i.e. through their own rose-tinted (or other colour) spectacles, through their own belief systems. It isn't about reality; it's about interpretation and perspective. There are a number of unhelpful thinking styles that people can have which can each have a huge effect on how they process experiences in life, affecting how they view and interpret events.

The key to taking control of how you experience the world around you is to know yourself, to know what you are like, to understand when you are likely to over-react, feel paranoid and get upset – we call this 'self-insight'. When you KNOW how your brain and body interacts, you can make adjustments accordingly, and have a more realistic perspective on events and experiences. If we don't have much self-insight and allow our limiting beliefs or unhelpful thinking styles to regularly distort our perspective on life, we can be affected in a number of ways. Limiting beliefs can cause you to suffer, for example, relationship break-ups, lack of success at work, anxieties, phobias and even mental and physical illnesses.

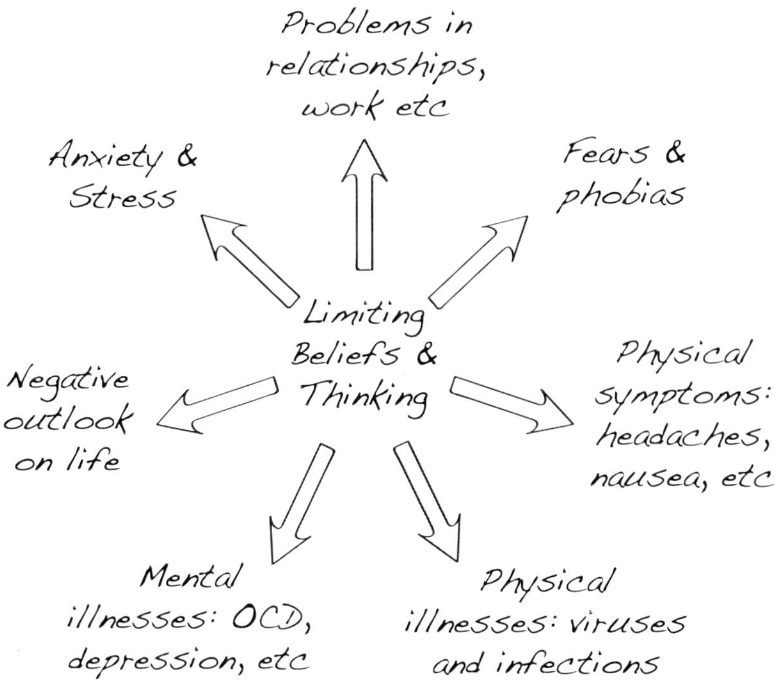


You may find it incredible that merely your beliefs and thinking can cause such a wide range of problems and even physical symptoms and illnesses. 'Ok', I can hear you say, 'I can see that your thinking could cause psychological symptoms such as stress, anxiety, phobias etc., but it can't possibly influence physical illnesses.'

If you think about it, this is not such a bizarre concept as you might first assume. There is plenty of research that suggests your beliefs and thinking have a real impact on factors such as: **how happy you are; your proneness to anxiety or depression**; **how much success you achieve**; **how innovative and entrepreneurial you can be; your ability to recover from a major illness such as cancer or a stroke** and even **your immune system.** (e.g. Dunkley *et al.*, 2003; Emmons and McCullough, 2003; Mirowsky and Ross, 1990; Nolen-Hoeksema, 1991; Clark, 1999; Taylor *et al.*, 2006; Mueller and Thomas, 2000; Tschuschke *et al.*, 2001; Watson *et al.*, 1999; Lewis *et al.*, 2001; Cohen and Doyle *et al.*, 2003; Lengacher and Bennett *et al.*, 2008; Yoshino and Mukai, 2003; Davidson and Kabat-Zinn *et al.*, 2003)

Question: *When are you most likely to come down with a cold, and when do you tend to get a really thumping headache?*

Answer: *When you are stressed, not thinking clearly and not managing your emotions.*

When you create and maintain high anxiety and stress levels, this not only contributes to psychological problems (such as fears, phobias, relationship problems, OCD etc.) but also affects your immune system. You become more susceptible to catching illnesses and find it harder to recover from them (Cohen *et al.*, 1993). We will be coming back to the effects of stress, and what is commonly known as the 'mind-body' connection (how your mind and the way you think can influence you physically) later on in this book in more detail.

## Reflecting upon your belief systems

Throughout this book we are going to be exploring many of the belief systems that you hold about yourself and the world around you. 'Easy' you're thinking to yourself, but it's not quite as simple as that! Most people reading this page have probably been thinking and acting the same way now for many years. Thought patterns and behaviours become normalised, and end up almost unconscious, similar to the way you learnt to ride a pushbike. Sometimes our beliefs and thought patterns are so ingrained that we don't even know they exist, they become implicit. 'Implicit' effectively means 'not needing or requiring conscious control'. Essentially, you have the thoughts but don't know where they came from and often do not even notice them. The opposite of implicit is 'explicit'. Explicit thought patterns are those that do require some form of conscious control; you are aware of them.

A quick example: *are you racist?*
You almost certainly answered with a loud 'NO'.

You're reading this workbook, and/or working through it with one of my trained colleagues, which means, that to a greater or lesser extent, you must be an educated person. What I'm getting at is this: surely in this day and age, an educated and intelligent person like yourself KNOWS that racism is just simply ignorance and prejudice? Would it shock you if I told you that, in all probability, despite your best intentions to hide it, you probably are quite racist?

If you go online, and go to this website: https://implicit.harvard.edu/implicit/research/, look for the link to 'Race IAT', and you can take Harvard University's five minute racism test (the links to this test seem to change every few months, so you may need to do a Google search to find it). As I said, you will, in all probability, be surprised to find that you are at least a little bit racist.

Where am I going with this? I just wanted to demonstrate to you that you have lots of beliefs and patterns in your thinking, which are beyond your normal conscious awareness. So, you are a bit racist, without even knowing it! How is this possible? Well, you have been through thousands of experiences in your life where there was some form of racist element to them. Maybe there was some racism in your school or job, maybe you have told/been told racist jokes, maybe when you grew up there were a disproportionate number of black 'baddies' or villains on your television, compared to white ones? Unconsciously you pick up on all of these racist cues, and they form a belief system, an unconscious prejudice - that you don't even know you have.

If you explained to a friend of yours, who suffers from any of the problems or symptoms or limiting beliefs mentioned in this book, what a 'negative or limiting thought' is, and then asked them how often they experienced them, they would probably nod their head in recognition and reply, 'yeah, I do that at least five or six times a day'. What your friend is admitting to is the five or six times a day they have 'realised' that they have had negative or limiting thoughts. These are the really big, obvious thoughts that stick out like a sore thumb. Your friend is not aware of the hundreds or even THOUSANDS of smaller negative or limiting thoughts that are going through their head almost constantly. These thoughts occur so often, that they have been 'normalised' into more of an attitude, rather than individual thoughts – they are the shit-tinted spectacles I mentioned earlier on in the book. Like racism, they have become implicit.

'But', you say to yourself, 'if our innermost thoughts and beliefs are implicit, and more or less hidden from our conscious thinking, how do we detect and change them?' Good question! Although our thoughts and beliefs tend to be 'normalised' and more or less hidden away, they often do make themselves very clear and obvious, in the way in which we talk to ourselves.

## Our 'inner voice' or self-talk

Question: 'Think back through your life, think of your parents, teachers, friends and partners - who do you think the most CRITICAL person in your life has been?'

I'm sorry it's a trick question really, because by far and away the most critical person in your life, is you. The person who *'tells you off'* the most is YOU. The person who *'puts you down'* the most is YOU. The person who places the most limits on your hopes, desires and ambitions, is YOU. In fact, you probably do far more damage to your own health, self-esteem, and your ability to deal with stress and anxiety than EVERYONE else in your life put together!

Test this out on yourself:
For just one hour, of any day, pay attention to that 'inner voice' of your own. When you think to yourself, 'It's going to be a lovely day today', what does your inner voice say? When you say to yourself 'I am going to get that job', what does your inner voice reply? When you tell yourself 'I am going to go on a diet', what is the reply?

Chances are that your 'inner voice' wasn't anywhere near as positive, helpful, supportive or caring towards you as you would like and expect it to be.

Your 'inner voice' isn't really an inner voice at all. Obviously, it's a metaphor for what is sometimes called 'self-talk' - the 'thought conversations' we have going on in our heads most of the time. It may be that we are thinking of someone in our lives who was very critical and 'always on our backs', criticising us, challenging us, comparing us: 'I can see my dad looking down on me, very disapprovingly'. Some people think of it as *the little devil on my shoulder.*

# A question of belief - Exercises

Please complete all the exercises within this book - none of them have been added to bulk the book out - they are all essential for you to complete.

## 1. How do you view yourself?

An important part of this book is about you getting to know yourself better and understanding the driving forces behind your problems, symptoms and possible lack of successes in life. It may be that you haven't yet really properly considered exactly how you see yourself. So, please write a paragraph here on yourself, including the things you like and dislike.

## 2. Recognising your 'Inner voice'

Pay attention to the way you 'talk to yourself'. Do you have positive, supportive thoughts that encourage you to get out and achieve whatever it is that you want? Or do you have a little 'inner voice devil' on your shoulder? Are you constantly putting yourself down and putting limitations on yourself and what you can achieve? Is your voice soft and gentle, or hard and strong? Does your voice remind you of a voice from your past - a parent, teacher, school bully or sibling?

Noticing the way in which you talk to yourself is a key step in making changes in your life. If you are not speaking to yourself and thinking in a constructive, supportive way then you are bound to be creating and/or maintaining problems for yourself. Recognising that this negative 'inner voice' exists allows you the option of change - if you haven't pinpointed a problem then how on earth can you alter it!

Once you have identified the sort of language you use, and how your 'inner voice' generally comes across to you, please write down some of the more common comments or phrases in the blank space. Include some specific examples of how you 'talked to yourself' throughout the day.

My inner voice:

Well done! Throughout this book, you will be learning how to create an empowering and positive inner voice.

## 3. What limiting belief systems do you have?

A LIMITING belief system is ANY belief system that does not help you to achieve the life you want. These can range from phobias and fears, to believing that you cannot get the job you want, to thinking that you will never find a partner, to believing that you can never recover from your illness. Have a think for a few minutes and just identify any limiting belief systems that you are aware of.

You don't need to pick these belief systems to pieces, analyse them or do anything else! Just acknowledge that they exist and write them down in the space below. As you work your way through this book you will slowly be able to break down your limiting beliefs and build ones that enable you to stop existing and start thriving!

## A question of belief - Recap

- ✓ Belief systems are sets of personal viewpoints, which provide us with a fundamental base of principles and 'rules' by which we view or base EVERYTHING we think, do, say, or believe.
- ✓ You view your life experiences through the rose-tinted (or maybe 'shit-tinted' depending on the belief) spectacles of your belief system. You are far more likely to see events and experiences that confirm your beliefs, rather than ones that challenge or negate it. Your belief systems are thus likely to always be reinforced.
- ✓ A limiting belief is ANY belief that DOESN'T help you to achieve the life you really want.
- ✓ Since we see everything through our 'belief system-tinted spectacles', one of the difficulties when challenging our limiting belief systems is that we often don't have very much perspective with which to view them.
- ✓ We experience events and situations through our rose-tinted (or shit-tinted) spectacles - through our belief systems and unhelpful thinking styles. Our experiences are not reality; they are our interpretation of reality, from our perspective.
- ✓ If we allow our limiting beliefs or unhelpful thinking styles to regularly distort our perspective on life, we can be affected in a number of ways. For example, suffering from relationship break-ups, lack of success at work, anxieties, stress, phobias and even mental and physical illnesses.
- ✓ We all have an 'inner voice' or 'self-talk' - the 'thought conversations' we have going on in our heads most of the time.

**Notes** - The blank area below is for you to make any notes.

# Chapter

# 2

# Your psychological foundations

Think about the town or city that you live in and picture in your mind one of the taller buildings. Look around and see how big and tall the building is compared to some of the other buildings, houses and businesses. Imagine how strong and deep the foundations of that building must be in order to confidently support the building built on top of them. I recently visited the 'Shard' in London, which is currently London's tallest building at 307 metres (87 storeys!) tall. There are other tall buildings tightly packed around it, and I remember thinking 'bloody hell, the foundations for that thing must be deep'! If you had built that building, you'd have wanted to make sure it was going to stay tall and strong and not sway around in the wind, or come tumbling to the ground in a storm. So, you would have built incredibly strong and deep foundations for it. Makes sense?

Well, you have foundations just like that building: you have psychological foundations. Your mind is like the Shard, and you want your psychological foundations to be as strong and deep as the Shard's, so you can put up with bad weather, a stressful environment, and even the occasional storm!

There are – essentially – two main components of a person's psychological functioning: their foundations, and their mindset.

Your psychological foundations - your concrete and steel - are your sense of power and control and your self-esteem. We will be exploring these in much greater detail shortly. Basically though, these two belief systems – your beliefs about how powerful and in control of your experiences you are and your beliefs about how worthwhile and likeable you are – have a huge impact on every aspect of your life. They are key to the way in which you perceive and experience everything around you. If these two attributes are strong and deep, you will have everything you need in place in order to thrive. If your foundations are strong, you can build a much bigger, taller, more durable building on top.

Your mindset comprises of the extent to which you have skills and techniques, which help you to manage the way you think, feel, and react on a day-to-day basis. Being positive, having the right attitude, being mindful and distracting yourself from unpleasant thoughts could all be skills within your mindset.

The stronger your foundations the less effort required to keep your mindset positive and functioning well. We all know people that are always positive, buoyant and happy, seemingly without putting any effort in… Equally we all know people who are forever trying some new faddy magical way to stay happy and manage their thinking – which usually requires an awful lot of effort – and they always seem to struggle to stay in their 'good place'. The first group have strong foundations and have to spend little time managing their mindset, the second have weak foundations and are continually having to fight off their depression, their anxiety, their doubts and worries, their social anxiety etc.

Our foundations are first created during our childhood, largely in relation to two things: how we are parented and taught, and the way in which we experience and process events. I say 'first created', because these things are ENTIRELY changeable and re-programmable, and this constitutes a major part of The Thrive Programme, and this book.

One of the unique elements to The Thrive Programme is the recognition that you can, in fact, build or re-build your foundations. Most therapies and interventions don't understand this, and hence cannot take this into account, and therefore solely teach people how to manage their mindset. When you focus solely on the mindset, it's like you are fire-fighting all the time. You are taught to wait for an anxious thought, doubt, worry, insecurity or problem to arise then get out your fire extinguisher (whatever technique you have been taught) and put the fire out. Don't get me wrong, these skills are hugely important, and I'm going to teach you the most powerful techniques there are. But, wouldn't it be better, smarter or even AMAZING to learn how to not build fires in the first place… if you didn't keep building little fires (your doubts, worries, anxieties etc.) you wouldn't have any fires to put out! You'd be like the first type of person I described in the paragraph above, who seems somehow 'naturally' more confident, positive, happy, strong and resilient. Well, there's nothing 'natural' about it, it's just that they have built strong foundations.

Many, many different therapies and interventions don't create lasting benefits because they only address the problems above the surface, and don't address the foundations. For example: it would be really hard to feel completely confident, if your self-esteem were really low. It's really hard to avoid depression, when you feel powerless. It's difficult to focus on success, when you don't believe you deserve it. It's hard to feel happy, when you feel haunted by your past!

Just as a plant won't flourish in bad soil, it's very difficult to thrive without strong psychological foundations. The stronger your foundations, the easier it is to thrive, and the more resilient you will be.

# Your foundations - Recap

- ✓ You have psychological foundations. You want your foundations to be as strong and deep as the Shard's, so you can put up with bad weather, a stressful environment, and even the occasional storm! Your foundations are key to thriving
- ✓ Your psychological foundations are your sense of power and control and your self-esteem.
- ✓ Your mindset comprises of the extent to which you have skills and techniques, which help you to manage the way you think, feel, and react on a day-to-day basis. Being positive, having the right attitude, being mindful and distracting yourself from unpleasant thoughts are all skills within your mindset.
- ✓ The stronger your foundations the less effort required to keep your mindset positive and functioning successfully.

**Notes** - The blank area below is for you to make any notes.

# Chapter 3

# How powerful do you feel?

# Your sense of power and control

The first component of your psychological foundations is **your sense of power and control** over your experiences in life. People can either have an **internal** sense of power and control or an **external** one: they either believe that **they** are in control of their experiences (**internal**), or they believe that **external forces** (such as fate, luck, their past or other people) control them. To clarify, I call it your 'sense' of power and control, and not your 'actual' power and control, because you are assessing the **beliefs** you hold about the different situations and events in life and **not** your **actual** skills. This is just about your beliefs.

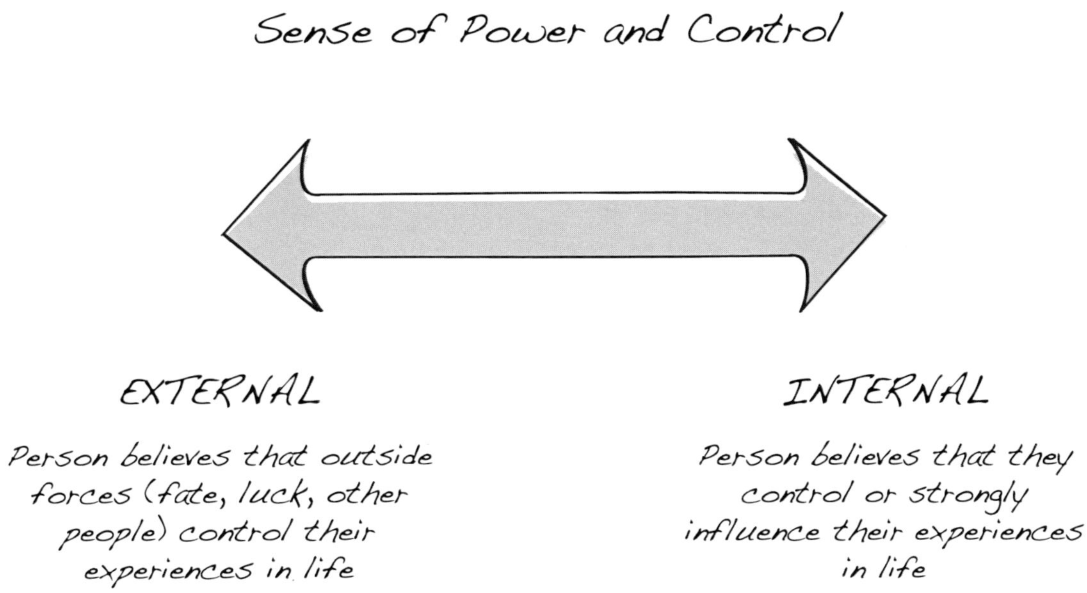


As I discussed in chapter 2, unless you have strong and deep foundations, you will find it hard to weather challenges and will struggle to flourish in life. Establishing and maintaining an **internal sense of power and control** is one of the two critical factors in your learning to thrive (the other being building your self-esteem, which we will come on to shortly). Please read that sentence again, slowly.

As a quick example, let's look at weight loss. Sense of power and control is a significant factor in a person's ability to stick to a diet or exercise plan. At the time of writing this book, there are more than 15 million adults in the UK who are considered to be 'clinically obese' and it's thought this figure will rise to 25 million over the next ten years (http://news.sky.com/home/uk-news/article/16056977). In the USA, the current adult obesity figure is a staggering 105 million, which equates to 33.8% of the adult population (http://www.cdc.gov/obesity/data/adult.html).

The vast majority of these obese adults are obese primarily due to the fact that they feel unable to lose weight, because they have an external sense of power and control. They have little belief in their own abilities to achieve and maintain a healthy bodyweight. Every time they attempt a new diet and fail (or succeed only to put the weight straight back on) they feel more powerless about their ability to lose weight. Sooner or later they just get to the point where they give up trying. Those in medical professions don't understand the situation (why would they, they are doctors, not therapists), they instead tend to believe that obese people are either lacking in self-control, or are just plain lazy (Price, Desmond, Krol, Snyder and O'Connell, 1987)!

A really good example of a person with an incredibly strong internal sense of power and control would be Jessica Cox. Jessica was born without any arms. As a small child, she was frustrated that she wasn't able to do things that other children were able to do easily. She had low self-esteem and felt angry and upset about being different. But Jessica has now learned to live her life to the full. She has stated that 'Life is 10% what happens to you and 90% of how you respond to it'. Jessica is now a black belt in Taekwondo, plays the piano, drives a car, and can even fly a plane - all using her feet. She works as a motivational speaker, helping others to see that they can achieve great things by being creative and determined.

Your sense of power and control over your experiences can be divided into your beliefs in relation to two domains: your **direct influence** and your **coping skills**. Your sense of **direct influence** refers to the extent to which you believe that you can exert direct control over the events in your life. Your sense of **coping skills** refer to whether or not you believe that you have the resources to respond positively to, tolerate and bounce back from events outside your direct influence.

To understand this further, let's look at a person's beliefs surrounding getting cancer. Someone with a very strong sense of direct influence would believe that they could prevent themselves from getting cancer. They might believe that through diet, exercise and living a psychologically healthy lifestyle, they will not get ill. A person with a low sense of direct influence would believe that there isn't a lot they can do to prevent illness; seeing it as determined by genes, bad luck, or other factors outside their control. Research has demonstrated that factors like diet, exercise and stress play a significant role in cancer (and plenty of other illnesses) but the reality is that, no matter how healthy your lifestyle, you cannot completely prevent yourself from getting ill. Most people realise this. Someone with a poor belief in their coping skills would view getting cancer as a disaster, believing that they would not be able to deal with it. A person who has a strong belief in their coping skills, however, believes that, if they were to get cancer, they would have the resources to manage the situation and still live a meaningful and worthwhile life.

So, people with an **internal** sense of power and control:

1) Have a **high** sense of **direct influence**, believing that they have power and control over many of the events and outcomes in their lives. In relation to this, they usually:

- Have a positive outlook on life and a 'can do' attitude. They believe that they have (or can learn) the internal resources needed to shape their lives and achieve their goals
- Believe that their successes and failures in life are largely down to internal reasons (i.e. ones that they can control). E.g. *"I passed my driving test because I practised lots"* or *"I did badly in my driving test because I didn't practise enough*." As a result, they are likely to put effort into achieving success in whatever domains are important to them
- Believe that they can strongly influence their physical and mental health
- Don't tend to have strong religious beliefs or, alternatively, believe that their religion gives them internal resources and strength
- Don't tend to believe in the paranormal, spiritual or magical
- Have faith in their own views, or seek to weigh up the evidence, rather than automatically deferring to other people's opinions.

2) Have a **strong** sense of their **coping skills**, believing that even when events are outside their direct influence, they have the skills and resources to respond positively, cope and bounce back. In relation to this, they usually:

- Don't tend to dwell on negative experiences or emotions

- Tend to employ their skills and resources in the face of challenges or problems, or use these as opportunities to build new skills and resources
- Show resilience: an ability to bounce back from challenging situations, traumas or misfortunes
- Tend to find it quite easy to manage stress, stay calm, be relaxed and feel happy.

People with an **external** sense of power and control:

1) Have a **low** sense of **direct** influence, believing that external forces determine most of the events and outcomes in their lives. In relation to this, they often:

- Tend to have a more negative outlook on life and a more helpless attitude towards certain situations. They don't believe that they have the internal resources to adapt, make changes and achieve their goals. They think that they need outside help, a significant partner, or some external support.
- Believe that their successes and failures in life are largely because of external reasons (i.e. ones that are uncontrollable). E.g. *"I was so lucky to pass my driving test!" or "I didn't pass my driving test because it was raining."* As a result, they are more likely to suffer from *learned helplessness,* where they do not take action, despite the fact that they have the power to alter their situation.
- Don't believe that they can do much to stay healthy and stress-free, or believe that they need a lot of external help (such as medication, doctors, therapists) in order to ward off or fight stress or illness
- Tend to believe in some sort of higher power or religion (they may score highly on the on The Revised Paranormal Belief Scale; Tobacyk, 1988)
- Tend to believe in the paranormal, spiritual or magical
- Are likely to listen and automatically defer to authority, experience, education and significant other people.

2) Have a **low** sense of their **coping skills**, believing that they do not have the resources to deal with events outside their direct influence. In relation to this, they often:

- Dwell on negative experiences or emotions, frequently worrying and creating anxiety, and/or often feeling depressed or lethargic
- Tend to be dependent upon other people or some sort of external 'crutch' (medication, alcohol, cigarettes, other drugs, comfort food) in the face of challenges or problems
- Find it hard to recover from challenges, difficulties or traumas
- Tend to create anxiety, stress, and frustration.

Remember, there is a spectrum running from a really internal sense of power and control to a really external one. So you may find that you identify with certain aspects of both internal and external descriptions. You may also differ as to where you fall in terms of your sense of direct influence and your coping skills.

## Locus of Control

A similar concept to 'sense of power and control' is 'locus of control' and many psychological researchers use this latter term. The word 'locus' is Latin for 'place', and the word 'control' refers to how much influence you believe you have over events in your life. Locus of control is a concept that was first developed by clinical psychologist Julian Rotter in the 1950s.

> *"Individuals who have an internal locus of control believe that a positive cause/effect relationship exists between their own behaviour and the outcomes they experience. People having an external locus of control, on the other hand, perceive a lack of a relationship between their activities and consequent outcomes. In these individuals, outcomes may be perceived as controlled by sources external to oneself such as powerful others or by chance factors such as fate or luck."*
>
> (Crisson and Keefe, 1988)

In a recent search of the PsycINFO database (April 6th, 2012), I found 16,913 research studies with the phrase 'locus of control' as keyword. That's nearly seventeen thousand research papers into this subject. I found that in relation to just about every illness, phobia, medical condition, habit, disability and lack of success, the research suggests that how in control you feel is really significant. It substantially affects whether a person is going to suffer a symptom in the first place, whether they are going to 'get better', whether they win the race or reach the peak, their happiness, their health... (The **really** sad thing here is that it isn't actually that difficult to change your sense of control.)

Here are a few examples of this research (there is more in the support section of our website):

A study by Abrahamsson *et al.* (2002), demonstrated that feeling powerless is a key factor in dental phobia. Those with panic disorder have been found to have a more external locus of control than those without, believing that events occur in a random and uncontrollable way (Cloitre, Heimberg, Liebowitz and Gitow, 1992).

In relation to depression, a number of studies have highlighted the importance of a sense of control. Burger (1984) found that those who believed that their lives were controlled by chance or powerful others, had higher levels of depression. Mirowsky and Ross (1990) determined that depression was associated with not feeling in control of either good outcomes or bad outcomes, or of both.

Abouserie (1994) looked at locus of control and stress levels in university students. It was found that those with an external locus of control had higher levels of academic stress than others who had an internal locus. So the students who believed that they were in control of their situations were less stressed than those who believed that their academic results were controlled by luck or outside forces.

One recent research paper (Gale *et al.*, 2008) examined the health effect of childhood locus of control. This report used results from the 1970 British Cohort Study where thousands of British adults were followed from birth. Those who had shown an internal locus of control at the age of ten were less likely to be overweight at age 30, and also appeared to have higher levels of self-esteem. Sturmer *et al.* (2006) revealed that locus of control was an important factor in heart disease. It was found that those with an internal locus of control over disease had a lower risk of heart attack.

A particularly interesting study by Rodin and Langer (1977) involved pensioners in a nursing home, who were divided into two groups. To one group of pensioners it was emphasised that the nursing home staff were responsible for their care and that these staff would try to make them happy. To those in a 'responsibility-induced' group it was stressed that they were responsible for themselves. This group was also offered plants to care for whereas those in the first group were given plants that the staff watered. Those in the responsibility-induced group became more active, reported feeling happier and appeared more alert. They were more involved in social activities with the staff and other residents.

Even more incredibly:

> *The most striking data were obtained in death rate differences between the two treatment groups. Taking the 18 months prior to the original intervention as an arbitrary comparison period, we found that the average death rate during that period was 25% for the entire nursing home. In the subsequent 18-month period following the intervention, only 7 of the 47 subjects (15%) in the responsibility-induced group died, whereas 13 of 44 subjects (30%) in the comparison group had died.*

Just to clarify that last line in the quote above, **half as many pensioners died when they were given a plant to look after and encouraged to feel responsible.** The act of looking after the plant gave them a sense of purpose - they realised that they weren't completely powerless, and so started to think more internally, which helped to develop a more internal locus of control.

I hope you are starting to see the importance of believing that you can influence your experiences, as this has a profound effect upon almost every area of your life.

## Why do we refer to sense of power and control rather than locus of control?

We are using 'sense of power and control' rather than 'locus of control' for several reasons. Firstly, as I mentioned earlier, I wanted to avoid using psychological or scientific language wherever possible, as we are in the business of 'de-mystifying' how the mind works. Many people haven't heard of 'locus of control' but it is fairly obvious what we mean when we talk about 'sense of power and control'.

Even more importantly, by referring to 'sense of power and control' we are actually talking about something subtly different to and more empowering than locus of control (though we should note that different researchers have understood locus of control in a number of different ways, increasing confusion!). Locus of control essentially refers to whether you attribute the cause of a particular event or outcome to internal or external factors. Sense of power and control does encompass this, but also refers more broadly to whether you feel internally skilled and powerful in the face of events that were caused by outside influences.

So, having an internal sense of power and control does not mean that you have to attribute EVERYTHING in your life to internal factors. Many events DO come about because of our beliefs, thoughts, feelings and behaviour. People with an internal sense of power and control realise this and take responsibility; they have a good sense of direct influence, which contributes to a 'can do' attitude. There are, however, aspects of life that are not always controllable. People you love die, friends move away etc. and often you haven't done anything to cause these things to happen. You cannot possibly be in control of everything that happens to you in your life. But people with an internal sense of power and control also have a high sense of coping skills. They believe that they have the personal power to overcome, tolerate, influence or respond to events and to take charge of their lives, even on the occasions when current events were not originally influenced by their own actions. This is really critical! Even if you have a high sense of direct influence, if your sense of coping skills is lacking, you are likely to still feel helpless and anxious in relation to certain aspects of your life.

Another very important point to note in relation to this is that having an internal sense of power and control and making internal attributions does not require you to 'self-blame' and berate yourself! Indeed, berating and blaming yourself can lead to the same sort of feelings of powerlessness that making external attributions does. There is, for example, a big difference between thinking, 'Ok I failed my driving test because I went too fast round a corner and didn't bay park correctly. I could have done a bit more practice before this test. I'm going to practise loads in the next few weeks so that I pass next time' and, 'I failed my driving test because I am useless'. The first thought leaves you feeling in control and motivates you to practise and change your situation, whereas the second probably results in brooding, misery and feelings of 'What's the point in trying again?' In Chapter 7 'Mind Your Language!' we will be looking at your language in detail and how to effectively use it in an active and positive way.

## How powerful do YOU feel?

Let's now take our first proper look at your TQ Report. A major part of the assessments you completed was the SPACE quiz.

The vast majority of (British and American) people have a significant (or worse!) external sense of power and control, i.e. most people feel powerless. (In fact, in relation to locus of control, American people have become more and more external over the last forty years or so, according to research undertaken on college students by Twenge, Zhang and Im (2004). The authors suggested that the average college student in 2002 was more likely to have an external locus of control than 80% of students in the 1960's.)

Don't panic if at this point the test shows that you have an EXTERNAL sense of power and control. You wouldn't be studing this manual if you were 100% internal (and no one is 100% internal!). Later on, I will show you how to create and then strengthen an INTERNAL sense of power and control.

### In what areas are your thoughts and beliefs external?

It can be really helpful to break your sense of power and control down into areas or types of belief, so that you can see if there is a specific type that is largely responsible for any feelings of powerlessness. Think about how you stand in relation to your sense of direct influence and your beliefs about your coping skills. Once you have ascertained where the bulk of your beliefs are coming from, you can put some effort into changing any areas that are particularly problematic. For example, if you have an external sense of power and control it may be mostly in relation to:

- A belief in luck/fate/chance
- A belief that your past still has a significant effect upon you
- Paranormal type beliefs
- A belief that powerful others (partners, parents, friends, doctors, politicians etc.) determine the course of your life
- A lack of belief in your own capabilities and capacity to take control
- A sudden or chronic illness you suffered (or still suffer) from
- Living through a time of great instability or unpredictability (for example having nursed a terminally ill relative, or living/working in a war zone).

In your TQ Report, we have broken down your overall SPACE score into the individual areas: have a look, where are you strongest and weakest? Are any of the areas surprising to you? What can you do to make improvements?

## Where does our sense of power and control come from?

Your sense of power and control is just a belief system. Essentially, you LEARN to have either an internal or external sense of power and control from your parents and your environment. Internal people tend to have grown up in families that valued education and learning and encouraged their children to apply effort and be responsible. These families tend to have been supportive, caring and consistent (McClun and Merrell, 1998). People with an internal sense of power and control have usually been taught 'problem-solving' skills as children. They probably grew up in an environment where they were encouraged to think for themselves. Rather than their parents (or other people) doing everything for them, they were taught how to resolve difficulties and overcome obstacles for themselves.

Those with an external sense of power and control may come from less affluent backgrounds, since many people living in poverty understandably feel that they have little or no control over their lives (Maqsud and Rouhani, 1991; Lever *et al.*, 2005). People who are external are also more likely to have grown up in an environment where parents (or care-givers) were overly controlling, very overprotective or did not give their children much responsibility (McClun and Merrell, 1998). Greater externality may also be associated with parenting that is excessively permissive and does not provide much support, consistence and encouragement.

Additionally, people in societies where there is instability or conflict tend to be more external, as their environment increases the expectation of being out-of-control and powerless. Could this, in part, explain why wars always seem to be fought in highly religious communities? Often people attribute wars to religion. Perhaps, though, this is not always the case. In a society where there is unrest, people feel more out of control and consequently become more external. In such societies, people are more likely to believe that God has more power over their lives than they do. Thus in countries where wars are ongoing, religion is highly prevalent.

### Cultural influences

Outside of our families, our culture and social environment has the biggest impact upon our sense of power and control. We are bombarded every day with advertisements, pictures, stories, experiences, sayings and beliefs that propagate our 'cultural externality'.

Interestingly our (British) society does, to some extent, promote the development of an external sense of power and control in our children, by propagating many paranormal and external types of beliefs. Our culture encourages our children to believe in all sorts of magical external forces: Father Christmas, the tooth fairy, lucky charms, superstitions, etc. Indeed you would probably feel like a bad parent if you didn't bring these things into your children's lives! A strong emphasis on anything 'magical' or out-of-control during childhood can, however, encourage a child to form an external sense of power and control, especially if the child is not actively encouraged to develop problem-solving skills.

A recent poll of some of my colleagues produced the following list of potential external cultural beliefs, sayings and influences:

- The weather and the common British desire to discuss it as though it is a significant factor in how good or bad your day/week is going to be
- Saying 'good luck' or 'that was lucky' or 'luckily' or 'bad luck' or 'unlucky'
- Sayings like: 'someone's just walked over my grave', 'my ears are burning - someone must be talking about me', 'you look like you've just seen a ghost', 'he's a natural footballer', 'it's a gift from God' and 'she's a born runner'

- Gambling and games of chance, like bingo, scratch-cards, horse-racing, fantasy football and playing the National Lottery. The lottery is seen every day on British TV in some way, shape or form. The symbol for the UK lottery is a picture of a pair of crossed fingers, as in 'keep your fingers crossed for good luck'. If you currently live in Britain and regularly watch TV, you probably see this sign at least five times every single day of your life! At the time of writing there is even a weekly lottery called 'The Health Lottery'. 'Health' and 'lottery' – there are two words you really don't want to associate together!
- Saying 'I'm addicted' - smoking, gambling, cream cakes, sex etc. - or people claiming they have 'an addictive personality' thus absolving themselves of responsibility for their actions
- Black cats, walking under ladders, unlucky number 13, broken mirrors, saluting a magpie, believing in the 'tooth fairy', and all other superstitions
- Making a wish when you blow your birthday candles out, or when you pull apart the 'wish-bone' from a chicken, dropping a penny in a well and making a wish, etc.
- Horoscopes, stargazing, fortune tellers, the power of crystals, mediums and psychics
- Celebrating Halloween
- That belief that everyone has a soul-mate 'out there' somewhere
- Customs, practices and celebrations surrounding religion, such as reciting prayers, singing hymns, christening a child, believing in biblical creationism
- The British class system
- Comparing siblings' abilities or giving them labels, therefore influencing their thinking e.g. she's the brainy one, she's the pretty one, he's the sporty one, he's the drama queen, she is the lazy one etc. This also equates to the role you play (and never stop playing if you are external) or your position within the family
- Endorsing stereotypes like 'blondes have more fun' or 'blondes are stupid' etc.
- Using magical or biblical terms such as 'miracle' (as in beauty face creams)

### Maintaining our sense of power and control

So, we are trained to have either an internal or external sense of power and control, trained by our parents, our carers, our teachers, our clergy, and our politicians. Trained, from birth, to either believe that we can influence what happens in our lives, or that we can't. It then becomes habitual for us to process events in a particular way (remember in chapter one, I talked about how we tend to reinforce our belief systems?). We don't tend to change our beliefs easily (though we could do so) because once you have your sense of power and control, be it either internal or external, you then interpret the experiences in your life in relation to this, further propagating your beliefs.

The following diagram shows this process occurring in relation to an event or situation.

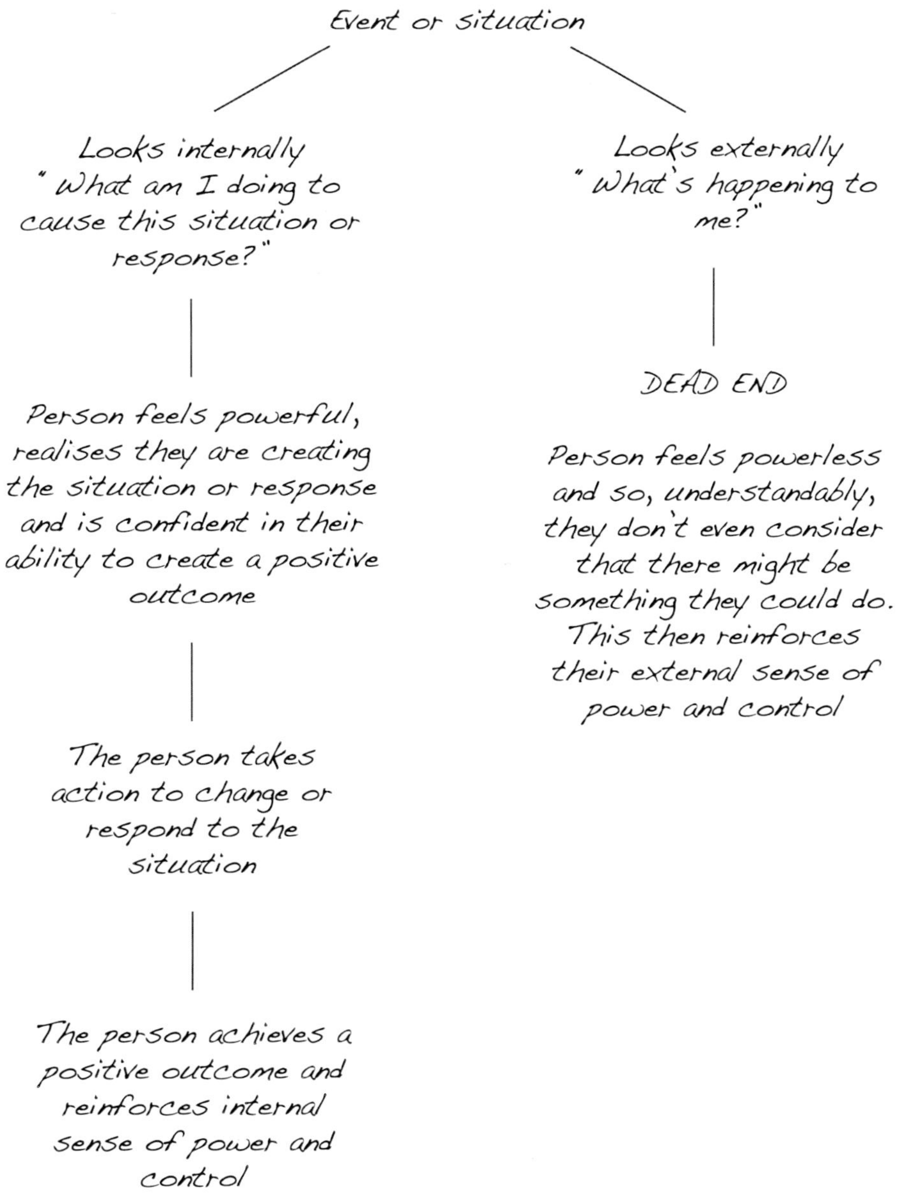


For example, let's look at people who have undertaken an exam. Those with a strong **internal** sense of power and control are likely to believe that their results were achieved through their own efforts and skills. They tend to feel that their successes, or indeed disappointments, are within their own control. Those with a strong **external** sense of power and control are more likely to believe that their results are due to good or bad luck. They may believe that they have only done well through fluke or that their papers have been marked incorrectly. Those with an **internal** sense of power and control are, therefore, likely to put more effort into their studies than those with an **external** sense of power and control. This is entirely understandable – after all, what is the point in working hard if you believe that you cannot really affect an outcome? As you can see, a person's beliefs lead to a bit of a self-fulfilling prophecy. Those who believe that they are powerless do indeed become more helpless, as they put less effort into gaining skills and achieving positive outcomes.

Think about what you, your friend or your parent said when they passed their driving test. Did they say, 'Well done me! I deserved to pass, I worked really hard on my driving skills!' or did they say 'God, I was lucky – I made three mistakes and they still passed me!' Every time you interpret and process an event in your life, which you do many times daily, you are further strengthening your sense of power and control.

A hugely important factor to remember here is that your sense of power and control isn't necessarily based upon reality. It's not a fixed or permanent thing, like the colour of your eyes, or the size of your feet. It's just a belief system. It's the way that you see things, it's the way you think things, and it's the way in which you process information. There are other ways of doing these things. You can change these things quite quickly and painlessly – like the OAPs looking after their pot-plants I mentioned earlier.

## There's always a cost

Although, we've already discussed some of the ways in which your overall sense of power and control can impact upon your psychological and physical health, it might be hard for you to understand the overarching impact of holding particular external beliefs. You might think that certain external beliefs seem harmless? Maybe you are thinking: 'come on Rob, it doesn't do any harm me reading my horoscope', or 'there's nothing negative about believing in fate', or maybe even 'there's nothing wrong in trying treatments like homeopathy – the worst that can happen is that they won't work'?

Well, I'm sorry but there is always a price to pay for holding a powerless, external belief... every single external belief you hold is disempowering you in some way, shape or form. Every belief you hold about external powers, fate luck and chance, 'magical' treatments, social pressures, the influence of your past experiences, your lack of skills, and such like you are paying for by feeling a little less powerful in some other area of your life. Every belief you hold about ghosts, life after death, mediums, homeopathy, fate, synchronicity, magic, playing the lottery, praying etc. is having a significant impact on how powerful and in control you feel, which in turn has a huge impact upon other areas of your life, such as how much anxiety and stress you create.

Just as a related aside for a minute, I've helped a number of white, middle-class, teenagers that consulted me after following fairly common, unhelpful paths. They developed symptoms such as school phobia, social anxiety or depression. Their parents had plenty of money to pay for their children to receive rapid help for their issues but, instead of being taken direct to the nearest psychologist or therapist for predictable, understandable and evidence-based help, their parents took them for acupuncture, reiki, homeopathy, herbal remedies or similar. Despite the fact that there is not a single shred of evidence anywhere on Earth that these 'treatments' (a) actually help the symptoms mentioned above, and (b) actually do anything at all other than act as a placebo, the parents tell their kids things like 'don't worry, I'm taking you to see the homeopath, that will sort your school phobia out'.

When the treatment – predictably – doesn't help, the teenage sufferer feels somewhat deflated and starts to believe their problem must be more serious and involved. This renders them more powerless and external and, of course, their symptoms then worsen (don't forget the sufferer's sense of power and control causes or influences – either directly or indirectly – most of these symptoms in the first place!). Next in line is the herbalist, then the acupuncturist... and so it goes on. By the time I see the poor kid they feel so powerless, so confused, and are usually quite pissed off! The moral of this story is that holding external beliefs always has a cost. In this example, putting faith into and trying out these magical treatments wasn't a harmless exercise that was just 'worth a try' in case it helped. It served to exacerbate a child's sense of powerlessness and consequently increased their anxiety and symptoms. (Another moral of the story is: as a parent, put your own magical external beliefs to one side, and Google 'what's the most effective treatment for xxx'? Find a treatment that has a – genuine – proven track record, and take your child there).

As I mentioned earlier, having an internal sense of power and control does not mean that you have to attribute EVERYTHING in your life to internal factors. There are aspects of life that are not always controllable. But you want to have a realistic and informed appraisal of a situation, based upon evidence and critical thinking. You then want to focus upon building your sense of coping power and control in relation to areas of your life that are genuinely uncontrollable. You definitely don't want to blindly believe in external powers, magic and luck, when actually you do have the power to control or influence a particular situation because there is always a cost to holding these external beliefs.

## The Stockdale Paradox

Jim Stockdale was a US naval pilot who was shot down, then held prisoner at the infamous 'Hanoi Hilton', during the Vietnam War. Throughout his eight-year imprisonment he was routinely tortured and beaten. When Stockdale was finally released, his shoulders had been wrenched from their sockets, his leg shattered and his back broken.

Despite the terrible conditions he and his men faced, he took charge and instigated many psychological survival strategies to help ease their burden, and to allow them to feel they had some control over events. He implemented a step-by-step plan for dealing with torture, so that the men could hold out from giving sensitive information away too quickly, and so that when they did eventually capitulate, they didn't feel bad about it because they had reached certain 'torture goals'. Because the men weren't allowed to talk, he created a system of communicating through tapping to reduce their sense of isolation (Collins, 2001). He also revealed intelligence information in his letters to his wife, and on at least one occasion beat himself up to the point of being disfigured, just so his captors wouldn't parade him on TV!

Stockdale, unlike many of the other prisoners, came out of the POW camp almost completely psychologically intact, and got straight on with his life. In his book 'Good to Great', Jim Collins discussed a conversation he had with Stockdale about how he coped during his period in the POW camp. Stockdale stated:

*I never doubted not only that I would get out, but also that I would prevail in the end and turn the experience into the defining event of my life, which, in retrospect, I would not trade.*

Perhaps even more interestingly, when asked who didn't make it, Stockdale is said to have replied:

*Oh, that's easy, the optimists. Oh, they were the ones who said, 'We're going to be out by Christmas.' And Christmas would come, and Christmas would go. Then they'd say, 'We're going to be out by Easter.' And Easter would come, and Easter would go. And then Thanksgiving, and then it would be Christmas again. And they died of a broken heart.*

At a first glance, it perhaps seems odd that those who were most optimistic were those who suffered most and did not survive. After all, a lot of research suggests that maintaining optimism is generally very helpful in living a successful and healthy life (see for example Scheier and Carver, 1993). According to Collins, Stockdale stated in relation to the death of the optimists:

*This is a very important lesson. You must never confuse faith that you will prevail in the end-which you can never afford to lose-with the discipline to confront the most brutal facts of your current reality, whatever they might be.*

Stockdale had absolute faith that HE had the skills and resources both to survive captivity, and to eventually escape. He didn't pray every day for the war to be over, he didn't keep hoping that someone would just appear and rescue him, he didn't lay awake at night agonising over whether friends and family back home were rallying around in support of him. He had an internal sense of power and control, and a belief that he could manage the whole situation. In particular he had a strong belief in his coping skills; he knew that he could deal with whatever was thrown at him. At the same time, he had '*the discipline to confront the most brutal facts of your current reality*' - what we call perspective.

Collins labeled this the Stockdale paradox:

> Retain faith that you will prevail in the end, regardless of the difficulties (internal sense of power and control)
>
> AND at the same time
>
> Confront the brutal facts of your reality, whatever they might be (maintain perspective)

We can understand 'The Stockdale Paradox' in terms of sense of power and control. Those prisoners who were blindly optimistic in the POW camp were likely to have had an external sense of power and control. Although they were initially positive (and probably hoping that they would be rescued soon, or that God would save them) they didn't have a firm belief in their abilities to tolerate and get through their situation (i.e. a poor belief in their coping skills). When they weren't rescued quickly and their situation didn't change, they felt really terrible and really powerless. Stockdale on the other hand was very internal, and in particular had a high belief in his coping skills. He firmly believed that he would get out of his terrible situation **but** he also strongly believed in his ability to deal with and endure his current circumstances. He knew that he didn't need to be rescued by Christmas or Easter to survive. He believed that he would deal with whatever he had to face and come out the other side ok. So whilst Stockdale had a strong belief that he would escape, he also faced up to the reality of his situation and did not just blindly hope that things would magically get better.

For our purposes I am going to alter the wording of Collins' Stockdale Paradox slightly and rename it 'Stockdale thinking'. Stockdale thinking is what you want to employ when meeting challenges in your life.

> Retain an internal sense of power and control: the belief that you have the skills to tolerate, influence, or overcome any challenges that you face
>
> AND at the same time
>
> Confront reality and maintain a realistic appraisal (perspective) of your situation

An example of doing this could be fighting or living with a major illness:

I recently met a lovely seventy-year-old man called James Reck (real name – he has kindly given me permission to tell his story). He won't mind me saying that he was, until recently, a bit of a wreck (sorry, pun too obvious to miss)! His partner had recently died and he was a heavy smoker. He went to visit one of my Thrive Consultants for some help. He, like most, completed the course in six sessions, felt much better, and stopped smoking. A couple of weeks later he was told the devastating news that he also now had lung cancer and had about six months to live.

Obviously this news completely set him back, he started smoking again, became depressed and gave up the will to live...

Actually, no he didn't. I just lied, sorry. He didn't do any of those things. He is in fact the happiest, most positive, most powerful, calmest, most thriving (and actually most charming) seventy-year-old I have ever met – DESPITE the fact that he started chemotherapy last week and has been told he now has around 12 months to live. Why is this? James understands that his cancer is happening to him (an external event), but also realises that by having strong foundations, being very positive, and having a strong immune system (internal) he can fight it as much as possible. Although he has cancer, he can, and is, exerting many coping skills. James is calmer about having lung cancer, than the average person is about receiving a parking ticket. He can't control the cancer (though he is putting in effort to fight it) but he can control how he reacts to it. Despite being told he doesn't have long to live, he is completely thriving and making the most of life.

When I made the mistake of asking him how he deals with negative thoughts and feelings, his response was to pull an ever-so-slightly confused and embarrassed face and say 'I don't create any negative thoughts and feelings'. He is thriving so much, that he doesn't even create negative thoughts and feelings! It's not that he has negative thoughts and feelings and manages them well, HE DOESN'T CREATE THEM! You can read more about James and watch his videos here: www.thriveprogramme.org/james

## Reflecting upon your sense of power and control

We've talked a lot about how having an external sense of power and control tends to mean that you reach a 'dead end' and don't even consider that you might actually have the power to influence a situation. This section is, therefore, designed to help you to consider more internal interpretations within several key areas of your life.

### Why it's not about the past

A key area in which people often have an external sense of power and control is in relation to their beliefs about the significance of their past. Most people believe that their past has a big impact upon their lives today.

- They believe that their self-esteem is created or affected by earlier events and experiences in their lives
- They believe that 'who they are' and their personality was fixed in their childhood
- They believe that their phobias, fears, anxieties or depression are caused by stressful or traumatic events from earlier on in their lives
- They believe their social anxiety or shyness was caused by embarrassing experiences from their past
- They believe that because they have had their habits for so long, that they must be deeply ingrained and very hard to change

***None of the above are true!***

Though many past events were significant and potentially traumatic at the time, they aren't a direct cause of people's problems and anxieties later on... **it's not about the past**. Earlier life events, no matter how conflicting or traumatic, have very little – if any – direct effect upon your life **now**.

Please put your pen and notepaper down, and just hold off from writing me your 'I needed twenty years of psychotherapy to sort my childhood out' complaint letter for now... just finish reading this chapter first.

No, I am not saying that those events and experiences weren't horrible, frightening, conflicting, scary, painful or life-changing... they WERE life-changing, but not for the reasons you probably think.

In one sense, there are many ways in which your upbringing and past experiences have contributed to who you are today. Your foundations were built as you interacted with the world around you. You developed particular beliefs in response to events and interactions in your life and you may have maintained these into the present. But the past itself isn't important **now**. You may have experienced traumatic and challenging events, which were frightening, conflicting and distressing BUT the really important thing to understand is that these events themselves are not having a direct effect upon you today. Traumatic experiences and memories aren't causing your symptoms in the here and now. It doesn't matter, for example, whether you developed a sense of powerlessness and low self-esteem in relation to being bullied, or your parents divorcing, or because your parents were over-controlling… All that matters is that in the here and now you have particular psychological foundations – particular beliefs about yourself and your sense of power in relation to the world around you – and it is the state of these foundations that is causing your symptoms. Most importantly, it's not difficult to change these foundations.

Let's look at a simple example: A person experiences a life-threatening car accident, whilst they were driving on a motorway, where they are injured and left with a scar on their leg. 10 years later, they have a huge phobia of driving. Every time they think of driving, get in a car, watch an accident on TV, they have a panic attack and feel terrible. To make it even worse, when they have their panic attack, they even have 'flashbacks' to the original accident.

Question: What is causing their phobia today?

You are probably thinking something along the lines of: '*well the accident was obviously really traumatic and the awful memory of the event is triggered-off somehow every time they think of driving. Then all the bottled up fear, anxiety and panic come rushing to the surface'*.

Based on my clinical experience, this is exactly the sort of thing that the majority of people believe.

Trouble is, this is completely wrong. The reality is nothing like the description above. The reason the person has their phobia of driving **today** is due to their beliefs, thinking, behaviours and habits in relation to driving **today**, such as 'driving is terrifying' or 'I'm a terrible driver'. Of course, the person's experience of the original incident contributed to the **initial** development of these unhelpful beliefs, thinking and behaviour. It is important to realise, though, that many people have been involved in life-threatening and potentially traumatic road accidents and many of these do not have a fear or phobia of driving. A person may interpret and respond to the event in a way that is powerful and resilient. I was just recently talking to someone who was telling me about a major car accident he had a few years previously, where he was happily driving again just a few days later. The state of a person's psychological foundations at the time and the way in which they consequently process and interpret the experience is critical. It's also important to realise that, even if a person does experience the event in a way that leads to a fear or phobia, at any time subsequently, they could change their limiting beliefs, thinking and behaviours in relation to driving (they don't because they feel powerless and do not have the insights and resources to do so).

Perhaps you are thinking 'Oh but that is just about a car accident, surely bigger, more traumatic events must be different'? No is the answer. They aren't. Not being bullied at school, not being abused, not being in a war zone and not having to deal with the death of a loved one. Not in any of these cases are the traumatic events or memories from the past directly affecting people today. That's not to say that people aren't affected – they do sometimes have terrible symptoms – but it's not about the past events themselves or the memories of such events *per se*. It's all about the world-views and self-beliefs that a person developed in relation to these events and the fact that they have maintained these into the present day.

Maybe that makes some sense to you but perhaps you are finding it hard to really believe that traumatic or conflicting memories of the past aren't impacting upon you today? Perhaps whenever you remember a particular past event you still feel scared, distressed and powerless?

To understand why 'it's not about the past' you need to understand two things:

1) Memory is entirely constructive

2) We do not store or bottle-up emotions

Think back to your wedding day, your last birthday celebration, a recent holiday, or just a nice time out with friends. You can probably bring to mind snapshots or a video of the event? In relation to important celebrations, you have probably browsed through 'snapshots' or watched – in your mind – a 'video' of the event dozens of times?

Trouble is, we don't actually store pictures, snapshots or videos in our brains. We don't actually have a huge mental filing cabinet full to the brim of photos and videos from our earlier lives. It FEELS like we do, but we don't. Ochsner and Schacter (2000) have stated that *"Cognitive psychology and neuroscience have impressively demonstrated that memory is an **active** process that involves **interpretation** and **construction** at all stages."* So, contrary to what it feels like, we DON'T have a photo or video vault in our brains that accurately stores all the events and experiences in our lives so that they can come back to haunt us at a later date. We reconstruct our memories.

You construct the photo or video – you re-create it, every time you think about it. When we experience something, we encode and store bits of information in lots of different areas of the brain in the connections between neurons (nerve cells). These little bits of encoded data are really **very** little bits. A brain neuron is about a thousand times smaller than a millimetre. No one neuron in the brain contains all the information needed to reconstruct a memory. Lots of neural networks in different areas of the brain are activated.

When you later recall an experience, you draw together **some of** the encoded bits of data and 'fill in the gaps' around them. It's like having a partially completed jigsaw puzzle, and filling in the blank spaces with what you think probably goes there.

Lots of factors affect how we encode and remember events. Firstly, things like how the person was feeling at the time of the experience, what belief systems they held then, what thinking styles they were using at the time, what sort of mood they were in, all affect how the event is encoded. You then have to factor in the same sort of variables at the time they reconstruct the memory.

A person's current emotional and physical state can influence they way in which they remember an event. For example, one study (Eich, Reeves, Jaeger, & Graff-Radford, 1985) found that people currently experiencing high levels of headache pain tended to recall the past headaches as having been more severe than they actually rated them at the time. People's current goals and desires can also alter their recall. Ochsner & Schacter (2000) have highlighted that: *"The constructive recall of affective events may at times be led by the desire to remember the emotional past in a way that helps create a particular view of the self in the present".* We actually see these effects quite frequently in our clinics. Imagine someone with significant anxiety issues or depression that are having a very limiting effect upon their life, and they, understandably, feel that their life is shit. When this person looks back to their past, to the memories and events that they believe caused their current anxieties and unhappiness, they are likely to construct, view and experience those memories as more emotional, more conflicting, and perhaps more damaging than they actually really were at the time. Just as they view current events through shit-tinted spectacles, their memories are likely to also be viewed through these glasses.

Let's also have a look at a hypothetical example. Someone might have felt fantastic at the time of their wedding, believed whole-heartedly about the sanctity of marriage, and felt that the world was a wonderful place... When thinking about the event a few weeks afterwards, their experience of remembering is still likely to be happy and rosy. Ten years later, they now look back at the experience, whilst going through a turbulent divorce and suffering from depression. Do you think the memory will be the same? Of course it won't. Their experience of remembering the event will be entirely different to when they thought about it two weeks after their wedding.

I think it's probably safe to say that most people also believe that we 'bottle-up' or store emotions with our memories, somewhere in our brains. Again, this is not true at all. We don't store emotions anywhere. All emotions we experience, we are creating **now** in the present moment. It may feel that emotions are 'bubbling to the surface', that you 'have a lot of anger bottled up', that you 'have all these feelings you need to express', or that you have 'buried the feelings deep down', but this is not how your mind works. Any emotion that you feel is formed in response to the way in which you interpret a situation, event or recollection. If you have a phobia of dogs, and react with panic and anxiety after being barked at by a dog today, your reaction stems from the beliefs you hold about dogs TODAY, your psychological foundations TODAY, and how well you are managing your mindset TODAY. It's not about the past! As Ochsner and Schacter have stated (2000) *"Our initial interpretation of a given event's emotional significance need not be the last one we ever have, and how we encoded it initially need not determine how we react to it at recall"*. Again, the emotions you create in relation to any event or memory are related to your current belief systems and thinking styles.

Let me give you an example. If you have been unfortunate enough to have experienced the death of a loved one, you will understand this easily. I imagine my experience of this will have been much like your own. After your loved-one dies, you understandably create lots of emotions and lots of pain. At that point, any memories of your loved one are likely to be distressing – even though the experiences themselves may have been fantastic, such as going on holiday or going out for a meal. But, because you are now viewing these experiences through the lens of your loved one having died, you feel emotional and unhappy when you recall these experiences. When you get to the point of acceptance and you've resolved the conflict, you feel totally different, at peace with yourself. At this point you can look back upon the life of the deceased and you find it much easier to think about the happy times.

## Religious beliefs

At some point it becomes necessary to talk properly about the potentially sensitive topic of religion. It is not my intention to offend anyone here, but to avoid the topic of religion for fear of upsetting someone would be overlooking one of the most important factors in helping you and would go against one of the major principles of The Thrive Programme.

As you have seen, having an internal sense of power and control is very important for psychological and physical wellbeing. One of the key aspects of many religions is a belief in the presence of a 'higher power' or god, i.e. a powerful external force. This does not necessarily exclude the possibility of having a relatively internal sense of power and control. One of my friends has dedicated religious beliefs but also feels generally powerful and in control. Some people with religious beliefs, however, have no belief in their own personal power at all. If you believe that your life is entirely 'in the hands of God' and, rather than taking any personal responsibility or action, you merely wait for God's will, then you are likely to feel quite powerless and helpless. This tends to result in an inability to adapt, make changes and deal with problems. Instead, believing that God enables you to make choices and take responsibility gives you personal control and empowers you. If you believe that God is acting through you or strengthening your inner resources, then you are likely to be more resilient and positive.

If you do have religious beliefs, it may be helpful for you to take a look at how your religion impacts upon your life. Is your religion a positive factor that enables you to take responsibility and make changes? Or have you relinquished all responsibility and control, believing that you have no personal power?

How did you come to have religious beliefs? I know it might sound like a daft question, but clearly not everyone with faith had an epiphany one day and found God. I was recently running a seminar in Ireland and I asked the delegates a question: 'did you choose to believe in God?' About forty out of the fifty people there said 'yes'. I asked those who said yes to think back to when and how it happened, none of them could.

When asked, 'well if you didn't CHOOSE to become religious, where did the belief come from?' Delegates started talking about their childhood: growing up in a very religious environment, going to a religious school, going to church each week, being told to pray, reciting the Lord's Prayer every day, having religious icons and pictures on the walls at home, being threatened with 'Hell' as a punishment for being naughty, being teased with 'Heaven' if they behaved well. Basically, the majority of delegates at the seminar hadn't really thought about this before. They had never really appreciated the effects of their upbringing upon their beliefs.

I had correspondence from a couple of the delegates after the seminar, who told me that they had given up their religious beliefs after realising that it wasn't their choice at all. It's probable that the vast majority of religious people around the world are religious because they were brought up to be so, and NOT because they chose to be so.

I am not suggesting here that you have to give up your religious beliefs. But I am suggesting that you want to make the choice surrounding whether or not to hold these beliefs. You do not need to have a completely internal sense of power and control. This gives you plenty of opportunity to keep any religious beliefs you wish – once you have given it some thought and made that choice for yourself. Reflecting upon your beliefs and making that decision, in whichever direction, is about giving yourself the power and control, rather than just automatically believing in something because of your upbringing.

I recently took a very strict Christian lady through Thrive, and she was a wonderful client. She challenged all her beliefs, overcame the problems/symptoms she was consulting for and felt fantastic. Not only did she maintain her faith but it was also stronger and clearer for her post Thrive. (On a side note, her priest was so impressed with the changes she had made to her life, that he is currently sponsoring her to undertake my 'Thrive Consultant' training course – so that she may help some of the other parishioners.)

### A lack of belief in your own capabilities and capacities

A person's external sense of power and control is often related to a lack of belief in their own capabilities and capacities. Very often this lack of self-belief is linked to a person's self-esteem, which we will be discussing in depth in the next chapter.

For now, you want to start challenging powerless beliefs about your capabilities. Are you really as incompetent or powerless as you are telling yourself? Aim to evaluate the situation realistically. Even in instances where you do not **currently** have the skills and capabilities needed to achieve a particular goal or aim, you want to remind yourself that you can develop them. You want to examine disempowering external beliefs such as 'people are naturally sporty' or 'intelligence is all down to a person's genes' or 'personality is fixed'.

The actions at the end of this chapter will help you to start building your self-efficacy and confidence in your capabilities.

### Powerful others

A final common area of externality is the belief that powerful others (partners, parents, friends, doctors, politicians etc.) determine the course of your life. I'm not going to say anything about this here – because there is too much to say! The way in which we interpret and respond to social pressures has a whole chapter to itself. This is coming up very soon in chapter 5 and, as you work your way through this book, you will learn how to interpret and respond to social pressures in an empowering way.

# Desire for Control

It is really important to recognise that your sense of power and control (the extent to which you BELIEVE you can control your life) and **desire for control** (how much control you WANT or feel you NEED over your life) are not the same thing. A great deal of research demonstrates that these are different concepts (for example: Burger, 1984; Dembroski *et al.*, 1984; and Gebhardt *et al.*, 2002). Most of us desire some control over our lives. As we have already mentioned, a sense of powerlessness is a huge contributing factor to depression, phobias and anxiety. Some people (you!), however, attempt to get a lot more control than others!

Desiring control over your life is a good thing, if it is teamed up with an **internal sense of power and control**. People that generally like to be in control and, additionally, believe that they do have the power to shape their lives, are likely to engage in active problem-solving behaviour and to positively seek out situations where they are in charge.

Those with a **healthy** desire for control **always** have a strong belief in their coping skills (p. 35). They believe that they have the skills and resources to cope with situations that are outside their direct influence. This means that although they like to be in control, they are not a 'control freak'. When you feel powerful and capable of dealing with challenges, even when you have a healthy desire for control and like to take charge of your life, you can afford to 'let go' sometimes. You don't feel the need to try to control every little thing, because you know that you can deal with external situations.

If you have a high desire for control and an **external sense of power and control**, you are likely to find yourself struggling. **Desiring** a great deal of control over your life while believing that you are powerless results in people anxiously attempting to control every insignificant aspect of their lives that they can; they become a **'control freak'**! As a result, people in this **'external high-desirability-of control'** category can often ***appear*** to have a lot of control over their lives, when in reality they feel quite powerless.

When someone has an **excessively high desire for control** (i.e. they try to control everything around them) it is **always** because they feel powerless in some way. People who have an excessively high desire for control **can** sometimes have a relatively internal sense of direct influence, but they **never** have a strong belief in their coping skills. Their attempts at over-control occur because they do not believe that they have the skills and resources to deal with certain situations. This means that they will often go out of their way to avoid feared scenarios, or may rely heavily on 'external' help in situations that they perceive as challenging. They may be very controlling in their inter-personal relationships.

Despite their efforts, the extreme attempts at control do not provide much relief nor really help the person to actually be in control of their lives in any meaningful sense. In fact, many *obsessive* rituals or actions (more later) may make the person feel temporarily more in control, but at the same time contribute to an **external sense of power and control** due to the *magical beliefs* that many of these acts are based upon. Here, I am not talking about someone who feels they need to vacuum the house every few days to keep it tidy (in control). I am talking about the person who scores highly on the *obsessional thinking* quiz (Kelly, 2008) mentioned in Chapter 6 'Unhelpful Thinking Styles'. Many of the avoidance behaviours and over-controlling actions carried out by 'control freaks' also reinforce their low sense of coping skills. By desperately attempting to control everything they can, they are essentially telling themselves 'I can't cope if I'm not completely in control.' This only heightens their sense of powerlessness and, in turn, further increases their desire for control.

One research study (Burger, 1984) found that depression was strongly related to a belief that life is controlled by chance (external locus), regardless of how much control people **desired**. Those depressed people who felt powerless and had a **high desire for control**, however, were significantly more likely to have had suicidal thoughts.

A good example of situations where someone is attempting to gain some control, but is inadvertently propagating a sense of powerlessness, is superstition. You might think that people who engage in self-oriented superstitions (such as touching wood, avoiding walking under a ladder or carrying out other protective rituals) are showing an internal sense of power and control, because they feel that their actions are controlling an outcome. In actual fact, although engaging in superstitious acts may temporarily make a person feel a bit more in control, they are really just reinforcing an external sense of power and control by emphasising the external factors of luck or chance. By engaging in superstitions, you are not looking at ways in which you can really influence your situation, but instead appealing to 'magical external forces'. This link between externality and self-oriented superstition is supported by research by Peterson (1978) who found that a belief in self-oriented superstition was linked to externality on Rotter's locus of control scale.

Common superstitions include not walking under a ladder, touching wood or crossing fingers when you want to be lucky, avoiding black cats crossing your path, being careful not to smash a mirror (and therefore avoiding seven years bad luck), throwing salt over your left shoulder if you have spilled some, saluting a single magpie, saying 'bless you' to someone who has sneezed (to prevent an evil spirit entering their body during a moment of weakness), saying 'that Scottish play' instead of 'Macbeth' inside a theatre (believing the only time you are able to do this without bringing bad luck to the play and the actors, is when the name 'Macbeth' is in a line in the play), avoiding the number 13, wearing or carrying a 'good luck charm', saying 'break a leg' instead of 'good luck' to a person about to perform, and the most obvious one: praying to your god.

All of these age-old superstitions, like 'old wives tales', were created to make people feel that they had some control over seemingly unknown or unexplainable events. Now that science and logic have explained away superstitions and magical beliefs, it's very surprising to find just how many people still are superstitious.

Prof. Richard Wiseman conducted a superstition survey in 2003, during the National Science Week, 2068 volunteers took part. Here are some of Wiseman's findings:

> *The current levels of superstitious behaviour and beliefs in the UK are surprisingly high, even among those with a scientific background. Touching wood is the most popular UK superstition, followed by crossing fingers, avoiding ladders, not smashing mirrors, carrying a lucky charm and having superstitious beliefs about the number 13...*
>
> *...People who tend to worry about life are far more superstitious than others - 50% of worriers were very/somewhat superstitious, compared to just 24% of non-worriers. People who have a strong need for control in their lives are far more superstitious than others - 42% of people indicating high need for control were very/somewhat superstitious, compared to just 22% of people indicating low need for control. People who have a low tolerance for ambiguity are far more superstitious than those with a high tolerance - 38% of those with low tolerance were very/somewhat superstitious compared to just 30% of those with high tolerance.*
>
> (Wiseman, 2003)

Have a look at your DFC score on your TQ Report. What did you score? People who have a very strong desire for control have always got an external sense of power and control and particularly a poor belief in their coping skills. If you believed you had the skills and resources to cope with anything in life, why would you need to over-control and avoid certain situations?

## The impact of your desire for control

As we have briefly mentioned already, the effects of desire for control depend, however, upon whether or not a person has an internal or an external sense of power and control. This is particularly important to understand in relation to overcoming challenging situations, as many people with a high desire for control put in a lot of effort into controlling situations that they perceive to be challenging but only end up becoming more external and feeling more anxious because of the nature of their efforts.

The following diagram shows how a person with a medium to high desire for control would respond to a challenging situation, depending upon whether they have an internal or external sense of power and control.

**In a difficult, uncomfortable or challenging situation...**

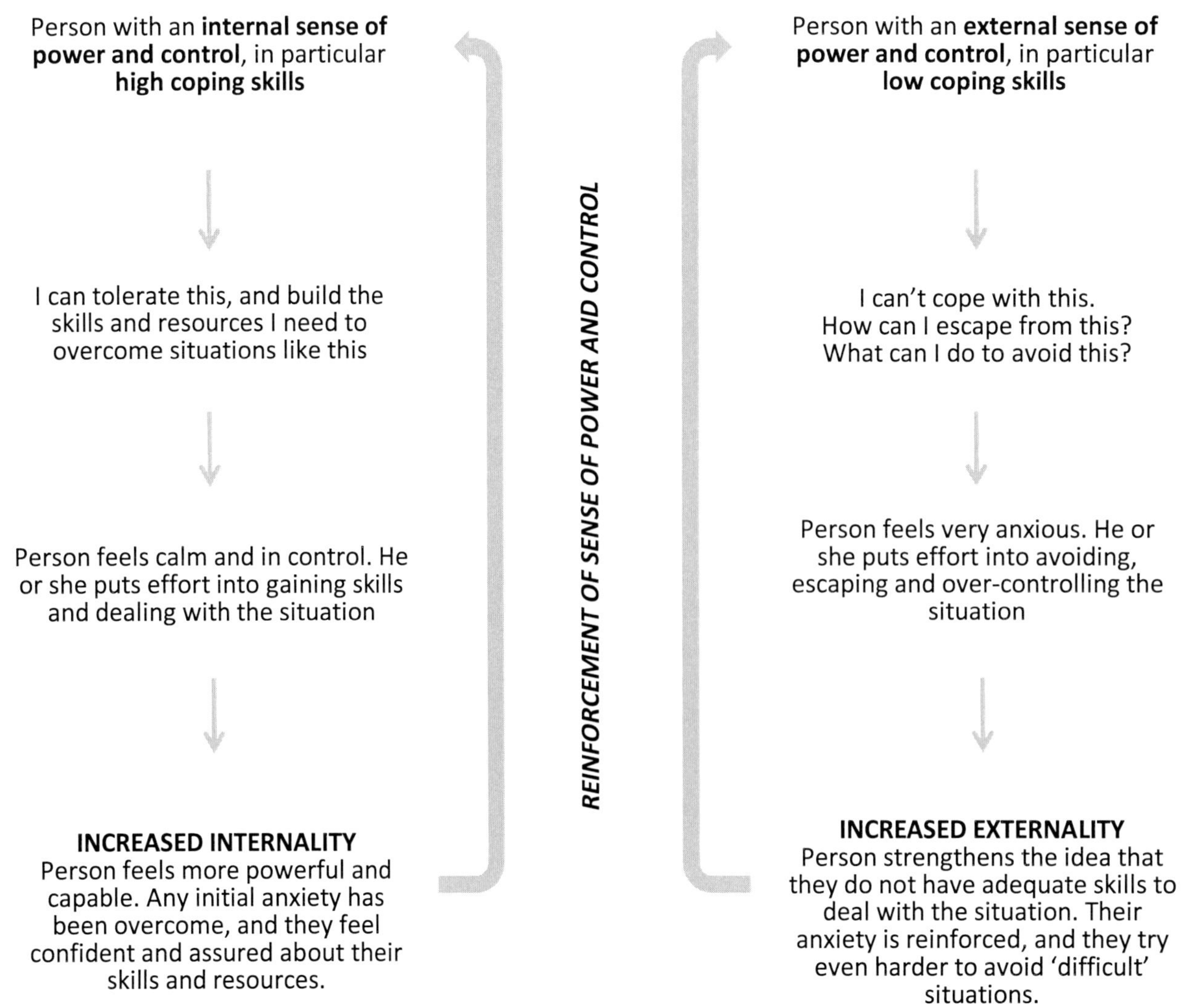

## 'Want' versus 'fear'

You have probably never heard of Émile Coué, but he knew rather a lot about you. Coué was studying 'the mind' around the same time as some of his well-known contemporaries, such as Sigmund Freud and Joseph Breuer. One of Coué's main interests was 'suggestion' and 'self' or 'auto' suggestion. Coué also formulated something that we call 'Coué's Law'.

*Coué's Law*, or more fully, ***Coué's Law of reversed effort***, is a pretty significant psychological discovery, but also, strangely, one of the least well-known. Coué's Law states, that **'When the imagination and the will are in conflict, the imagination invariably gains the day'** (Brooks, 1922).

So what does that even mean? Psychology, like all other sciences, possibly due to the number of obsessive people the subject attracts, seems hell-bent on creating a hundred different names for the same thing, then making these names incredibly hard to understand, and even harder to write! It's really quite simple to understand though:

Coué's Law relates to the times where you **want** to achieve a particular outcome, and are perhaps even putting lots of effort into making that outcome happen, but you, additionally, **fear** that an alternative negative outcome might happen. You might, for example, be really determined to present a speech at a wedding in a confident and calm manner BUT you also keep worrying that it might go wrong, imagining that you might forget your words or stutter, visualising blushing or everyone laughing at you. Your 'inner voice', that little devil always sitting on your shoulder, your fears, worries, doubts, your 'imagination', conflicts with what you would actually like to achieve.

You could be stating determinedly what you WANT to happen ('I'm going to go on a diet and lose weight'), then your inner voice replies with what you FEAR will happen: *'you won't stick to it - you never stick to a diet'.*

'It's going to be a lovely day today' = *'no it's not, it's going to be really stressful'*
'I am going to get that job' = *'you're not good enough to do that job, don't be daft'*
'I am going to go on a diet' = *'there's no point, you never stick to a diet anyway'*

Your fears and anxieties can often win against your desires and goals. A good way to illustrate this is to pretend that you are walking along a plank of wood about thirty centimetres wide, suspended about three metres off the ground. You know that you can do this, it's easy. Just keep putting one foot in front of the other. Walking this plank requires no special skills - anyone could do it, IF the plank were on the ground. So you are walking along this plank, feeling confident, feeling positive, all you have to do is walk to the end (say, ten feet). Half way along the plank though, you glance down at the ground, and suddenly your heart starts to beat faster as your startled inner voice says, 'God that's a long way down, I would really hurt myself if I fell now!!' Almost as you are thinking this, your legs start to tremble a little bit, and this trembling is fed back to your brain as 'I am going to fall'. The more you become 'fascinated' with the idea of falling, the more you shake and tremble - your body reacts on your mind, your mind reacts upon your body, and then you fall. You fall, because you imagine yourself falling. If you don't imagine falling, you don't fall.

There was a famous Derren Brown episode on television (search for it on YouTube), where he asks Henry, the world's top skipping-on-a-high-wire-artist who has never fallen off the high-wire whilst performing, 'Can you perform your act for us now, but just make sure you don't wobble and fall off?' At the same time Derren says this a huge airbag is inflated under the high wire (Henry, like most high-wire artists, wouldn't be seen dead using an airbag), which clearly makes Henry question either his confidence, or Derren's ability to 'psyche him out'. Either way, the world champion and Guinness record holder falls off into the airbag, to his great surprise.

Another example of Coué's Law in action is the Ouija board. Many teenagers 'play' with Ouija boards at some time or other, quite often in the days after watching a horror film, and many adults use one to make contact with dead people (or so they believe). Basically, an Ouija board is a piece of board about the same size and shape as a Monopoly board. Instead of famous streets and train stations though, it has the alphabet and a few words printed on it. The people using/playing with the board have one finger gently placed on a piece of triangular plastic that rests on top of the board. This flat plastic triangle has a hole in the centre so that you can read the letters and words that 'it' spells out as 'it' moves freely around the board, driven by the spirits of dead people. Forget the teenagers playing - they are just teenagers playing. The adults who want and believe they are contacting the dead though, are *deadly* serious about it! The idea is that you rest your finger on the triangle VERY lightly so as you couldn't possibly 'cheat' and move it consciously. The triangle is then moved around the board by the dead people, spelling out stuff like 'the wedding ring is under the bed' or 'don't worry, Granny is in a happy place now'.

The people using the board would swear on their lives that they are not (knowingly) moving the triangle. In fact, they could sit and PASS a polygraph (lie-detector) test - because they are not lying, they really BELIEVE that they are not moving the triangle around. Think of it in terms of Coué's Law though. Consciously, they don't want to 'cheat', they really believe that this manufactured piece of cardboard and plastic can contact dead people, so, they really WANT to hold their fingers perfectly still on the triangle in order not to influence it in any way, BUT (and it's a very big but) they FEAR or IMAGINE 'a spirit coming through' and the triangle shooting all over the place and spelling out fascinating words and phrases. The people 'using' the board don't even know that they are moving the triangle around. (Ironically, the Ouija board wasn't invented by a spiritual person wanting to find a way of contacting the dead. It was, in fact, invented as a parlour game to find out what people were thinking about unconsciously! The trademark owner, and game producer, is Hasbro - who also produce 'Mr. Potato Head', 'Twister' and 'Monopoly' - to name just a few.)

A final non-therapeutic example could be when sports people 'choke' and lose their game/race. If you were living in the U.K. during the summer of 1993 and you were a sports fan, you couldn't have missed the year's Wimbledon tennis final between Steffi Graf and Jana Novotna. Graf was the favourite to win, but by the final game Novotna was ahead, and was outplaying Graf big time. This was going to be one of those amazing 'horse comes out from the back of the pack to win the race' type situations that we all love. But, with just minutes to go, Novotna 'choked'. 'Choking' is what athletes and sportsmen call it when they panic due to pressure, and make silly and disastrous mistakes. Novotna was poised to win the biggest and most prestigious tennis competition in the world, she suddenly realised it, and Coué's law took over and made sure she lost. She made mistake, after mistake, after mistake, as if she were in some kind of daze. Only after she went up to collect the 'loser's trophy' from the Duchess of Kent and burst out crying on her shoulder, did the enormity of what she had done sink in. Interestingly, it's worth noting another of Novotna's behaviours: she is very superstitious. She wouldn't let her mother attend the first two of her Wimbledon matches because she thought it would be 'bad luck'. Think about 'bad luck' for a minute, and you'll realise it immediately invokes Coué's Law – what's another way of saying 'bad luck'? Try: 'If I do this thing, something bad might happen'.

In a therapeutic setting we often see Coué's Law having a devastating effect on people. It's not about negative thinking, which can and does affect people. This 'law' specifically relates to when you want a particular outcome but you fear that something else could happen. A classic example would be premature ejaculation: the man initially feels confident and expects success, but thinks/worries/imagines something along the lines of 'What if I don't last?' or 'I hope it will work properly this time', which fulfils Coué's Law to a 'T'.

What about the vocal tics of a Tourette's sufferer? What do YOU think is going through the mind of a

Tourette's sufferer just before they completely embarrass themselves by shouting out 'bollocks' (or similar) at the top of their voice? Could their thought pattern be **'whatever you do, DON'T shout out the rudest thing you could possibly think of - you would look really stupid!**' The more they think about it, the more they worry it will happen, until sooner or later their fuse blows and they go 'pop'.

I've just spent four sessions going through this book with Maddy, a very positive and friendly lady in her early sixties who lives in Cambridge. Before working through this book with me, the poor lady hadn't slept properly for forty years. Forty years! I'm shattered and grumpy if I have one bad night's sleep and Maddy had suffered from chronic insomnia, not sleeping for more than a couple of hours each night, for forty years. You can only imagine the impact this would have had upon her life. She had tried numerous techniques and interventions over the years to try and help her sleep, but nothing really helped. Coué's Law was the reason Maddy hadn't slept properly. There was a good reason forty years ago why she didn't sleep for a few days, then that cause went away, but not before she had started to worry about not getting any sleep.

She would get ready for bed, determined to have a good night, but would then lie in bed thinking '**God I hope I sleep tonight, I'm going to be in a terrible state tomorrow if I don't**'. The moment she thought that she was doomed not to sleep that night. She had been thinking more or less the same way for forty years. Maddy's testimonial can be viewed on Amazon, or the Thrive website.

Don't believe me?

Don't believe that your imagination is THAT powerful, and that it can overrule what you determinedly want to occur? Make sure you complete the following exercise.

## Exercise: Chevreul's pendulum

Many people find it hard to complete this exercise when another person is watching them, as performance anxiety kicks in and they feel unable to relax! So it is probably best for you to find some time to do this exercise alone.

You will need:

- a piece of card or paper, about 40cm square
- a knitting needle or 30-40 cm long twig
- about 30 cm of cotton (string is too thick)
- a wedding ring/small weight to suspend on the cotton, from the end of the rod.

Draw a big circle and two dissecting lines on the card, as per the following diagram. Label the four ends of the lines as A, B, C, and D.

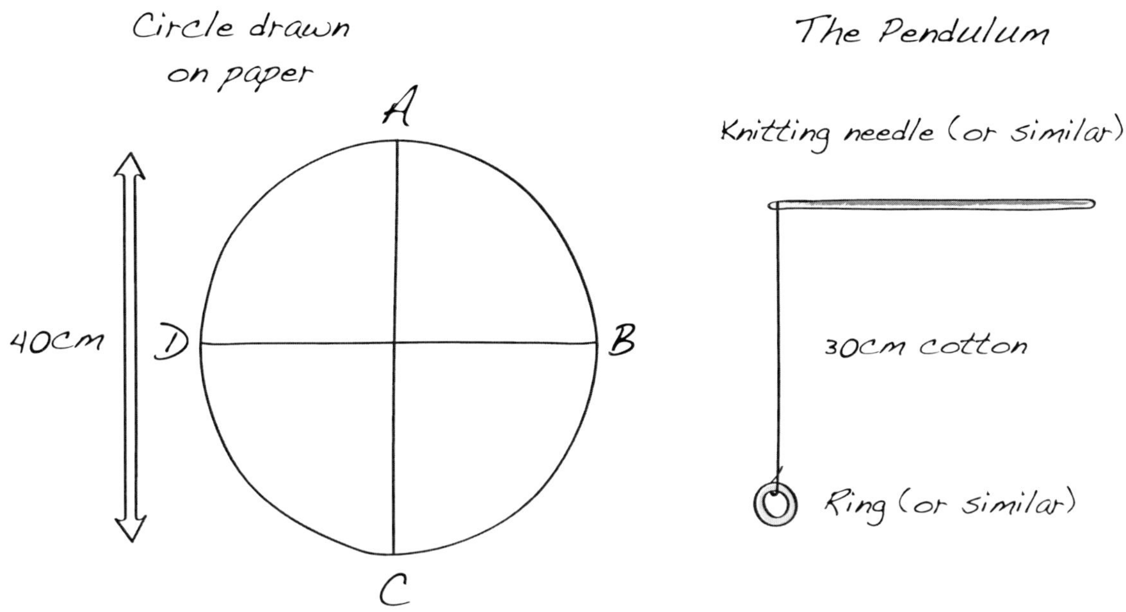


Now put the diagram on the floor at your feet and stand above the paper with the 'pendulum' held like a tiny fishing rod. Line up the bob with the centre cross of the diagram as you look down upon them. With your hand and arm as still as you can hold them, simply concentrate on one line of swing along that line. The less you think of the bob and the more you concentrate on the line - the more the bob will swing in that direction. Change your concentration to line B-D and in due course the bob will dutifully follow. Likewise, change your concentration to the full circle A, B, C, D and, sure enough, the pendulum will commence a circular clockwise action (anti-clockwise if you concentrate on the sequence D, C, B, A).

Repeat the whole exercise a few times and prove to yourself that, like Pavlov's dogs, your subconscious mind is becoming trained by repetition, and becomes more adept each time.

Finally, attempt to cancel the effects by intervention of your conscious will - by saying to yourself that the action will not happen, whilst still imagining that the pendulum is swinging - and watch yourself repeatedly fail to stop it.

## Why do people fear things going wrong?

So why don't we all 'naturally' imagine what we WANT to happen anyway - why do some of us focus our attention on what might go wrong instead?

Basically, those who worry about ' 'what might go wrong' are those with a strong desire for control and a poor belief in their coping skills. They are ironically, trying to get more control of the situation by looking at the worst-case scenario. If I know in advance what might go wrong, I won't be shocked or startled if the worst-case does happen. In other words, the person is attempting to get an idea of whether they could cope with the situation if it all went wrong. This is a great idea in theory, if people were able to calmly and dispassionately identify the worst-case scenario in order that they could be totally prepared for a situation. Great for fighter-pilots, firemen and, perhaps, politicians. If, however, your belief in your coping skills is poor, knowing what the worst-case scenario is just means you have so much more to worry and fret about!

## Visualisation or rehearsal

A great way to avoid this situation is easy: you want to be training your imagination so that you are always imagining/rehearsing/anticipating what you WANT to happen, and NOT what you fear will happen. What you imagine or rehearse happening in your mind is incredibly powerful.

Maybe you have children, or maybe you can think back to when you were a child at school, where like me, you took part in a school play at some time or other? If not, you at least remember other children in a play? Good. Do you remember how the play came about? Did the teacher just say one day, 'Children, tonight we are going to put on a play'? Probably not. Almost certainly what happened was that the teachers announced the school play and asked for volunteers to take part. Once all the parts had been allocated, everyone read through the script together. After that everyone took their scripts home to learn their parts. After that came lots of rehearsals, then rehearsals on the stage, then rehearsals on the stage in full costume, then rehearsals on the stage in full costume with a small audience, then, finally, the first proper performance. The important lesson here is that you practised and rehearsed exactly what you wanted to happen, and you kept on practising and rehearsing and visualising what you wanted to happen, so that 'on the night' - bar Santa getting stuck up the chimney - it all went swimmingly well. You had anticipated it happening so many times, that on the night, it just happened. All you need to do in life is what you did when you were at school (NO, not that!), rehearse what you want to happen 'on the night'.

Maddy, mentioned above, for example, wanted to have a good night's sleep, but imagined tossing and turning. She learned to imagine having a wonderful night's sleep, and wake up in the morning feeling completely refreshed. If you want to walk along a scaffolding plank and not fall off, don't look down and imagine falling! Look ahead and imagine walking easily and calmly along the plank, stepping off the other end feeling completely calm. If you have a vocal tic, imagine shouting out things like 'daffodils', 'world peace', or 'love you' - you won't offend anyone, and you might make some new friends! If you consider yourself clumsy, imagine walking carefully and easily up the caravan steps, carrying the hot coffee without spilling it, eating your spaghetti without getting it down your new jumper, and weeing into the toilet without getting it all over the seat!

There is an abundance of evidence that supports just how effective rehearsing or 'positively visualising' something happening, really is:

Martin and Hall (1995) were studying how much mental imagery could enhance motivation. They found that people who practised 'performance imagery' (positive visualisation) spent significantly more time practising their skills (in this case, golf), set higher goals for themselves, had more realistic expectations, and adhered more to their training programme. Driskell *et al.* (1994), were studying whether 'mental practice enhances performance'. The research showed that *'mental practice had a positive and significant effect on performance'*. Blair and Leyshon (1993) were studying the effects of positive imagery on footballers and they found that *'Performance on the post-test, as measured by response time, revealed a significant improvement for both the skilled and novice players in the imagery group'*. Liu et *al.* (2004) were researching the effects of mental imagery on patients relearning how to use their limbs and muscles effectively after suffering a stroke. They found that: *'Patients engaged in mental imagery-based intervention showed better relearning of both trained and untrained tasks compared with the control group'*.

Proof of just how negative your thinking and visualising has been about a certain subject or situation, is how unusual it feels to visualise it in any other way. Let me give you an example. I have worked with many people who have had a fear of flying (including myself!) and when asked how they imagine a particular flight is going to be for them, they usually say something like, 'It's horrible and frightening and I feel completely out of control. The plane is bumping all over the place and people are getting thrown around and then it crashes and we all die'.

I then say to them 'Ok, what would it be like if this was your easiest and best flight ever?' They reply, 'What do you mean?' (They don't even understand the question!), I say, 'Ok, imagine you have landed in Geneva (or wherever) and you have had such a great flight that you phone me up to thank me for helping you. I then ask you, what was great about the flight?' Client now looks puzzled, so I ask again 'What, specifically happened during your flight that made it great?' The response is 'I don't know'.

The point I am making is that the client had NEVER thought about flying in a positive way, and found it really strange to imagine flying as anything other than terrifying. It's not surprising that they had a fear of flying, if they only ever visualised and anticipated flying to be a terrifying experience. This resistance to seeing something as 'easy' when you are used to seeing it as 'hard', is called 'cognitive dissonance'. It's as if your brain is saying to you, 'hmm, I'm sure this used to be terrifying'. The sufferer is so used to being terrified of flying, so used to feeling powerless in relation to their fear of flying, that whenever they think of flying they immediately feel completely helpless. The great thing is though, that the person with a fear of flying doesn't need to challenge their fear whilst they are terrified, stuck on board a 747 heading for Australia. They can challenge and rid themselves of their fear of flying from the comfort of their own living room by visualising/imagining what they want to happen, rather than what they fear will happen.

The dissonance that I described above disappears very quickly once you start to positively imagine/visualise a different outcome. What you need to remember is that the first couple of times you visualise something new, it might feel a little strange and unusual (dissonance). However, if you continue through this 'rough patch', the new visualisations and feelings will become much easier very quickly. After a little while your default response to the issue you have visualised will always be positive.

# How powerful do you feel? – Exercises & ACTION!s

## Creating a more internal sense of power and control

Remember your 'sense of power and control', is not your 'actual' power and control. It refers to the beliefs you hold about the different situations and events in life, and not your actual skills. You are very likely to be far more powerful and in control than you currently believe. This section is going to start to show you how to develop a more internal sense of power and control.

### ACTION! Re-thinking your quiz answers

Locate your SPACE quiz answers (towards the end of your TQ Report) and highlight any statement which you scored less than three points for. Now, go through all these marked/external answers and find five that you think it would be easiest to change your beliefs about. For example, you may have thought 'when you read it in black and white, it does sound daft that I read horoscopes - how can they possibly affect my life?' In which case, as you are already beginning to doubt your earlier belief, this might be an easy one to change. So put a big circle around the statement. Now find another four. Once you have your five, mark them from one to five in order of easiest to hardest.

Now, pick your number one, and start working on it. Think about how you came to have the belief. Did you develop it yourself, or pick it up from a parent or friend? Did you start to 'think that way' after a period of stress or uncertainty in your life? Think about the implications of your belief. In the horoscope example above, do you REALLY believe that the current position of the planets, millions and millions of miles away, is actually going to affect your day? Have a realistic appraisal of your belief, look at the evidence for and against, go onto the Thrive website and read some of the research papers. The previous section helps you to do this in relation to some of the main areas in which people often hold external beliefs.

In other words, come to some intellectual and scientific understanding of your belief. If you still want to keep the belief, then keep it. Bear in mind that ideally you want to lower your sense of power and control score to five or below. If you have changed your mind about the belief, make sure you remind yourself every time you come across it, and remind yourself of the evidence for/against it. In the example above, every time you come across a horoscope in a magazine or newspaper, remind yourself what the whole thing is about and turn the page. Don't read it 'just in case' or because 'it's still interesting even though I don't believe it', you want to be actively promoting an internal sense of power and control, not dancing on the thin line between externality and internality! Now go to number two on your list.

Once you have completed this process, pick another five external statements and go through the process again.

### ACTION! Thinking more internally

You've already completed an exercise on noticing your inner voice (chapter 1), so you are starting to have a good idea about your thought processes. In the next chapter you're going to be shown the very best way to boost your self-esteem quickly, and this will also have a profound effect upon your locus of control - making it more internal. On top of this, you want to consciously start to think and process experiences more internally. Start to think and act the way an internal person does.

1. Think: 'I can do this, I've got the skills to get through this, I can make this work, I've worked through this before and I can do it again, this is a molehill, not a mountain, there is a way around this situation, I just need to apply myself'.

2. When you are in a situation think to yourself 'I know the way in which I would have viewed this in the past, but what is the reality?' For example, if you are feeling panicky in the dentist's chair/on a plane/ at the doctor's/ up a tall building etc. tell yourself 'this anxiety is not happening TO me, I am creating this anxiety myself. I can calm myself down, I can do this'.

## ACTION! Challenge yourself

One of the very best ways in which to create a more internal sense of power and control is to challenge yourself and process the whole experience internally. By setting yourself and overcoming a challenge, or achieving an aim, you are building up evidence that you DO have control over the direction your life takes and showing yourself that you are a capable and successful person.

A challenge or aim can be anything you want to do or achieve, regardless of what that is. You could, for example, take up a new hobby/sport/pastime or work towards overcoming something you find a little scary. Getting fit is a great way to increase internality and any of the sports that increase your body-confidence (like martial arts, yoga, pilates, using the gym) are really good. Undertaking combined physical and mental challenges: long-distance running, triathlons, assault courses, endurance sports etc. can also be particularly effective. Doing something you find slightly scary helps you to show yourself that you do have or can develop the skills you need to overcome other more significant challenges.

In relation to this though, you want to make sure that you set yourself realistic aims. It is no good deciding that you want to earn £1,000,000 this month when you have just been made redundant, or telling yourself that sometime in the vague and fuzzy future you are going to ask the person you really fancy out on a date. These aims are pretty unlikely to be achieved. The first is completely unrealistic and the second allows you to put it off indefinitely.

So let's take a look at the best ways in which to go about setting challenges or aims.

Your challenges do not need to be big. Indeed, to start with you want to set yourself small, easily achievable aims. The purpose of these is to start building up that belief that you are able to affect the course of your life and that you can achieve the things you want. As you build up more and more confidence in yourself, achieving bigger aims becomes easier and easier.

When you have long-term bigger goals, you want to split these into smaller, short-term aims anyway. These short-term objectives help you to keep motivated, as well as moving you towards your target in simple steps.

Recording your challenges is a good idea for several reasons. Firstly, taking the steps to actually write down your aim makes the point to yourself that you are serious about achieving it. It also makes it a lot easier for you to take stock of your progress and record your achievements. You could buy yourself a little notebook rather than just writing on scraps of paper that could easily get lost. Having a specific notebook to set out your goals additionally emphasises the fact that you mean business.

### Focusing upon performance versus learning and effort

Performance oriented aims are those that are focused on gaining a particular achievement related outcome, such as lose X amount of weight by Y, or gain a B at A-level in French. Looking at performance outcomes is an easy way of measuring progress and sometimes achieving a particular performance outcome is important in some way. For example, an individual may need to obtain a B in A-level French to get into university. Yet it is essential to not only focus on the performance outcome, but also skills you have learnt along the way and the effort you have put in. Rather than focusing solely upon what you have achieved, what you have mastered and learnt is really important. In fact, this is often more important than the outcome, since it is these skills that will enable you to thrive in life.

The main thing to keep in mind when setting your challenges or aims should be that you want to gain from the process of doing something (such as wanting to gain more knowledge relating to a particular job, or learning how to push yourself physically and getting fit). You don't want to be too fussed about how well you perform, but you instead want to be focused on your efforts and and the skills you gain.

The type of goals people choose to set themselves can often be linked to the beliefs they hold and specifically how in control they feel. Carol Dweck is a famous American psychology professor who has investigated this area. Dweck and her colleagues (see, for example, Dweck, 1999) have looked at the sort of goals students set when they hold different beliefs about their intelligence. Some students believed that intelligence was fixed; they felt that there was nothing they could do to change the amount of intelligence they possessed (i.e. they had an external locus of control with respect to intelligence). Others believed that their intelligence was changeable and that they could improve their intelligence through effort (i.e. they had an internal locus of control). When given a choice between setting either performance or learning goals, those with the external 'intelligence is fixed' mindset tended to set themselves performance goals, wanting to prove that they were intelligent. They saw performance outcomes as reflective of their innate ability, so believed that they had to do well to show that they were clever and, consequently, felt very judged in relation to their performances. Those with the belief that intelligence was changeable tended to set learning goals - they wanted to gain new skills and improve their intelligence. They challenged themselves far more than those who believed intelligence could not be changed, and showed much less social anxiety in relation to their performances.

Elliot and Dweck, (as cited in Dweck, 1999) divided a sample of children and gave half the children performance goals and the other half learning goals, before getting all the children to carry out a task. Some children in each group were told that they had the ability to do really well at the task and others were told that their level of ability was not so high (but only temporarily). The task first involved a number of easy problems, which everyone did well on. Then came some much more difficult problems. Those children that had been given learning goals persisted in the face of the hard problems, they did not worry about their intelligence and they maintained good problem-solving strategies. For the learning-goal children it didn't matter if they had been told that their ability was not that high beforehand, they still persisted in the face of challenges and employed useful strategies. The children who had been given performance goals showed a helpless response to the challenging part of the task, their problem-solving abilities decreased and they criticised their intelligence. This was particularly the case for the children who had been told that their ability at the task was not very high beforehand.

A good example of this sort of helpless response can often be seen in people trying to lose weight. Normally people losing weight set themselves a performance goal in relation to weight loss, such as 'I am going to lose a stone by April' or 'I am going to cut out all chocolate and sweets from my diet' or 'I am going to stick to only eating 1200 calories every day'. They start their new regime enthusiastically and things seem to be going well. But then they have a wobble or a setback. Maybe they don't lose as much weight as they wanted to one week; maybe they eat a bar of chocolate one evening whilst watching TV, or maybe they go to a party and eat more than their daily calorie allowance. Now if this person has a strong belief that they can lose weight they will probably persist in the face of their setback. But many people don't have that much faith in their ability to lose weight. Their setback is seen as evidence of this and they will tend to immediately give up. But if these individuals had initially set themselves more learning-oriented goals (such as 'I am going to learn how to eat healthily and maintain this in my everyday life') either instead of, or in conjunction with, their performance weight loss goal, they would have been far less likely to immediately feel helpless at the first signs of a mistake or difficulty. After all, learning goals are about learning how to do something, so mistakes and challenges are to be expected!

Just to highlight again, there is nothing innately wrong with wanting to achieve a particular performance outcome, and as I have mentioned earlier, this may often be desirable. It's not that you shouldn't set yourself aims or challenges that relate to performance, just that it is helpful to make sure that performance outcomes do not become your main focus. Many people reading this book will instinctively want to focus upon their performance because they have an external locus of control and social anxiety (see chapter 5). If this is you, then you really want to remind yourself that learning skills and processing your efforts is your main aim.

## Processing your goals

You want to reward yourself when you have completed your challenge or aim. This is so important that I am going to expand upon it further here. When you have been seeing yourself through 'shit-tinted spectacles' you tend not to even process the positive things about yourself or the things you have achieved. You do, in fact, have many experiences evidencing the fact that you are a worthwhile, competent person, but (until now) you have probably dismissed, explained away or not even noticed them. So, it is really important that you now make sure that you do process your achievements. Realise that on achieving a challenge or aim you have done something significant and that you are allowed to reward yourself and give yourself praise for your success. Even if you do not attain a particular desired performance outcome, you want to focus upon what you have learnt and the efforts you have put in, and process these.

## Set yourself a challenge!

At the moment, you want to start by setting yourself a small challenge or aim. You can build up to larger challenges or aims over the next couple of months. Your challenge could be as simple as reading the next chapter of this book and making sure that you put effort into completing all the exercises.

There is a table on the next page for you to write down your first challenge or aim, but for the future it is a good idea to buy yourself a notebook as suggested. I have also added an example to help you!

| Challenge or aim | Steps to achieve this | Processing my achievement |
|---|---|---|
| I am building a more internal sense of power and control | 1. To work through the next chapter of this book<br><br>2. Completing all the actions within this chapter over the next two weeks<br><br>3. Decide upon a new hobby that I would like to take up by exploring online. | I'm feeling more in control and have realised that many of my external beliefs are not based upon evidence. I feel proud of the effort I have put in over the last few weeks. I have also decided to go to a drawing class, which runs every month, to have fun, gain more new skills and meet new people. I am looking forward to continuing to build up my sense of power and control as I continue to work through the programme. |

| Challenge or aim | Steps to achieve this | Processing my achievement |
|---|---|---|
| | | |

## ACTION! Use your imagination

Start training your imagination to work FOR you. Use your imagination to rehearse situations/experiences before they happen, so that they happen and you experience them, just the way you wanted them to be. This works really well for social events and performance-related situations (going for an interview, giving a speech, overcoming a sexual inhibition, asking someone on a date etc.) but also for fears and anxiety-triggering situations (flying, darkness, being alone, spiders, knives, snakes, lifts, tunnels, hospitals, needles etc.). Choose a couple of events or scenarios that you have either been worrying and thinking negatively about, or that you feel you would like to work on. Find a quiet place (e.g. just as you go to bed, or when you are on a train to work, or when you are in the bath) and spend five or ten minutes on each scenario really visualising/rehearsing what you want to happen. Remember the more you practise/rehearse visualising, the easier it becomes.

# Sense of Power and Control - Recap

✓ Sense of power and control refers to how much control or power you believe you have over events in your life.

✓ An internal sense of power and control is where you believe that the events and experiences in your life are mostly controlled by your own thoughts and actions (high sense of direct influence) and that you also have the resources to deal with situations that are outside your control (strong belief in your coping skills).

✓ An external sense of power and control is where you believe that the events and experiences in your life are mostly controlled by external forces (low sense of direct influence), such as powerful others, luck, fate or chance, and/or you believe that you do not have resources to deal with those situations that are outside your control (poor belief in your coping skills).

✓ Having an internal sense of power and control is important to both mental and physical health, and is particularly key when making changes in your life.

✓ Your sense of power of control isn't necessarily based on reality - it's just a belief. It's the way that you see things, it's the way you think about things and it's the way in which you process information. You can change it!

✓ Desire for control refers to how much control you WANT or feel you NEED over your life.

✓ Those with an external sense of power and control and a high desire for control are likely to feel particularly powerless, and as a result attempt to gain control of their lives in any way they can - often to little or no avail.

✓ People who have a very strong desire for control have **always** got an poor belief in their coping skills. If you believed you had the resources to cope with anything in life, why would you have a strong desire to over control and avoid certain situations?

### What should I be working on from now on?

1. Remind yourself that your symptoms are not happening TO you, you are creating and/or maintaining them yourself and you can undo this easily.
2. Keep working on your sense of power and control quiz answers, challenging any external ones and changing them to more internal beliefs.
3. Start thinking and speaking in an internal way.
4. Set yourself a small challenge and process the whole experience internally.
5. Visualise what you want to happen rather than what you fear will happen.

**Notes** - The blank area below is for you to make any notes.

# Chapter

# 4

# How do you feel about yourself?

# Self-Esteem

The second key component of your psychological foundations is your self-esteem. Have a look at your TQ Report: what did you score?

## What is self-esteem?

Self-esteem or self-worth essentially refers to **how you feel about yourself**. It is your *perception* of how worthy and likeable you are. If you have high self-esteem you feel positively about yourself, believing that you are a deserving and good person. You like yourself. For those with low self-esteem the picture is somewhat different.

## How do we develop and maintain our self-esteem?

Our sense of self-worth develops as we process and store our experiences in life. If, for example, you grow up in a family where you are constantly put down and belittled, you are likely to begin to believe that you are fairly worthless (unless you perceive other positive experiences in relation to who you are). If you grow up in a loving, accepting family you are much more likely (although not guaranteed) to develop high self-esteem. People with a negatively distorted sense of self do not, however, need to have been regularly put down or abused by others during childhood. The source of negative experiences can be internal. In fact, many people who I have treated with self-esteem issues have come from loving, caring families and it is largely their own self-criticism that has caused them to build up such limiting beliefs about themselves.

Your self-esteem can change throughout your life in relation to how you process your experiences. Young children tend to have a fairly fluctuating sense of self. They have not had time to build up a permanent picture of who they are, so their sense of self varies depending upon the environment they are in. Young children are also not yet particularly discerning of the truth of the information presented to them, so are more likely to automatically believe in the reality of whatever they are experiencing in the moment. When a child has just been severely told off he may believe that he is very bad, but when he has just been praised he is the most fantastic child in the world!

By the time you get to adulthood, you have many more experiences contributing to your picture of who you are. Most people have developed a very strong sense of self, positive or negative, by the time they are adults, they know exactly who they are and this does not change significantly in different environments. They have built up a solid 'belief system brick wall' about themselves. This can be a good or bad thing depending on how positively or negatively the self is viewed! If you have developed low self-esteem you are likely to have a persistent feeling of 'not being good enough'. You may feel worthless, as though you are a 'bad' person or as though you do not deserve to be happy. Someone with low self-esteem has no trust in their ability to achieve the things they want in life. This kind of limiting belief system often pervades all aspects of someone's life.

Many people do have a slightly different perception of exactly who they are depending on the environment they are in and the role they play within it. You may feel a little differently about yourself depending on whether you are at work or with your family etc. Your sense of self can also change gradually over time as you take on board new significant experiences.

For some people, (usually 'externals') their perception of themselves is still extremely unstable, because it is almost entirely based on external events. For this sort of person, his or her self-esteem depends entirely upon the situation experienced at the time. This means that the person constantly experiences a roller coaster of emotions. If you can identify with this, then there are likely to be times when you feel fantastic, but there are going to be many times when you struggle with very low self-esteem. In an extreme case a person may fluctuate from believing he/she is worthless, stupid and pathetic one moment to thinking him/herself valued, intelligent and powerful in another. If, for example, you are at a party, surrounded by friends, fun music playing, drinks flowing, then you are on top of the world! Alone in your bedroom after a stressful day at work, however, you feel lonely, miserable, unloved, insignificant.

Your perception of yourself may be very different to others' perception of you. Your self-image may indeed have become a little distorted and lacking in true perspective. You may have built up a negative picture of yourself but other people may see you as a lovely, intelligent, friendly person, although you do not see this at all.

Low self-esteem causes you to constantly view your life and the world around you with respect to your low opinion of yourself (those shit-tinted spectacles again). You don't need to have **very** low self-esteem for it to have a profound effect upon your other belief systems and your life, just **lower** than it could or should be.

You may be surprised that I am describing low self-esteem as just a belief! As I said earlier, many people tend to think that self-esteem is a fairly rigid and inflexible part of our 'make-up', maybe something genetically predisposed, like the colour of our eyes or hair, or whether we are left or right handed, but it is not. We often believe that the amount of self-esteem we have is entirely dependent on our upbringings: how much love, nourishment and security we receive from our parents and the society around us, that it is fixed at the point we become adults, and it doesn't change once we have grown up. This is also not true. I have indeed taken people through therapy who have suffered a terrible childhood and had very low self-esteem, but I have also taken people through therapy who experienced a wonderfully supportive and loving childhood who also had low self-esteem. Equally, there are people who have had an awful, abusive childhood that have relatively high self-esteem. It is not about the reality of a person's forming experiences that matter, but rather their perception of them, and how they 'process' them (more about this later). In other words, what they believe about them.

Think about it - you have a view of yourself as a certain type of person, who has a certain type of friend, who does a certain type of job, who likes certain types of food, who knows what you are capable of, and what you are not capable of. This is EXACTLY what a belief system is! A friend suggests going into town tonight to see a show, and you think to yourself 'that's not really my type of thing.' You talk to friends who are going skiing, and you think, 'I'd love to do that, but I'm not that type of sporty person.' These are all beliefs. Beliefs are not facts; they are just what we believe.

Low self-esteem is not having a great opinion of yourself, not liking yourself very much, believing that you don't 'deserve' the great things in life. This is just a view, a belief; it's not a 'fact'.

Trouble is, like any belief, we look for 'evidence' that supports and nurtures it because we feel safe and comfortable in the knowledge that our life is predictable and makes sense. All new information is seen through 'belief system tinted spectacles'. All new experiences are interpreted so that they make sense to us, i.e. so that they fit with our belief systems. This is why many limiting belief systems are often maintained, despite overwhelming evidence to the contrary. Think of someone with anorexia, who weighs only five stone (32 Kg) and who believes she (around 90% of anorexia sufferers are female according to my clinical experience) is fat. Her friends, family, doctors, psychiatrists and nutritionists ALL tell her that she is life-threateningly thin, but she believes she is fat, so she 'IS' fat. These clashing experiences are interpreted in a highly distorted way so that instead of contradicting the belief system they reinforce it.

You might find it incredible that it is possible to back up a negative self-image with positive experiences but people do so all the time! When people with low self-esteem do well in exams, they think it's just that they have been lucky. When they receive compliments, they assume that these compliments are not really meant and people are just being nice. When they have a lovely time out at a party they feel guilty because they should have been doing something else far more important. If you think about it, I bet you can conjure up many times where you have twisted your own positive experiences in the same sort of manner.

### Your self-esteem 'battery'

It might be helpful to think of your self-esteem as being a little bit like a rechargeable battery. Most people have got some rechargeable batteries in their house somewhere, they're really useful and when their power starts to fade, you can just put them on charge overnight and hey presto, they're fully charged again. Your self-esteem works in a very similar way. Positive, pleasant, rewarding, validating, ego-boosting thoughts or experiences fill your self-esteem battery with 'positive charge' and you feel good about yourself. If your battery is completely full you feel mentally very robust and resilient; you can take a few knocks, experience a few setbacks, be disappointed by a partner, friend or work colleague and not be reduced to feeling like a shivering, worthless wreck.

At the same time, negative or limiting thoughts, criticisms, bad experiences, the lack of validation or the withdrawal of love or care, is going to 'reduce the charge' in your self-esteem battery.

***Positive thoughts, experiences and feelings charge the battery. Negative thoughts, experiences and feelings deplete it.***

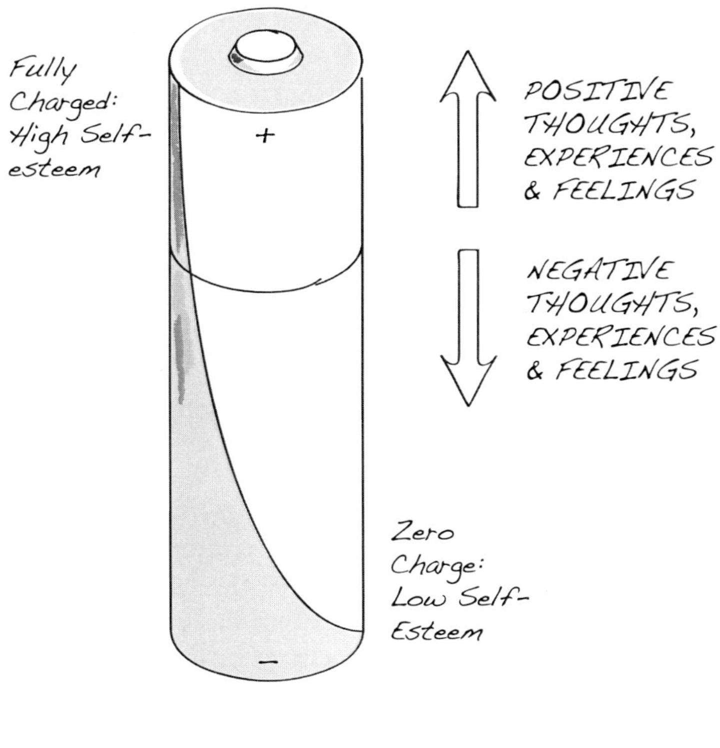


So the reason why our self-esteem seems to fluctuate from day to day is because it does! A person who has lots of pleasant, validating experiences, who tends to be quite a positive person, has more of an internal sense of power and control and who tends to see the proverbial glass as 'half full', will, most likely create robust, high self-esteem. A person who tends to always see the glass as half empty, has an external sense of power and control, and who experiences many negative, limiting, critical, and self-deprecating thoughts, will tend to have low self-esteem.

Remember, these experiences don't have to be actual real experiences that you go through; they can just be your thoughts or your 'inner voice'. Some people are very self-critical and, unknowingly, put themselves down hundreds of times every day.

**In terms of your self-esteem, you are what you think!** Remember that 'self-esteem' is what YOU currently think and feel about YOU. It doesn't necessarily reflect the reality of how good you are, how nice you are, how loveable you are, how pretty or handsome you are, or how clever you are. Your self-esteem is just what YOU currently think or feel about YOU.

Put to one side the results of the self-esteem quiz for just a moment, and ask yourself a question:

'How high is my self-esteem at the moment?'

It doesn't matter what the answer was, I just wanted you to ask yourself the question. When you asked yourself the question, what went through your head? I'll bet you actually asked yourself another question: **'hmm, how do I feel about myself today?'**

How do I **FEEL** about myself **TODAY**? You probably didn't think of your school days, you almost certainly didn't think of your childhood, you wouldn't have thought about that time when you were bullied, or the ex-partner who dumped you, you just asked yourself 'how do I **FEEL** about myself **TODAY**?'

How you 'feel about yourself today', is entirely related to what you have been thinking about yourself, and your life, today. Not last week, last month or last year. Not when you were seven, seventeen or twenty-seven, but **today**. If you woke up this morning and immediately thought in a positive, happy, loving, powerful and charitable way about yourself and your life, then you probably **FELT** very good about yourself this morning. In which case, your self-esteem is probably high today.

If, on the other hand, you noticed the weight you have recently put on; the bags under your tired eyes; the cellulite around your hips; the grey hair on your head or chest (men only, probably, hopefully?); your stressful day ahead and how hard you were going to find it; how much pain you were going to be in; how angry you were going to be; how phobic you were going to be, then don't be surprised if your self-esteem is very low today. If you scored more than say five on the sense of power and control quiz, then you are quite external in your thinking. You are probably now validating your current low self-esteem by recalling something that happened in your past - you certainly won't be thinking: **'I am creating low self-esteem today by the way I am thinking, I'm going to change that right now!'**

Try it this way - imagine, for one week, that you have some sort of mental tab or scoreboard that records the number of positive and negative thoughts that you have each day. Every time you have a positive, pleasant, rewarding, validating, ego-boosting thought this is noted on your tab. Equally, every time you have a negative, critical, powerless or limiting thought it is also recorded. The percentage of positive and negative thoughts on your tab reflects the charge of your self-esteem battery. If you have 70% negative thoughts and 30% positive ones then your self-esteem battery is only 30% charged, and you only have 30% self-esteem. You can change this by just changing the positive/negative balance of your thoughts.

## The relationship between sense of power and control and self-esteem

Your self-esteem, as we have already discussed, is what you currently think, feel and believe about yourself, and your sense of worth. People with high self-esteem tend to be more internal and not judge themselves by external standards, such as what others think, because they feel good about themselves and believe that they are competent and able to make decisions. If you have low self-esteem you are less likely to believe that you have the personal power to affect your life - you are unlikely to think that you are capable of taking control or even that you deserve to, and thus tend to have an external sense of power and control!

Again the relationship is not one way and sense of power and control significantly affects self-esteem. People with an external sense of power and control tend to always look outside of themselves for validation and to create their sense of self. This is why people with lower self-esteem also tend to have more fluctuating levels of self-esteem - it is because they are external. When they have had a good day at work, been out with friends, been chatted-up by a lovely person, or just been 'made' to feel good, they feel better about themselves and their self-esteem increases for a while. These self-esteem increases tend to be temporary though, as these experiences are not processed internally. If every time you experience something positive you attribute it to external forces (such as luck, other people, a higher power) rather than internal ones (such as your effort, abilities, personality) it is very hard to feel more than temporarily positive about yourself and truly build up your self-worth. For example, if you have an external locus and you successfully pass your driving test, you are quite likely to believe that you passed because of luck, because the examiner was nice, or because 'they have recently lowered their standards.' Either way, you are unlikely to process the experience 'internally' by thinking to yourself, 'Well done, you can achieve anything that you put your mind to, you studied hard for that test and really deserve a full driving licence.'

## Building your self-esteem

In reality, you have had trillions of experiences in your life: some good, some bad, some happy, some sad, some you regret, some you wished you could do again and again. You have enough experiences to corroborate just about any belief system you care to adopt. Anyone can think back through their life and think of something they wished they hadn't done or said, something that 'proves' to them they are a bad person. Or they can think back to a time when they helped an old lady across the street, which confirms to them that they are a good person.

Or a time that they really worried that their partner was having an affair, which confirms for them that they are a paranoid person. How much self-esteem you have, how much self-worth you have, how 'good' you think you are is all just a belief.

This is good news, no, GREAT news, because it means that you can change it if you wish. You can change your view of yourself; you can change what you believe about yourself, you can change your level of self-esteem. Until you do though, you will view every experience in life through the rose-tinted (or shit-tinted) spectacles of your self-esteem beliefs. How long does it take to build high self-esteem, even if you are doing it from scratch? **About two weeks!**

Let me say that again, just for clarity - it only takes about two weeks to build yourself good self-esteem, even if previously it had always been low.

### Two weeks to build a good level of self-esteem, am I mad?

Think about it . . . your self-esteem is what you currently think of you, right? It's a belief based on your most recent (or relevant) thoughts and feelings about yourself and your life. So, during a day or week where you are, for whatever reason, having lots of positive, happy, powerful and kind thoughts about yourself, your self-esteem is higher. With me so far?

Ok, so we have trillions and trillions of thoughts and experiences in our lives, so many that we cannot possibly have all of them, or even one percent of them, in our mind at any one time. Even when we have very powerful experiences, they soon drift away from our conscious mind and into memory. Think back to when you last came back from a holiday, trip, or time spent with friends. For the first few days of being home, you were probably still in 'holiday mode', the holiday still fresh in your mind. How long after you came home and settled back into normal life, did the experiences of the trip drift away from your conscious thoughts and into your memory? About two weeks. Our recent thoughts, experiences and feelings tend to stay in our conscious minds for a couple of weeks, your self-esteem is (to a greater or lesser extent) based upon the thoughts you have in your conscious mind.

Now think back to a different time, think back to a date, an evening out with friends, a nice meal with your partner or something different, a time when your were chatted-up by someone, maybe even your wedding day - but think of a specific occasion where you felt really good about yourself. Now, ask yourself this: how high was your self-esteem then? If your self-esteem on that occasion was 80%, and your general self-esteem (as tested at the beginning of this chapter) is 50%, then how else do you explain the sudden rise in your self-esteem from 50-80% in the space of just a few hours, if your self-esteem isn't based upon your thoughts and feelings at any given time? I bet, on the occasion you just thought of, you felt great, happy, powerful, confident and positive?

## Building your self-esteem (and creating an internal sense of power and control)

Have a quick glance at your self-esteem quiz score in your TQ report. When you have your benchmark, it is very easy to come back and complete the quiz again at a later date, and see just how much you have increased your self-esteem.

Try and see self-esteem as really nothing more than a self-evaluation: it's what YOU currently think about YOU. It's not based on any sort of reality at all.

Let me give you an example: say you scored 35% on the quiz above. This figure represents what YOU think about YOU. You believe that you are '35% good enough', 'trying 35% hard enough', 'being 35% nice enough' or 'are only 35% loveable'. I wonder, what percentage would your friends and colleagues give you? If I got, say, twenty of your friends and colleagues together and asked them to secretly 'evaluate' you, what percentage would THEY give you? I'll bet you a bottle of Jack Daniels whiskey that THEY would give you at least 90%. How is this possible? Either you are 35%, or you are 90%?

Remember, your self-esteem is NOT a reality. It's just YOUR current evaluation, your current OPINION, of you. Your friends and colleagues won't 'see' you in the same negative, uncharitable, judgmental light as you do - they won't be wearing your 'shit-tinted spectacles'. Don't believe me? Try it. Ask them! When they come back to you with phrases such as: 'lovely person', 'hard working', 'a great friend', 'really clever', 'really supportive', 'very sexy' or 'caring and un-judgmental', be prepared to be shocked.

Why shocked? Well, people tend to be quite egocentric and think that everyone else thinks the same way as they do. Therefore if I think I am not very clever, I assume that most other people would think the same thing. Only when you look outside of yourself and get some perspective, are you forced to realise that people think differently about you than you do. Your friends and colleagues take a much more balanced view of you than you do: they know you are not perfect, and that you sometimes make mistakes. They know that you are sometimes grouchy or snappy first thing in the morning. They know that you usually get a little bit drunk at the office party but they like, love, respect, adore, look up to, value, cherish you, they think you are a great worker and care for you regardless. They are not continually berating you, putting you down, comparing you to others, criticising you, or thinking that you are not good enough. This is what clouds your judgment when you evaluate or assess yourself.

As I stated earlier on in this chapter, it is my firm belief that your self-esteem is actually only about two weeks old. That's right! Your current level of self-esteem is NOTHING WHATSOEVER to do with: your childhood, your teenage years, your failed marriage, your poor exam results, your lack of career progression, or anything else that happened more than two weeks ago.

Why two weeks? Well, because it actually doesn't take very long to change a belief system - once you have the motivation to do so. In fact, the 'moment of change' actually takes about a second. You might deliberate over a decision for a number of minutes, hours or days, but the actual moment you make up your mind takes just a moment.

So the moment that you recognise you have been assessing yourself through shit-tinted spectacles, and decide to take them off, you are going to feel a whole lot different. In my experience, once you start to complete the exercises in this book, it only takes about two weeks to see a significant difference. All the people I have worked with, whether consulting for depression, chronic fatigue, low self-esteem or something else entirely, once they have read and understood this book (or talked through the book with one of my consultants) have taken less than two weeks to actually resolve their issues. If you go to www.amazon.co.uk and search for this book, you can see what some of these people have to say about this process.

So, are your shit-tinted spectacles a fixed and permanent part of you? No, they are just a habit. You look at yourself this way because you are used to looking at yourself this way. The behaviour, like many others talked about in this book, is cyclical.

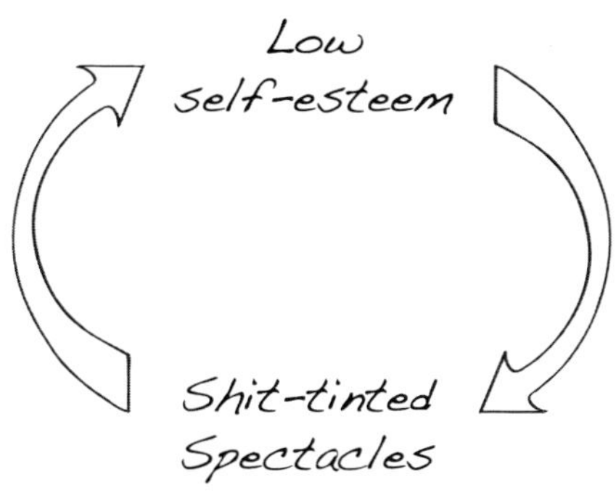


Because you view yourself through your shit-tinted spectacles, you see yourself as not very good, not very nice, not very clever, not very fit, not very pretty etc. This then leads to a poor evaluation or assessment of you, and this, in turn, creates low self-esteem.

Because you have low self-esteem, you tend to view yourself very critically: always looking for what you have done wrong, seeking out where you are failing, checking for 'crows feet' or cellulite in the mirror, rather than complimenting yourself on how good the rest of your looks are; thinking about recent mistakes, rather than recent successes; generally looking at yourself in a negative, critical and hostile way - through shit-tinted spectacles.

Think about your current level of self-esteem, and then think about the last time you had a great time and felt really good. I recently asked Brenda to do this. Brenda worked out that her current level of self-esteem was just 15% (she scored 17 on the self-esteem quiz) and then I asked her to think about a time when she had felt really good. She thought back a couple of years to her thirtieth birthday when she was out for the evening in London. She was expecting just a quiet meal with a few people but another friend had secretly organised a big party, so Brenda found herself having the time of her life with around fifty friends. I asked her, 'Ok, if I had been in London that night, bumped into you and asked you 'How high is your self-esteem right now, what would your answer have been?' Brenda replied, '110%'.

I asked her, 'How is it possible to go from having just 15% to over 100%, in just a few hours?' She thought about this for a moment or two, then answered, 'I guess it's impossible to feel worthless and stupid when you have fifty friends around you making you feel lovely.' She then went on to say, 'Also, when you are out and doing something or having a good time, you are not brooding about life being shit!' I think Brenda explained this almost perfectly.

Think back now to a time when you felt really good. It doesn't matter how long ago it was, what you were doing, or who you were with, just remember what it was like. Now ask yourself: 'why did I feel so good?'

Going back to Brenda's comments for a moment, I think the only insight she still lacked (at that point) was that she was still processing the bit about her friends 'making her feel lovely' externally. Was it Brenda's friends who made her feel lovely? No, it wasn't.

We believe something, as in Brenda's case, 'I'm worthless and stupid'. We then look around for 'evidence' to support our belief, as in Brenda's case, she would think about how much weight she had put on, about the mistakes she had made at work, and about how her last boyfriend had dumped her. We ignore any other evidence that might disagree with our beliefs. In Brenda's case, she had put on weight, but she was still quite slim; she had made a few mistakes at work, but she was generally very successful, in fact she had recently received an unexpected pay-rise and promotion; and although she had recently been dumped, two or three other guys had already asked her out.

Her shit-tinted spectacles had stayed firmly in place until she was faced with OVERWHELMING evidence to the contrary - fifty people had secretly got together and travelled all across London to spend some time with her. How could she possibly dismiss this? How could she, even with the darkest of tints in her glasses, maintain her beliefs about being worthless and stupid? One or two people could be lying. Another one or two might have only come along because their partners were there. Another couple maybe only came for the food. Possibly another two because they felt sorry for her, but that still left another forty-plus people who only attended because they liked and cared for her. This overwhelmed her natural defences, and she then had to view the experience differently.

It still wasn't her friends though, that made her feel good about herself that night; she made herself feel good. It wasn't so much a case of 'you're making me feel good about myself', but more 'I must be nice and lovely, because all these people are here'. Trouble is, she didn't realise this.

Forgive me if I am sounding just a tad pedantic at the moment, but this is a really BIG issue. It's a HUGE issue. Imagine an issue so big, that it had snow on the top, chairlifts, and a big sign at the bottom saying: 'this is a big issue'! Brenda was processing the experience externally, up until the point where it challenged her thinking enough when she had to actually allow herself to briefly process it internally and recognise 'I must be nice and lovely', at which point, she felt good. Brenda didn't recognise this process going on in her head though, she still thought that it was her friends making her feel good, so when the party was over and she went home again, she went back to feeling shit.

Brenda and I 'cured' her of her low self-esteem, by getting her to recognise the fact that she had felt better, when SHE had stopped thinking: 'I'm stupid, I'm fat, I'm worthless etc.' and instead thought to herself 'I must be nice and lovely'. Once she realised that SHE could make herself feel better and raise her self-esteem whenever she wanted to, she understandably did it all of the time. She started using active, positive and internal language (more later), both in her thoughts and when she spoke. She also remembered that when she was out with her friends enjoying herself she wasn't brooding and worrying about things, so she started to keep herself busy, and got on with something interesting whenever she started to think negatively about something.

One thing that Brenda still found hard, because of the habit of always thinking of her failures, mistakes and insecurities, was processing her day-to-day positive experiences and achievements, they always seemed to be left by the wayside. For example, she had almost forgotten that she had recently been given a pay-rise and promotion, it hadn't really 'sunk in'. So, I set about designing a simple technique for processing achievements, in order to help people build their self-esteem and feel more grounded.

## ACTION! Processing the positives

People who suffer from low self-esteem, and/or have an external sense of power and control, tend to either not process their positive experiences at all (because either they don't recognise them, or they mitigate them down into nothing e.g. 'yeah, I know the boss said it was a great piece of work, but he's bound to say that - that's his job'), or only process them externally, which effectively means they receive little or no psychological benefit from the experience at all, they might as well never have experienced it. Have you seen the film 'Groundhog Day'? Imagine waking up every morning as if it was your first morning - nothing that you have experienced before has actually happened, and you are starting each day afresh. Your self-esteem battery would be empty and you would feel flat. This is what happens when you don't process your positive experiences. You may be a lovely, caring, powerful, knowledgeable person, but if you don't process these experiences, they never become a part of you and they might as well not have happened.

'Processing' is what takes place when your experience becomes a memory. Remember back to the chapter on cognition when I talked about how people experienced my consulting room differently? Some people think of it as big and airy, others think of it as small and dark. We don't process reality, we don't process the actual experience, we process the experience as viewed through our belief systems, our unhelpful thinking styles, and our tinted spectacles, and this is what then becomes 'memory'. If you experience a movie as boring, then your memory of that film will be that it is boring. If you only process the negative elements of your day yesterday, then your memory of yesterday will be that it was negative. If, instead, you processed all the good, positive, happy and healthy experiences, your memory of yesterday would be good, positive, happy and healthy.

REMEMBER: What you experience in life is not reality, it's reality as experienced through your belief systems, unhelpful thinking styles, tint of spectacles etc.

I know I am labouring the point, but your self-esteem is what YOU currently think and feel about YOU. Even though external people look outside of themselves for reasons why things happen in their lives, the reality is that your self-esteem is entirely based on what you currently think and feel about you. What you currently think and feel about you, is based on your most recent (processed) experiences. If, over the last couple of weeks you have processed lots of negative, powerless, critical thoughts about yourself and your life, then you will have low self-esteem. If you have just come back from a two-week cruise around the Bahamas, where all the Michelin-quality food and the exotic cocktails were free, then you probably currently feel pretty bloody good (apart from the hangover and bulging tummy).

Your self-esteem forms one part of your psychological foundations and is, therefore, one of the most important things for you to improve if you want to take control of your life. I'm going to challenge one of your limiting beliefs right now, and tell you that significantly increasing your self-esteem is actually a very simple, easy and fairly quick thing to do. Forget what you have read in 'pop psychology' magazines and books, and what your natural instinct probably suggests. Improving your self-esteem is NOT a difficult and laborious thing to do: it's quick and easy.

Here's how:
Cast your mind back over the last few days (weeks if necessary) and think of ten positive experiences you have had. If you cannot think of ten you probably have very low self-esteem and are just not recognising these experiences because you are looking back through your shit-tinted spectacles. If this is you, then imagine taking your spectacles off and viewing these experiences neutrally - as if they are someone else's - this should give you more clarity.

Now, on the following page, you will see a table that has room for you to write down these ten positive experiences. It doesn't matter whether you experienced all these things yesterday, or that they are spread over the last few days or even weeks. We are not looking for huge, or significant, experiences here - yes, of course you can use those if you have them though - we are looking for the day-to-day positive experiences that often pass us by.

Examples of day-to-day positives could be: going for a run, doing a good piece of work, helping an old lady across the road, biting your tongue when you were upset or angry with someone, being chatted-up, making yourself look nice, doing a favour for a friend, putting effort in to change your life or simply reading this book! As a general rule, a positive experience is anything that you feel good about or anything that if your friend had achieved the same thing you would say 'well done!' in response to.

For each of your experiences please first write down why it was positive. Secondly, you are going to think about what you would say to someone else if you heard he/she had achieved the same success. Finally, you are going to think about what the previous columns show you and what you have learnt. When you have finished writing these ten things, really THINK and FEEL about a great sense of reward and accomplishment. Tell yourself 'well done mate - you are really starting to change your life'. Treat yourself the way you would treat someone you love.

To make things even easier for you, I have given you a few examples:

| Positive Experience | What made this a positive experience? | What would you say to someone else who had this experience? | What does this show you/ What have you learnt from this? |
|---|---|---|---|
| I have worked my way through this book so far | It shows I am committed to making changes to improve my life.<br>I have looked at myself and my personality honestly and faced things that were challenging | Well done!<br>You should be proud of yourself for showing this determination | I can help myself<br>I can overcome difficulties |

| | | | |
|---|---|---|---|
| I passed my driving test | It was a big challenge to overcome my nerves<br>Passing takes a lot of effort, practice and concentration | Congratulations!<br>Good job, that shows you can overcome many things you find tricky | I can achieve things even if I don't find them easy |
| My friend gave me a hug for getting her lunch | It felt really lovely | You are lovely for getting someone's lunch. | I'm a decent person and I good have friends. |
| | | | |
| | | | |
| | | | |
| | | | |
| | | | |

| | | | |
|---|---|---|---|
| | | | |
| | | | |
| | | | |
| | | | |
| | | | |

Great. Well done.

Please don't go past this point until you have completed the exercise for ten different positive experiences. DO NOT berate or criticise yourself if some of your positives don't seem very big. Remember: treat yourself the way you would treat someone you love.

Now, here is where this technique can become really powerful. . .What I want you to do is to carry around with you, for the next few weeks, a small list of your latest ten positives so that you can have easy access to them, in order to process them several times each day. The very best way to do this is to have your list on your mobile phone (most mobiles now have a diary or a notes section, if yours doesn't, just text your list to yourself). You don't need lots of details, as in the table you filled out above, you just need a couple of words to remind yourself what it was you achieved. Make your list from 10 to 1, as in the example below:

10. Went running
9. Paid tax bill

8. Took kids away
7. Finished Thrive book
6. Completed project
5. Painted spare room
4. Bought a copy of 'Big Issue'
3. Bought pressie for Jane
2. Thinking positively
1. This list!

Notice, I have only listed enough information to remind myself about what the positive experience was. Now, several times each day, I want you to read through your list, spending only about 30 seconds on each one. As you remember each remind yourself why it was a positive experience, remember how it felt and what you thought at the time, really 'be there' again. Remember the effect it had upon your mood and how it enhanced your self-esteem. If your positive experience was something that you achieved - like cooking dinner for your friends - you can also make sure you process the experience internally (helping to build an internal locus) by reminding yourself that YOU achieved it. Tell yourself something like: 'I cooked dinner for five friends - I worked really hard at it and it turned out to be lovely. I'm good at cooking and I can achieve anything I put my mind to.'

This whole process should only take 5 minutes to complete (10 x 30 secs).

When should you do this? As often as possible! Ideally, when you wake up in the morning; before you get out of bed; during coffee and lunch breaks at work; when you are sitting on the toilet (you've got nothing better to do for five minutes, and you always have your phone on you!); when you are relaxing in the bath; before going into a meeting; before writing a report; before going to bed, at the very least, 5 times every day. Once you get used to it - like cleaning your teeth - it becomes second nature, and is really VERY rewarding.

Once you have something else to add to your list, i.e. when you have another positive experience, add it as number 10 in your list, then everything else moves down the list one place, with the old number 1 disappearing off the list altogether. Below is my new list, after adding a new number 10:

10. Helping lady in car park
9. Went running
8. Paid tax bill
7. Took kids away
6. Finished Thrive book
5. Completed project
4. Painted spare room
3. Bought a copy of 'Big Issue'
2. Bought pressie for Jane
1. Thinking positively

It doesn't matter whether you add three new positives each day, or just one per week, just add one when you have one.

You DON'T need to add each new positive into the original table above that I started for you. This was only for your first ten, so that you understood fully how to process them.

By the time my experience of 'helping the old lady get her car out of the snow in the car park' has gone all the way down my list to number 1, I will probably have processed it more than sixty or seventy times. There will be NO DOUBT in my mind about this experience and it WILL affect my self-esteem. The experience will really be HARD-WIRED into my memory, and not forgotten easily. My mind, on a day-to-day basis, will be filled with my thoughts and experiences about me achieving things, being successful, creating an internal locus, and changing my life.

If, whilst completing this exercise you find it hard to think of positives to add you are probably either: (a) looking too hard and missing the obvious, or (b) dismissing smaller positives and searching for more significant events. In the case of (a), stop looking so hard - we're just after normal day-to-day positive events or experiences. In the case of (b), you are probably a bit of a perfectionist (see Chapter 6 'Unhelpful Thinking Styles') and not allowing yourself to 'celebrate such a ridiculously small event'. In which case, stop being so bloody hard on yourself! Some of the sorts of things you can put on your list are:

- When you've stepped outside your comfort zone
- When you managed to calm yourself down.
- When you confronted a situation, rather than avoided it.
- When you noticed yourself brooding/worrying, and put a stop to it.
- When you motivated yourself to start a task or goal you've been putting off.
- When you did something to improve your life, even in some small way.
- When you made an effort to improve your social or work life.
- Receiving and accepting a compliment you would normally disregard.
- Allowing yourself to relax or do something you enjoy, just for the sake of having fun.
- Not beating yourself up about something that you've not done well or could have done better.

If, whilst completing this exercise, you realise that you are sometimes actually really horrible to yourself, then please realise that this is just a habit you have got into and you can get out of this pretty quickly. It's likely you have some of the perfectionist thinking mentioned above, but also some of the 'black and white', and 'catastrophic' thinking that will be discussed in Chapter 6 'Unhelpful Thinking Styles'. For the time being, and for the benefit of this exercise, please PLEASE stop being so hard on yourself! Cut yourself some slack - if you still feel the same way about yourself once you have completed this book, feel free to go back to self-flagellation. In the meantime, please just try to be nice.

I recently had the pleasure of working with one of the most anxious, insecure and panicky people I have ever worked with. We went through this book together and he COMPLETELY changed his life - in just four weeks. This is his testimonial from the Amazon website:

*'Hi all, over the last 12 years I have been battling with anxiety and panic attacks. I have visited doctors and other therapists always looking for an answer to my problem (none of which helped me at all. Medication isn't the answer it just made me feel like a zombie). I was always looking on the negative side of life and would regularly worry about situations that hadn't even happened, I was even losing sleep over these imaginary situations! So when I visited Rob and we went through the book together, my thinking started to change. I started to change for the better and I can honestly say my life has completely turned around. All you have to do is WANT the change for yourself! It's that simple. I'm the happiest I have ever been and I feel now there is nothing I can't achieve.*

*I really want to pass on the tools to help people now with anxiety and panic because I feel so passionate about helping people who are in that unbearable situation that I once was.*
*Thanks a million Rob. John'*

Why have I added his testimonial here? Well, because the change in John (not his real name) was really quite remarkable - he completely changed, COMPLETELY, in just a few weeks. I asked him why he had achieved so much, so quickly, and this was his reply:

*'I live in Harrow, and work in the City (London) and I spend 30 minutes every morning, and every evening on*

*the train. For the last four weeks I haven't been surfing the web, playing 'Angry Birds', or chatting to friends on Facebook on the train, I've been processing my positive experiences.'*

He had gone from rarely having a powerful, positive thought, to having hundreds every day. His self-esteem had no option than to shoot-up, his sense of power and control had no option other than to become more internal, and his social anxiety just disappeared. Last time I spoke with him, he was setting up a rock band!

## Self-Esteem - Recap

- ✓ Self-esteem is the way that we feel about ourselves. It is our beliefs how likeable we are and our sense of worth.
- ✓ If you have high self-esteem you feel positive about yourself, believing that you are worthy, interesting and likeable.
- ✓ If you have low self-esteem you believe that you are not very worthy, not very likeable, not very bright, or a not a very good person.
- ✓ Your self-esteem is NOT necessarily based upon reality.
- ✓ It's a belief based on your most recent or relevant thoughts and feelings that you have had about yourself. It's just YOUR current evaluation, your current OPINION, of you.
- ✓ Your friends and colleagues almost certainly won't 'see' you in the same judgmental light as you do.
- ✓ You can change your self-esteem significantly in only two weeks, if you start processing your experiences differently.
- ✓ It's important to have good/high self-esteem as it affects many other areas of your life.

### What should I be working on from now on?

1. Process your positives - this is something that you want to do at least five times **every single day!**

2. Keep working on the **ACTION**s from previous chapters, in particular focusing upon building an internal sense of power and control.

**Notes** - The blank area below is for you to make any notes about the chapter.

# Chapter

# 5

## How do you respond to social pressures?

# Our Social World

Humans are social and cultural animals. We develop and learn about the world around us through our interactions with other people. Think about how a baby learns to talk – it' all about how they interact with their parents and siblings. As a society we have many values, rules and laws and our beliefs about ourselves and the world around are shaped by these social norms as we develop through life.

We've talked a bit already about how social influences, such as parenting, schooling and culture contribute to the development and maintenance of your foundations (sense of power and control and self-esteem). We are now going to think more about the social influences and pressures that exist in life and how you respond to these.

Love, to a child, is about being truly accepted, being valued, being loveable, being an equal member of the family unit and fitting in. A growing and maturing child wants to please mum, dad, other family members, teachers and friends. They want to fit into their group, be a part of this group, share the same values and beliefs as this group; they want to be socially accepted.

Social influences can be both positive and negative. All communities have certain values, norms and shared moral values, which can impact upon us in various ways. Different levels of social pressure exist within different communities and cultures, with some being more restrictive and judgemental than others.

At one extreme end of the spectrum, there are some societies and communities that celebrate difference and individuality and encourage autonomy. No community, however, is free of social pressure and influence! Even more liberal societies promote certain moral values and 'rules' and uphold legal systems (most people would argue that having a legal system is a good thing; though the ways in which people believe that this should be implemented differ). At the other end of the spectrum, you have some societies where very rigid norms and standards for behaviour exist. There may be severe consequences for transgressing these rules.

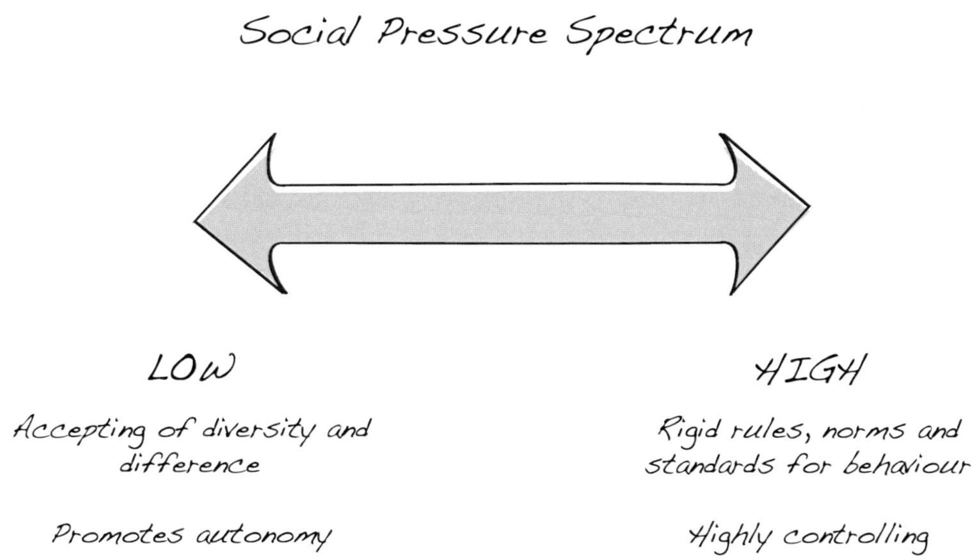


Britain is a relatively liberal and accepting society. Yet, there are still a myriad of ways in which social pressures exist. There are many means by which we are taught to conform, 'fit in' and follow particular rules. There are plenty if cultural values and traditions that contribute to children developing poor psychological foundations – think back to the chapter on your sense of power and control. There are still socio-economic divides and judgements made based upon the 'class system'. Racism, gender based discrimination, homophobia, transphobia, and other prejudices still exist. In some other parts of the world, the social pressures and judgements are far stricter. In some countries, for example, women are not allowed to drive, drinking alcohol is prohibited, homosexuality is illegal, and capital punishment exists.

## Parental influence

There are many ways in which our parents contribute to the development of our belief systems and thinking styles, both positively and negatively. As parents, we all influence our children. We all persuade our kids to work hard, be kind, watch their manners, clean their teeth every day etc. Most of the time we do this honestly, clearly and state why our children would benefit from doing what we suggest: 'clean your teeth twice a day and you should always have good, nice teeth'. We are asking our child to do something they don't really want to do (which kid really likes cleaning their teeth?) but for something that will ultimately benefit them. However, the line between what solely benefits our children and what benefits us, their parents, is sometimes very blurred.

If you go to a magic show and the magician performs some amazing tricks, you know it isn't really 'magic', you know it's really a trick and that through sleight of hand, distraction and the clever use of language, you are carefully manipulated into seeing and believing exactly what the magician wants you to. That's fine, though, because that's what you expect at a magic show. You are going there to be tricked and conned. In fact the more skilled the magician is at tricking and conning, the more we like them! Similarly, we expect to be conned, OK, maybe not conned, just manipulated a little bit, when we speak to an estate agent, car salesman or even go out on a date. We don't expect these people to be honest with us, so we are on our guard a little bit, or we take what we are told with just a pinch of salt: 'a rustic, DIY opportunity', usually means the building has been condemned, 'average fuel economy', usually means that you need to get a mortgage just to fill the car up with fuel', and 'stunning blonde, 6ft tall, PhD from Harvard' - don't even go there! We expect to be manipulated and persuaded by some people in order to meet their needs and desires, but our own friends? But our own parents?

There can be a myriad of ways in which parents (along with society generally) 'groom' their children to hold particular views. To be fair, most parents probably aren't intentionally manipulating their children. Usually parents believe that they are acting in the best interests of their children. Additionally, they may struggle to consider perspectives that differ from their own, due to the fact that they are viewing life through particular spectacles! Yet, in many contexts, parents aren't encouraging their child to develop an internal sense of power and control, allowing them a diverse range of experiences, helping them to consider different perspectives and develop critical thinking skills. Instead, they are influencing the child to share their beliefs, without really giving them a choice to think differently.

We've talked about this earlier, in relation to religion. Kids that are brought up in a religious manner even though they are at an age where they cannot possibly begin to comprehend any aspect of religion at all, tend to be just 'automatically religious' as adults. I use the word 'automatic' because they have no say in the matter. As sure as night follows day, if you guide your child to believe in some sort of god, they will do. They may rebel against you later in life and stop going to church, but their deep-down fundamental beliefs remain affected by the religious upbringing. They didn't choose it, it was chosen for them. For good reason? To give the child the best life possible? Or because the parents felt under pressure by their family, their society, their church, or their culture?

Religion is by no means the only area in which a child can be 'groomed' to hold particular beliefs. Beliefs about fate, ability, relationships, marriage, gender, race, class, homosexuality, and a myriad of other things are all regularly conveyed to children by their parents and society in ways that make it difficult for them to consider different interpretations.

You will have developed particular belief systems as a result of your upbringing. You will hold beliefs and will have never even considered how you came to do so, or whether there might be other ways of viewing the world. The good news is, that as you read through this book, you are developing a greater awareness of these beliefs. You are building a more internal sense of power and control, enabling you to make choices and view the world differently.

# How do you respond to social influences and pressures?

How do you respond to social pressures? How do your psychological foundations impact upon your responses and how can you develop strong and deep psychological foundations in spite of negative social influences?

## Social Anxiety

People who have poor foundations often create substantial social anxiety. Before we discuss what this means, let's get an idea of how much or little social anxiety you have... have a look at your TQ Report: what did you score?

### What is social anxiety?

'Social anxiety' (sometimes called 'social phobia' or 'social anxiety disorder') is essentially a fear of being judged and evaluated by other people. People with social anxiety worry about others' opinions of them and fear embarrassment, humiliation or rejection. Social anxiety can manifest as a fear of talking to other people, an avoidance of social situations, a fear of intimacy in relationships, blushing, stuttering, many sexual problems, difficulty in maintaining eye contact, 'shy bladder' (not being able to urinate in public toilets), fear of public speaking, panic attacks, or just a constant worry about what other people think about you. Wherever you are, whatever you are doing, you are worrying about what the other people around you are thinking about you. Do they think I'm clever? Do they think I'm stupid? Do they think I'm a good lover? Do they think I have a silly sense of humour? Do I look ridiculous in this? Does my bum look big in this? Most people care, to a greater or lesser extent, what others think of them. With severe social anxiety, this can become incredibly debilitating. Some people have so much social anxiety that they shy away from life completely and avoid relationships (of any kind) and all social situations, in order to minimise their exposure to their horrible feelings of being judged. Other people set very high standards for themselves in order to avoid perceived judgment. These people often describe themselves as 'perfectionists', but they are not really driven to be perfect, rather they are driven to avoid being judged for being a failure.

Most mental health professionals treat social phobia/social anxiety as just one of the spectrum of 'anxiety disorders' that exist (see DSM V, The Diagnostic and Statistical Manual of Mental Disorders, Fifth edition, 2013). They don't seem to realise that most people suffer from it to a greater or lesser extent.

### Where does it come from?

Social anxiety isn't "real". What do I mean by that? What I mean is that social anxiety happens inside a person's head – it's not about the reality of other people judging them. Although genuine social pressures and judgements do exist to varying degrees, social anxiety doesn't happen 'to you'; you create your anxious thoughts and feelings. Social anxiety is just an unhelpful reaction due to the beliefs that you hold about yourself and other people.

Social anxiety typically starts to develop in childhood, and is underpinned by a combination of different influences:

- Parental and other social influences
- Our psychological foundations
- Habitual thinking

Let's explore each of these in turn.

### Parenting and other social influences

We talked earlier about the fact that all societies have certain norms, values and rules. To a greater or lesser extent, we all want to form social bonds and be accepted by groups of people. It would be reasonable, therefore, to view social anxiety as 'the fear of not being accepted by your group', whether you are talking about your family, your friends, your religious group, your community or even your country. The first and most prominent way in which we are exposed to particular beliefs and ways of thinking is through our parents.

There is plenty of research that points to social anxiety being something children learn from their parents. Lieb, Wittchen, Hofler, Fuetsch, Stein and Merikangas (2000), found that *"There was a strong association between parental social phobia and social phobia among offspring."* Whilst Cooper and Eke (1999) studied 867 four year-old children who lived and went to school near Reading, UK and concluded:

> *Compared with the mothers of the children in both comparison groups, the mothers of the children who were purely shy had a significantly raised lifetime rate of anxiety disorder in general, and social phobia in particular. The odds ratio of a social phobia in the mothers of the purely shy children was raised over the normal control group by a factor of* **more than seven**. (My bolding)

If you are thinking 'maybe the parents passed it on to their children via their genes', Plomin and DeFries (as cited in Cooper and Eke, 1999) found that:

> *...an important role for familial environmental transmission has been suggested by the fact that the correlation for shyness between biological mothers and adopted-away children has been found to be low, whereas the correlation between adoptive parents and their adopted children has been found to be moderately high.*

I'll translate this statement from psychobabble into English for you: children tend to learn their social anxiety from the parents who bring them up on a day to day basis, whether or not these are their natural parents. As we have already discussed, parents can contribute to the development of a child's foundations – their sense of power and control and their self-esteem – in general. We are now going to explore parenting specifically in relation to the development of a child's beliefs about other people and social situations.

A growing and maturing child wants to please mum, dad, other family members, teachers and friends. Socially anxious parents, because they fear being judged themselves and believe that they need to firmly stick to social 'rules' to be accepted, tend to be more judgmental towards their children. They tend to fear being thought of as bad parents, so they are far more likely to want their children to be 'perfect', 'model' children. Parents may, consequently, hold the child to very high standards of behaviour. You can imagine the impact this could have on a child who wants to please mum and dad (as most children do)! It can significantly impact upon a child's self-esteem and their fear that other people will judge them. The child may come to believe that their parents' love is conditional upon the child meeting certain goals and standards of behaviour. All of these things increase the likelihood that a child will end up judging themselves harshly and will want to hide any mistakes from their parents (and friends, teachers, etc.).

Socially anxious parents are likely to also communicate the constant message that other people's opinions are really important, rather than teaching the child to have an internal sense of power and control. They are likely to convey a greater sense that making mistakes, behaving badly (especially in public!), and transgressing social and cultural 'rules' will have substantial negative consequences, suggesting to the child that other people do have a lot of power over their lives. Children may also notice their parent's own anxiety in social situations, which may suggest to them that these are difficult and to be feared. Finally, socially anxious parents, due to their own fear or avoidance of social situations, may not allow their children the opportunities to develop good social skills, again reducing their children's sense of power and control in relation to social situations. Parents may also be overprotective and worry about the child feeling embarrassed, scared or judged in social contexts (because that's the way that they would feel). When a parent conveys a message (either implicitly or explicitly) to their child that they believe that the child does not have the skills to cope with a particular social situation, it is, understandably, difficult for the child to feel confident in their abilities to manage the situation!

### Psychological foundations and social anxiety

Our foundations underpin whether or not we CREATE social anxiety. In turn, social anxiety can feed back into our foundations. As you probably noticed within the previous section, the ways in which socially anxious parents 'teach' their children social anxiety occurs in relation to the child's foundations. They inadvertently encourage their children to develop unhelpful beliefs about their self-worth and their sense of power and control in relation to other people and social situations.

Let's explore the influence of your sense of power and control and your self-esteem in more depth...

1) An external sense of power and control and social anxiety

Cloitre, Heimberg, Liebowitz and Gitow (1992) found that, compared to a control group, those with strong social anxiety had a significantly greater belief in 'powerful others' controlling the events in their lives. Having an external sense of power and control means that people look outside of themselves for causes and attributing factors for what they experience: they think 'what's happening to me'? They are more likely to believe that other – more powerful – people can hurt them, embarrass them, or affect their lives in other negative ways.

Having an external sense of power and control over your experiences means that you tend to look to other people for information and judgments about yourself. If your sense of self is entirely based on others' opinions, it is understandable that you worry about being judged. People with an internal sense of power and control worry less what other people think because their sense of self comes from internal sources (their own thoughts and experiences) rather than external sources (what others think of them). So, the more 'internal' you are, the less you will fear social situations and being judged generally.

Social anxiety is also about feeling powerless (or less powerful) in social or 'on the spot' type situations. It's about believing that you do not have the necessary skills and capabilities and thinking 'I can't do this,' 'I'm not good enough,' 'I would make a fool of myself' or similar. People with a poor belief in their coping skills feel less able to tolerate the judgement of other people (because they aren't very good at managing their emotional responses to events) and therefore worry more about being judged by others. They don't believe that they could cope with the consequences of others' negative judgements.

Remember what I just said about social anxiety happening inside a person's head, rather than being about the reality of other people judging you? Think about it for a moment: if you had a strong internal sense of power and control and a) looked internally to determine your views of yourself rather than turning to powerful others, b) felt that you had the skills and resources to influence and manage social situations and c) believed that you could tolerate and respond to any negative judgements from others, you wouldn't be particularly bothered about other people judging you. Even if there were genuine judgement coming from other people, you would feel that you had the power to ignore, tolerate or respond to this – you would show resilience in the face of any actual judgement.

The relationship between sense of power and control is not just one way. Social anxiety tends to feed back into an external sense of power and control. Experiencing anxiety can often feel out of control and tends to mean that you do feel less competent in social contexts (and even that you are less competent because you come across as shy, awkward and embarrassed). So every time you do create social anxiety, you are reinforcing your notion that you don't have the skills to cope with social situations and that other people's judgments matter.

Secondly, as someone who suffers from a little social anxiety, ask yourself why you might WANT to have an external sense of power and control? Social anxiety is, essentially, a fear of being judged and evaluated. This fear can sometimes mean that you WANT to attribute certain situations or symptoms to external causes as a way of protecting yourself. That way, the situations or symptoms are not your fault and you can't be judged for them. People are less likely to judge you, and be far more sympathetic towards you, if, for example, you are seen as being addicted to smoking rather than just choosing to do it. Or, that your depression is caused by a chemical imbalance in your brain rather than the fact that you are brooding, worrying and generally feeling hopeless. Or, that you are feeling ill because of a virus, rather than anxiety.

You can get caught in a cycle: The more external you are, the more you are likely to fear social situations. The more social anxiety you suffer, the more external you become.

**Note:** It is possible to have scored as having little or no social anxiety on the social anxiety quiz, but to have still scored as external on the sense of power and control quiz. People with a strong desire for control often don't appear to have much social anxiety because they developed the skills to avoid showing it. If you have an external sense of power and control, but didn't score as particularly socially anxious on the quiz, you probably fit into this category. It is, however, quite likely that you still experience social anxiety in certain contexts of your life (but you probably avoid them as much as you possibly can!).

2) Low self-esteem and social anxiety

Low self-esteem is about holding negative self-beliefs and perceiving ourselves as not being likeable or good enough. If you believe that you are an unlikeable person you are likely to be concerned that others might share your views of yourself. You are likely to worry that other people will spot the flaws in your character and the mistakes you have made. You worry that other people might be judging you because you are (consciously or unconsciously) judging yourself. YOU believe that you're a terrible person and you project those fears onto other people and worry that they will think you are terrible too. So, generally speaking, the lower your self-esteem, the higher your social anxiety. Conversely, if you feel good about yourself and are secure in your belief that you are a nice, deserving person, you tend to worry less about what others think of you.

Additionally, social anxiety can feed back into your self-esteem. Perceived hurtful and judgmental comments can affect how we see ourselves (if we have an external sense of power and control) and hence lower our self-esteem. Additionally, if you are continually worrying about how others see you, you tend to only process your strengths and achievements in relation to your perception of what others may think of you, rather than looking at what these mean to you. Take, for example, a student who has just passed a difficult exam having worked really hard. Now this student has done well and achieved something significant but she has gained a much lower mark than her friends. If this student has little social anxiety she is likely to process the achievement and congratulate herself for her hard work. If instead the student has high social anxiety she is likely to worry about other people's opinions of her score ("do my friends think that I'm stupid?") and focus on how she 'should' have done better compared to others, rather than processing her achievement.

So again you can get caught in a cycle: The lower your self-esteem, the more likely you are to feel socially anxious. The more social anxiety you suffer, the lower your self-esteem becomes.

## Habitual thinking

People who have social anxiety are also - quite simply - in the **habit** of thinking in a socially anxious way. Have a quick glance again at the diagram in the 'maintaining an internal sense of power and control' section on page 40. When someone is in the habit of reacting to events and experiences in life in an external way, they lose their critical faculties and don't ask themselves questions like 'why am I reacting like this'? 'Is there another way I could respond'? 'Is this really happening to me, or am I just doing this to myself'?

In other words, they don't ask any of the questions that would allow them to (a) recognise that thing wasn't actually just happening TO them, and (b) challenge their response and create a different outcome. Because of poor self-views, an external sense of power and control and a strong desire for control, people get into the habit of worrying about things that might go wrong. In social situations, they habitually project their own insecurities onto other people.

If you have social anxiety, you will view all social events and situations through 'socially phobic eyes'! In order to be worrying about other people's judgements, you have to keep asking yourself the powerless question: 'I wonder what they are thinking about me doing this?' The question is always phrased slightly differently – obviously – but it always follows the same format: 'I wonder if they think I'm too young for this job'? 'I bet he thinks I'm too fat to wear this'? 'I'm sure they think I'm an idiot'? 'I know they are thinking 'what on earth is she doing here"?
The point I'm making here is: the feelings of social anxiety one experiences are not passive, they may FEEL like they are happening to us out of the blue, but they are not. A person just does exactly the same thing, i.e. asks the same kind of powerless question, whenever they find themselves in a particular social situation: they react automatically, habitually.

### Gaining perspective on your social anxiety

We all want to make connections with other people and be accepted. That's normal and healthy! Social anxiety isn't about a healthy desire to form social relationships and acceptance though. Social anxiety happens when you have low self-esteem and feel powerless in relation to other people and social situations, so you worry excessively about what other people think of you.

Remember, social anxiety happens inside a person's head – it's not about the reality of other people judging them. Although genuine social pressures and judgements do exist to varying degrees, social anxiety doesn't just happen 'to you'; you create your anxious thoughts and feelings. The situation itself isn't automatically causing your social anxiety. There are different ways of responding to social pressures, influences and judgments. When you have good self-esteem and an internal sense of power and control, you evaluate your decisions and behaviour internally, you believe that you have the capabilities to manage social situations, and you know that you have the skills to tolerate and respond to any negative judgements.

You want to gain a realistic appraisal of the genuine social pressures, influences and judgements in your life. Remember earlier we discussed that different levels of social pressure exist within different communities and cultures, with some being more restrictive and judgemental than others? You want to gain a realistic appraisal of the actual social influences in your life. In many cases, the reality is that the judgement from others is far less significant than you believe. Much of the time, you are viewing yourself far more harshly than other people would! Where genuine social judgements do exist, you want to build up your coping skills, so that you are able to deal with and bounce back from these. You want to start making internal judgements of yourself rather than looking to other people. Remember, you are no longer a helpless child, who is being unknowingly groomed to hold particular beliefs. You do not have to conform to the views of your family or your immediate family – you have the power to consider other views and seek out other social bonds and new communities.

## Obedience to authority

Social anxiety isn't the only unhelpful way in which we can respond to social pressures…

Stanley Milgram and Philip Zimbardo were at the same school together in the Bronx (New York) during their teenage years. The Bronx was, and still is, a very poor area with high unemployment, a big gang culture, and hence lots of gun and knife crime. Milgram was Jewish (I say was because unfortunately he died in 1984) and Zimbardo was brought up a Catholic. With their religious upbringings, and in such a poor and unpredictable community, it's perhaps not surprising that – being both very bright and driven – they became social psychologists. They both conducted famous experiments that really shocked the world.

Milgram wanted to know whether the Holocaust could happen again. He wanted to know whether 'all Nazis were bad', believed in what they were doing or were just following orders. So in 1963 he set up his 'blind obedience study' at Yale University where he was a professor. He advertised for volunteers for an experiment studying how to 'improve memory', and around 1000 local people were screened to take part. They were told that they would be randomly split into two groups: one group were going to be 'teachers', and the other group were going to be 'students'. The teachers were (one at a time) led into a room on the Yale campus and sat at a big desk where there was a purpose-built electric shock generator, and a microphone. The teachers were told that the students (one at a time) were in another room, strapped to an electric chair (I'm sure you can see where this is going). The experimenter - in a white coat - just relayed the rules to the teacher, in a cold monotone.

He told the teacher that he/she was to ask the student in the next room a series of questions (via the microphone) and every time the student got the answer wrong they were to give them an electric shock. Every time they get one wrong the power of the shock went up by 15 volts to a maximum of 450! (On the shock generator dial were markers which said 'average shock', 'dangerous shock', 'deadly shock' and 'xxx'.)

The teacher started asking questions and when the student got some wrong he received some low-level shocks. As the shocks started to get bigger the teacher heard the student start to moan and yelp (through headphones), and the moans and yelps soon became shouts and screams. If the teacher turned to the experimenter and started to protest, the experimenter just said things like, 'Please carry on with the experiment, you have signed a contract, I will take responsibility'. Finally, at about 400 volts, as the teacher shocked the student, a loud thud was heard through the headphones and the student was unresponsive over the headset. The teacher asked the experimenter, 'What should I do?' and the experimenter replied, 'No answer is the same as a wrong answer, so please carry on the experiment and give the appropriate shock.' Again, if the teacher complained the experimenter just stated, 'You have your instructions - please continue with the experiment'.

I know what you are thinking right now - you're thinking 'I wouldn't have shocked him, that's just not right, I'm a nice person'. Yes? Did some teachers go all the way to 450 volts? (Milgram later presented his findings to 40 psychiatrists, and asked them 'what percentage of normal people would go all the way?' The psychiatrists said that only one percent of people would do such a thing.)

The first teacher stopped shocking at 285 volts. When it got to 330 volts another two teachers refused to go further. However, a massive two-thirds of teachers went all the way to 450 volts, despite knowing that the experiment could not possibly still yield useful results, as the student was already unconscious! This experiment has been undertaken many times all over the world, and the results are almost always the same: about two thirds of people, both men and women, would go all the way.

At the end of each experiment the student comes into the teacher's room and explains that he wasn't really hurt or shocked at all, and that he is an actor. This experiment has attracted some criticism, with some stating that the teachers could have guessed that they weren't really shocking people. So another couple of psychologists, Sheridan and King, in 1971 replicated the experiment, but this time the victim was a real, live, cuddly puppy. Could you? Would you? In this experiment the teachers see the puppy in front of them in a wire-mesh coated box. The puppy is supposed to walk from one end to another, and if it doesn't you press the button and give it a shock. As before, the shocks go all the way up to 450 volts. In this experiment, slightly fewer men went all the way - only around 50% of men shocked the yelping, shrieking puppy. What did the women do? (There were 13 men and 13 women taking part.) Did the lovely, cuddly puppy bring out the caring, mothering side of the female participants? Nope. 100% of the women went all the way! 100% - every single one of them shocked the puppy all the way to 450 volts.

These experiments demonstrate how normal people can do terrible, harmful, out-of-character things when (1) someone in authority instructs them to do so, (2) they get something out of it (teachers got paid to take part in Milgram's experiment and promised good grades – they were psychology students – in the puppy one), and (3) a diffusion of responsibility takes place (the experimenter or someone else took responsibility for the outcome of the experiment).

Zimbardo is most famous for his 'Stanford Prison Experiment' where he advertised for some volunteers - half were told they were 'prison warders', and the other half 'inmates'. A makeshift prison was erected underground on the Stanford campus and the experiment was due to last for two weeks. The experiment was designed to see what would happen when you gave some people (the warders) absolute power and when you took all the power away from some others (the inmates). Again, the volunteers were normal people taken from normal walks of life.

Within hours of the experiment starting the warders began 'throwing their weight around' and exerting their power over the inmates. They started punishing and ridiculing the inmates, dehumanising them and basically abusing them. Zimbardo stopped the experiment after only one week, because his girlfriend - who was also a psychologist and observing the experiment - said she would leave him if he didn't!

What have these two experiments got in common with people who smoke, kids in gangs, religious groups, people who follow a certain pop band and people who walk past a homeless person and not offer some money or help? There are pressures on these people, pressures on all of us to conform, to behave in a certain way, to follow the flock, to fit in with our friends, family and peers. We are taught from an early age to recognise the authority of others - particularly our parents, of course - and to defer to those more senior/of higher standing/in a position of authority. If the man in the white coat tells us something, we believe him.

In the puppy experiment described above, why did 100% of women shock the puppy all the way to 450 volts? Is it because women aren't nice? Is it because, deep down, women are more 'evil' than men? Though these two explanations are possible, it's far more likely that the women did it because (a) they were told to, and (b) they wanted to get good grades. Look at the year the study was carried out (it wasn't published because of the pain and misery inflicted upon the puppy - no ethics committee would support the research): 1971. Women were far more likely to be obedient to (male) authority back then because greater sexism existed. The women were all very upset and crying when they shocked the puppy, some were furious, others even complained to the Dean, but they all shocked the puppy - they believed that they couldn't say no.

Building stronger psychological foundations will help to respond to authority in a more helpful manner. When you have a more internal sense of power and control and good self-esteem you do not automatically defer to others, you instead consider whether or not it is right to do so.

## Unhelpful relationships with other people

People with poor foundations are also much more likely to form unhelpful social relationships with significant others – relationships that in some way reinforce their symptoms or maintain their poor foundations. A 'significant other' is any person who is important to an individual's life or wellbeing. Sociologically speaking, it is any person with a strong influence on an individual's self-evaluation, who is important to this individual.

### 1) Symptom-reinforcing relationships

A significant other, understandably, shows love, encouragement and support for their friend/partner/child. They listen to their worries and fears, help and support them through painful, emotional, or other difficult times. They mop their brow, fetch and carry, take them to their appointments, speak to the doctors and therapists, learn all about their friend/partner/child's condition, and, importantly, rarely challenge them.

This 'significant other' is just what we would all want if we suffered a heart attack, stroke, broke a leg or suffered some other similar setback - who doesn't want a little tender loving care when they feel lost, in pain, or unhappy? The difficulty is, that there is sometimes a fine line between 'giving support' and 'colluding and validating' (reinforcing). The significant other can (usually unintentionally) help to provide reinforcements for the person's belief systems and symptoms.
Think back to the very beginning of the book where I talked about belief systems. We know that to maintain any belief takes effort, especially one that isn't true (e.g. being sick isn't actually terrifying - it's just a bit unpleasant). You have to keep thinking about your belief, and interpreting events through distorted spectacles, in order to maintain it. If you stop thinking about your belief, then other experiences in life will slowly force you to change it – sooner or later the 'weight of evidence' would just be too much for you and you would HAVE to change the way you think.

Every time you have a conversation with your friends/partner/parents/doctor/therapist about your sense of powerless and difficulty in relation to your symptoms and they DON'T gently challenge your belief, they are inadvertently colluding with it. They have just helped you to add another brick into your 'wall of belief'. (Remember? - where every brick in the wall is another thought or experience that confirms your belief, the more bricks, the bigger the wall).

Let me ask you a question: Do you still believe in Santa?

No, I'm not taking the piss, it's a genuine question. Do you? I'm guessing that, if you are over the age of say, 12, you don't believe in Santa anymore? (If you are under the age of twelve and do still believe in Santa, then please give this book back to mummy and daddy, and certainly don't read the next few paragraphs! Oh, and sorry about the odd swear word in here, I know it's neither big nor clever). How did that happen? For ten years or so you believed in Santa, then suddenly you didn't?!

What went wrong? How did that happen? Why the sudden change of heart?

I'm guessing that, despite the want to carry on believing, the weight of evidence against the existence of Santa (not to mention the accompanying beliefs that he can visit every child in the world, and get down every chimney, whilst being towed through the sky on a magic sleigh pulled by a bunch of reindeer, the lead one having an over-sized red hooter) soon forced you to realise that it was a bit unlikely.

So, most kids stop believing in Santa by about the age of 10 or 12. Think about children who are brought up in a religious household. Do they stop believing in God by the age of ten or twelve? Some might, but most probably carry on believing, at least until their late teens. Why? Both stories are equally unlikely. If anything, the Santa Claus story is actually more plausible than the Jesus one. Santa only has one miracle to perform, and the other fella has loads. So, why do kids find it comparatively easy to drop the Santa belief, but not the God one? The answer, in a nutshell, is significant others. Your parents stopped colluding with your Santa beliefs, and started to let a wry smile cross their face when talking about leaving milk out for the reindeer, or stopped running out of excuses for the fact you don't have a chimney. They stopped colluding with you and the weight of evidence overcame your previously held beliefs, and you stopped believing. Not so with the God belief.

If you did grow up in a religious household, it's unlikely your parents stopped colluding with your God beliefs when you were age 10 or 12, because they wanted you to carry on believing them. When you questioned them about the existence of Santa, they probably said something like 'ah, you got us, you sneaky little devil, it was your dad in a red coat with a fake beard.' But when you asked a similar question about Jesus, they probably replied 'actually this fella did save the world, and his mum was a virgin, and he could walk on water - when he wasn't turning it into wine, could heal lepers, make the blind see, and come back again once he was dead'. So you carried on believing, because you had people around you that 'helped' you to carry on believing. (Please don't email me complaining about my comparison between the belief in Santa Claus and the belief in God. I'm describing how a young child might think when being told strange magical stories by their parents!)

A very similar thing is true for many psychological symptoms and problems. This is particularly the case for children. It's actually pretty difficult for a child to maintain a significant fear or phobia, for example, without at least one parent or caregiver colluding with them. Nowadays, when treating kids and teenagers at my clinic, I always work with at least one of the parents as well as the poor child. If mum (or dad) stops colluding, and instead starts to gently challenge their child's beliefs, they can help reduce the number of pro-belief thoughts that their child has by hundreds if not thousands of thoughts PER DAY. Sometimes, stopping colluding is alone enough to help the child overcome their symptoms. Let me say that again: if the parents stop colluding, and start to gently challenge their child's beliefs, then this alone can be enough to enable the child to challenge their limiting beliefs and overcome their issue.

McMurtry, McGrath and Chambers (2006) have written an interesting commentary called 'Reassurance Can Hurt: Parental Behavior and Painful Medical Procedures', illustrating this. They discussed how parents commonly try to reassure their children during medical procedures but that, perhaps counter-intuitively, research has suggested that this reassurance actually **increases** children's distress levels and perceptions of pain, rather than decreases them, i.e. rather than actually reassuring the child, often 'comforting' comments only serve to validate the child's anxiety about the medical procedure. The fact that mum or dad is trying to comfort them must mean that the procedure is really awful!

Another striking example of this type of reinforcement occurred with a recent client of mine, Ronnie. Ronnie was a 22 year-old who attempted suicide after losing his job and splitting up with his girlfriend. When Ronnie was discharged from inpatient psychiatric care he went to stay with his parents. Ronnie's family was really kind and sympathetic towards him – but this (understandably) highly concerned and sympathetic care only served to increase Ronnie's depression. Ronnie told me that the fact that his family was so worried and kind, only served to validate his beliefs that his life was really shit and there was something really wrong with him, so he got worse.

In relation to symptoms, illnesses or anxieties, people often seek out or create an environment, both the physical environment and the people in it, that support and collude with their thinking and belief systems. Typically we surround ourselves with people who share the same view of our situation and that don't question or challenge our beliefs and thinking about it. When your situation is normalised you feel much better about it. A good example of this is a smoker. In social and work situations smokers tend to seek out other smokers to share their smoking times, so they don't feel isolated, stupid or judged. Their smoking buddies validate their feelings and beliefs about smoking, and this provides a sort of 'intellectual comfort'.

With the advent of the Internet, it has become increasingly easy to get support from other people who have the same viewpoint as you. In 2007, Yahoo alone had just under nine million online 'Yahoo Groups' (Source: Yahoo). Online support groups/forums exist for depression, anxiety, emetophobia, social phobia, other fears and phobias, eating disorders, self-harm, IBS, CFS/ME, cancer, stroke, heart attacks and pretty much anything else you would care to name! Whilst these online groups may help you to feel a little bit better about living with your problem or condition, they rarely help you to actually recover! Because of the way most of these groups are set up (by someone suffering a certain problem and wanting to talk with others in a similar situation), they tend to back-up and support your limited thinking, rather than gently challenging it or giving you some perspective. If, for example, you are suffering from depression and join an online support forum you will be surrounding yourself with others suffering in the same way. It becomes normal for you to talk about and think about how depressed you are feeling and to hear similar stories from others. Rather than getting rid of your depression, you get to feel a bit better about being depressed.

When a person feels powerless and has low self-esteem, social support in response to symptoms can be reinforcing. Sometimes, people's symptoms result in their gaining support, attention and love that maybe they didn't get when they were well. It's sometimes difficult to comprehend how significant 'a little bit of attention' is to a person who (deep down) feels worthless, useless and powerless. Here I am not suggesting that the sufferer is being deliberately manipulative or 'attention seeking'. But in many cases there are gains that do provide some (unconscious) reinforcements and contribute to maintaining problems and symptoms.

It is, understandably, often very hard for people to admit that they may be gaining something 'positive' (e.g. love, care, attention, sympathy, etc.) from their symptoms. When you have a debilitating or distressing problem that you have been trying to overcome for years, it can be very difficult to think that you may in some way gain something from it. Additionally, if you have some social anxiety, you are going to fear being judged by others (because deep down you judge yourself very harshly) and thus you shy away from thinking about potential gains.

People tend to respond to the suggestion that they may be gaining something from their symptoms in one of two ways: 'How dare he suggest that I am getting attention or other gains from my symptom, this book is a load of offensive crap and I'm not reading anymore!' or alternatively 'Shit he's right - I am such a stupid, worthless, pathetic, attention-seeking idiot, it's all my fault I've got problems, I hate myself'. Yet if you are gaining something from your symptoms and on some level this is helping you to maintain your problems, then this does not make you in any way a bad person. Almost all of the clients that I have treated, regardless of their problem, have identified with receiving some reinforcements to at least some extent.

If you think about it, it's actually really common for people to receive *something* positive from situations that are unpleasant, traumatic, painful, upsetting or frightening. A good example of this is a kid with a broken leg. Having a broken leg is often scary, painful, might involve operations and injections, prevents the kid from running around with friends etc. But at the same time the kid probably does gain something from it. He/she may receive cards and presents, extra fuss from mum and dad, when he/she goes back to school all the other kids want to sign the cast and try out the crutches. Or take the example of having the flu. When you've got the flu you are likely to feel pretty crap and for the first day or so you are probably a bundle of misery who wants to curl up and cry. But again, there are some gains to your illness. Once you're cuddled on the sofa with a blanket and some paracetamol, watching TV, rather than going to work, you don't feel quite so bad. Perhaps your partner/friend/parent runs around after you, attending to your every need (or perhaps not). Perhaps they are really sympathetic, make you chicken soup or bring you cups of tea, offer to do all the shopping. . .

Now if you have high self-esteem and an internal sense of power and control you tend to feel positive about yourself and your interactions with others generally in life. The attention gained from others, when ill or in difficulty, is probably nice and makes your unpleasant situation a bit better, but it isn't particularly significant when you frequently perceive lots of positive experiences in relation to yourself. As such, attention from others doesn't tend to strongly reinforce problems and symptoms in those with high self-esteem and an internal sense of power and control. But if you have low self-esteem, high social anxiety and an external sense of power and control then any attention gained is likely to be quite meaningful.

An interesting piece of research (Walker, Claar and Garber, 2002) investigated whether or not social consequences, such as attention from others, contributed to maintaining illness symptoms in children with recurrent abdominal pain. It was found that higher levels of positive attention and a restriction of activities were indeed associated with greater symptom maintenance several weeks later. But this was only true for those children who had low self-worth and low academic competence beliefs. Children with high self-worth and competence beliefs tended to have low symptom maintenance at follow up, regardless. So in those children who felt they were worthless or incompetent, any extra attention gained from being ill really meant something. Maintaining a 'sick role', perhaps unconsciously, seemed like an attractive proposition, despite the negative consequences of feeling ill, because it allowed them to feel a bit more likeable and special. These children may have also found activity restriction reinforcing, as it may have allowed them to escape from participating in activities that they felt displayed their incompetence.

EVERYONE wants some care, love and attention and indeed deserves to receive some. If, however, you have low self-esteem and an external sense of power and control you may (wrongly) believe that you do not deserve to have any love and attention, but at the same time (understandably) desperately want some. You may, on some level, believe that the only way in which you can justify having some love and care is by having a legitimate 'excuse' such as being ill, being depressed or having another 'uncontrollable' symptom, problem or condition.

Have a think about it. There are likely to be many factors involved in your symptom and this section may not apply to you particularly. But if you have low self-esteem and an external sense of power and control then it may apply to some extent. Remember this is not about blaming or berating yourself, but exploring your ways of thinking and underlying beliefs that are causing you problems in your life, so that you can change them.

If you're reading this from the perspective of a significant other who is, perhaps unwittingly, providing some reinforcements for a loved one's symptoms, you may be feeling somewhat uncomfortable (especially if you have some social anxiety!). You probably don't want to think that you may have been contributing in any way to your loved one's problems, even if inadvertently. Think of things this way…

You are probably very close to your loved one and you obviously care for them a great deal. This has undoubtedly provided many benefits for them, BUT it may also have validated their problem or illness and perhaps provided reinforcements or gains for maintaining it. As someone who loves a person in distress or difficulty, it is often very difficult to not be concerned, worried and sympathetic. And equally, if you had instead ignored them, been really unsympathetic, judgmental or negative towards them, this would likely have caused problems too (Research by Walker, Claar and Garber (2002), for example, has shown that in addition to positive attention being reinforcing, negative attention, also, helps to maintain illness symptoms in children with low self-worth and low competence beliefs).

Ideally you want to be able to take a step back, maintain some perspective and support your loved one, without validating their negative beliefs. Gently challenging any limiting beliefs that a person may have, whilst still showing your unconditional love for them, is much more beneficial than just being sympathetic. So how do you do this?

When we love, or even just care for someone, we don't want to see them upset or in pain. We can empathise with them, we can feel sorry for them, we can feel guilty because we believe their situation/symptom is somehow our fault, we can even feel their pain. When your loved one is feeling anxious or unhappy, it's really hard to not let your emotions get in the way. You want to be 100% supportive: you're human. Trouble is, if you are blindly supportive, then you are supporting both the emotions/pain your loved one is going through, AND also their powerless beliefs about it. What you want to do is be loving, supportive, to ease their pain and suffering a little WITHOUT agreeing to their powerless beliefs about WHY or HOW they are suffering.

An example could be if your child said something like, 'I'm so anxious about tomorrow, I don't think I can cope'. Rather than responding with something like, 'You poor thing, this must be awful for you' a better response might be, 'I'm sorry you're feeling anxious, but you do have the skills to cope. You're creating that anxiety and you can change it. Let's look at what you have been thinking in order to wind yourself up.'

Remember: you want your loved ones to support you, love and care for you, WITHOUT colluding with your beliefs about HOW and WHY you need their love and support. They want to help you to realise that your symptom isn't happening to you (external cause) but is in fact something you are unintentionally doing to yourself (internal cause) and that you are in the process of training yourself out of it. It might feel like hard work but every day you are making some headway.

### 2) Taking too much responsibility for others' emotions

People with poor foundations can also end up taking far too much responsibility for other people's emotions within relationships. Many people would like others to take responsibility for how they feel – after all it's much easier than taking responsibility for these feelings themselves! Significant others (often parents, but can be partners or friends) can make statements such as:

"I don't want you to ever be unhappy"
"My life wouldn't be worth living without you in it"
"Don't ever leave me"
"Don't die before me"

Unless the person on the receiving end has a very internal sense of power and control, these kinds of statements tend to place them in an impossible position because they are being asked to take overwhelmingly responsibility for the other person's emotions. Even less obvious statements can have a similar effect:

"You've really upset me because…."
"I hope you're feeling guilty about making me feel…"
"I'm really worried about you when you do…"

You can imagine the effect upon children growing up in households where they are being encouraged to take responsibility for their parents' emotions.

What you want to be able to do is to take responsibility for your own thoughts and feelings, but not other people's. Yes sometimes we all do things that are wrong, thoughtless, dishonest or unkind, etc., which end up hurting other people. In these cases it is appropriate to think that you have been unreasonable or thoughtless and to think about what you could do to make things better. But if you are the sort of person who continually takes responsibility for other people's feelings, then, most of the time, there is absolutely nothing that you have done wrong! Here the other person's anger/fear/hurt is not about YOU, it is about his or her own external sense of power and control and low self-esteem. In a situation where you are taking undue responsibility for someone else's emotions, you need to start recognising this and take a step back.

**3) Placing excessive responsibility for your emotions onto others**

The reverse of the above is asking others to 'blame' other people for your emotions and feelings. Indeed most people are projective from time to time. For those with social anxiety, it's often easier to pass responsibility for any negative feelings over to another person, as that way you feel that it isn't your fault that you feel bad and people won't judge you for it. For example, 'you've made me so angry/embarrassed by having a tantrum in the shopping centre,' 'you make me so worried when you don't text me back for a few days,' 'I'm depressed because so-and-so doesn't care about me'.

If you have low self-esteem and an external sense of power of control you might also pass on responsibility for positive feelings as well as negative ones. Remember the example of Brenda in the previous section thinking that it was her friends who were making her happy, rather than the way in which she was thinking?

The problem with 'blaming' other people for your emotions is that by telling yourself that someone else is making you feel a particular way you believe that you are powerless to alter your emotions and feelings! You're stuck feeling unhappy/embarrassed/angry or feel unable to create positive emotions in yourself.

By taking responsibility for your own feelings it doesn't mean that you aren't ever allowed to think that other people are wrong or have behaved badly towards you, or that other people are nice and have done something kind for you. But you want to step back and gain some perspective if you are frequently handing over responsibility for how you feel to someone else. Are your feelings really about the other person's behaviour, or about your own insecurities and thinking? You can take charge of how you respond to events and experiences and be in control of your own emotions.

## ACTION! Challenge your social anxiety

Remember that the social anxiety you experience isn't real - it isn't coming from the situation you find yourself in (talking in front of a group of people, for example) it is coming from you. YOU are creating the anxiety by the way you are thinking and reacting to the situation. So, start to challenge your thinking whenever you feel some social anxiety. You will be able to do this more deeply by the time you have finished this book, but for now do this:

Whenever you experience some social anxiety (or any other kind of anxiety) tell yourself 'I'm doing this, this isn't happening **TO** me, I'm doing this, and I can stop it'. Be aware, or rather 'detect' what it was that you were thinking in order to create the anxious feeling, then change or 'amend' it. What did you actually think, in order to create the fear/anxiety? For example, if you had to talk to a group of people, you may have thought 'oh god, this is going to be so tough!' in which case, amend that thought to something more helpful such as 'I can do this, I don't need to create anxiety about it, I have the skills.'

Regardless of the nature of the situation you find yourself in, if you detect the negative/unhelpful thought you were having and amend it to something more helpful the anxiety you created will lessen significantly. Do it really well and the anxiety will disappear.

# Social Pressures - Recap

- ✓ Social Anxiety is a worry or belief that other people are judging you.
- ✓ Social Anxiety doesn't happen 'to you' - you create your anxious thoughts and feelings.
- ✓ You worry that you will fail/say the wrong thing/not pass the test/embarrass yourself, and then you imagine what others will think of you in that situation. The reality is that, most of the time, nobody really cares if you say or do the wrong thing, but in your mind they are noticing and judging you for your cock-up.
- ✓ People may also automatically defer to authority – building a more internal sense of power and control and high self-esteem helps a person to build a sense of autonomy
- ✓ People with poor foundations are also much more likely to form unhelpful social relationships with significant others – relationships that in some way reinforce their symptoms or maintain their poor foundations.

## What should I be working on from now on?

1. Challenge any social anxiety by reminding yourself that you are creating your feelings and the changing of your unhelpful thoughts to more constructive ones.

2. Keep processing your positives - remember this is something that you want to do at least five times **every day**!

3. Keep working on the other ACTIONs from previous chapters, in particular focusing upon building an internal sense of power and control.

**Notes** - The blank area below is for you to make any notes.

# Chapter 6

# Unhelpful Thinking Styles

# Unhelpful Thinking Styles

Now we are going to look at some 'unhelpful thinking styles'. Your thinking styles are part of your 'mindset' mentioned in chapter 2.

Again, most people tend to view the following thinking styles as parts of someone's personality that are fixed and unchangeable. This couldn't be further from the truth. These unhelpful thinking styles are basically just habitual styles of thinking: habits, mostly created in our childhoods, due to an external sense of power and control, social anxiety and/or low self-esteem. If the 'sufferer' stopped and thought about what they were doing for three seconds before they did it, they could stop the habit easily (I'll show you how to do this later). So an unhelpful thinking style, of all the pieces that make up the jigsaw of a person's symptoms and problems, is one of the easiest and simplest things to change, which is great news because the bloody things cause havoc!

An **unhelpful thinking style**, for our purposes, is a way of thinking that has become exaggerated or dramatised over time, usually because the person has felt powerless to change it. It is an exaggeration of a normal characteristic that we are all capable of displaying but some people have 'travelled further down that road' and turned a minor characteristic into a full-blown trait.

Thinking styles, like most symptoms, are directly related to your stress and anxiety levels, and your stress and anxiety levels are directly related to your foundations. People with an internal sense of power and control and high self-esteem, score much lower on the unhelpful thinking styles quizzes. These thinking styles **can** be helpful: most inventors have to be quite obsessive, therapists and police officers find it helpful to be hypervigilant, and impulsive thinkers tend to be good fun! However, for the purposes of this programme, these thinking styles are mainly unhelpful.

Much in the same way as our language does, our unhelpful thinking styles can validate our limiting beliefs and help to maintain our externality and low self-esteem. By challenging and managing our unhelpful thinking styles, we are again helping to create a more internal sense of power and control and higher self-esteem. We are also lowering our social anxiety and other symptoms.

The following styles of thinking seldom appear on their own. Usually, if a person has one of these unhelpful thinking styles, they've probably got a couple more hidden away somewhere. I have described them separately just for clarity. There are probably many other different thinking styles but the ones I have included here are the more common ones.

When you read this chapter, you may need to keep in mind what you have already learnt about yourself. You should now know whether your sense of power and control is external or internal and have a good idea about your self-esteem and social anxiety levels. If you have an external sense of power and control and low self-esteem and you tend to create high social anxiety, it may be that you find it challenging identifying some of these unhelpful thinking styles in yourself. Remember that this book is about really getting to know yourself and that in order to help yourself most effectively you will need to be honest with yourself.

You've already completed the thinking styles quizzes, so keep your TQ Report to hand as you work through this chapter, and compare your scores.

## The negative style

There is plenty of evidence to suggest that people who think negatively, or who have negative expectations in life, don't share the same successes, experience the same levels of 'happiness' and don't maintain as good health as people whose tendency it is to 'always look on the bright side' (for example: Goodhart, 1985; Gil *et al.,* 1989; Peden *et al.,* 2000).

'Negative Thinkers' are those people who always focus on the 'bad things', always assume that things won't go well, always assume they are going to fail, always assume the worst-case scenario. For them, the glass is half empty - 'it won't work', 'I can't find love', 'it's bound to get worse', 'I'm bound to get found out by the tax-man' etc.

We are not talking here of people who are *sometimes* negative, as everyone is capable of being negative from time to time. We are talking about people whose entire outlook is negative. If people who are really positive are thought of as: 'full of energy', 'full of life' or 'full of the joys of spring', then people who are very negative are seen (as one of my friends describes them) as 'energy vampires' who will suck all the energy and positivity out of you. (Keep some garlic handy!)

A negative person works hard to: find the faults in everything; spot the things that will probably go wrong; assume the worst case scenario; see how 'breakable' a toy is, rather than seeing how much fun it would be; think how expensive a holiday is, rather than how relaxing and revitalising it could be.

### Why be negative?

The negative person really does WANT and NEED to see the negative in everything because they have a negative belief system. We already know, from chapter one, that once you have a belief system you need to prove it to be correct. So when someone is a negative thinker, they need to be proven correct as well.

As an example, someone who feels achy and tired one day might worry 'oh shit, I am getting ill'. If they do come down with something later, the sufferer might in some way be PLEASED because he was right. Even though he now feels really shit, he was right. This way, at least he feels his life is predictable, he feels he has some control: 'I know what is going on with my own body'.

As I said in the introduction to 'unhelpful thinking styles', they are seldom seen alone (in a clinical setting anyway). Usually, if someone has a strong negative style, then they quite often have the **brooding**, **catastrophic** and **paranoid** styles also (see below).

I'm going to talk in detail later about 'secondary gains' but, for now, a secondary gain describes what a person may be getting out of something (an illness or a symptom) that at first may not be obvious. Perhaps a better name for secondary gains would be 'hidden gains' or 'hidden benefits'. When I mentioned the person feeling 'pleased' that he was correct about being ill on, you may have thought 'that's a bit bonkers, being glad that you feel like shit!' but there would have been some payback for him somewhere. He would have GAINED something from it. But what?

The most commonly associated symptom with the negative style is strong social anxiety. I'll say that again: **'negativity' almost always goes hand in hand with social anxiety**.

The negative person is fearful of many things in life: being judged, being let down, being rejected, feeling not good enough, feeling sad (to name but a few) and will go to great lengths to avoid these fears. Think of yourself as sixteen years old again (I do appreciate that this might be a long time ago for some readers!) and your best friend suggests that you ask out on a date the best girl or boy in the school. If you think that 'they wouldn't want to go out with me' and you 'don't dare' to even dream that they might, this is the feeling that people with a strong negative thinking style are trying to avoid. They don't want to dream/imagine/fantasise that things COULD be better, that they COULD get a nicer partner, that they COULD go on a wonderful relaxing holiday, that their symptoms could be cured because if they DID dare to dream it and it wasn't true, then they would feel REALLY bad, REALLY let down, REALLY stupid, REALLY rejected.

One side-effect of always thinking negatively is that if you don't think that something is going to work, be fun, be interesting, be challenging, be helpful or just be nice, then you don't do it. Hence, strong negative thinkers don't tend to do much in life - as they can always find a good reason not to. Negative thinkers tend to choose predictable, unchallenging work and tend to have over-empathic partners who buy into their spouses' negativity, making it even harder for the negative thinker to get out of their thinking. We call this spouse a 'significant other' - we'll talk about this later.

Can you imagine the impact that negative thinking would have upon someone who has cancer, or even a common cold? What about someone whose business fails, or someone who gets dumped by their partner? As you can imagine, these things would just be 'predictable' to the negative thinker; they were expecting it! If 'being negative' is all about not seeing the good, the nice, the fun, or the positive in anything, then it is not surprising how often negative-thinkers are ill.

One piece of research I stumbled across was talking about a thinking style that is the opposite of being negative - being grateful in life, even for the smallest things. Being grateful or positive about life resulted in better overall well-being for those involved in the study.

> *A grateful response to life circumstances may be an adaptive psychological strategy and an important process by which people positively interpret everyday experiences. The ability to notice, appreciate, and savor the elements of one's life has been viewed as a crucial determinant of well-being.*
>
> (Emmons and McCullough, 2003)

One thing that is particularly common to the negative thinker is the fact that, unsurprisingly, they don't smile very much. Now, I'm sure that YOU wouldn't smile very much if you didn't have anything to smile about but it goes deeper than that. Smiling isn't just a physical response to a thought or stimulus, it works the other way round too. Someone who smiles more feels happier (because they smile more), they feel more grateful in life, they see things more positively, they expect more out of life, they are less anxious, they are less prone to depression and they are more resilient.

They feel that life is easier, which makes sense if you think about it. Try frowning for a minute and just experience how it feels. Now smile and experience how it feels. It feels much easier to smile than it does to frown. It's not surprising therefore that people who frown a lot feel that life is harder and tougher than people who smile a lot, regardless of whether life IS actually harder and tougher for that person. Researchers have studied how different it FEELS to perform a simple task, first when smiling, then when frowning:

> *In one now classic study, two groups of people were asked to add up a list of numbers. During the task, one group were asked to furrow their brows (or, as the researchers put it, 'contract their corrugator muscle') while the others were requested to adopt a slight grin ('extend their zygomaticus muscle'). This simple act of facial contortion had a surprise effect on how hard they found the number-adding task, with frowning participants convinced that they had expended far more effort than the grinning group.*
>
> (Wiseman, 2009)

I mentioned resilience just now - resilience is the ability to 'bounce back' or recover from difficulties and challenges. It could be described as having an internal sense of power and control, a positive attitude and a strong feeling of self-belief.

> *Researchers have explained resilience in terms of hardiness, and proposed that hardy individuals have a strong commitment to self, are willing to take action and to deal with problems, have a positive attitude toward their environment, hold a strong sense of purpose, and develop a strong internal locus of control which enables them to see life's obstacles as challenges that can be overcome.*
>
> (Hebert, 1996)

*Resilient individuals are those who, despite severe hardships and the presence of at-risk factors, develop characteristics and coping skills that enable them to succeed in life.*

(McMillan and Reed, 1994)

*They appear to develop stable, healthy personalities and are able to recover from, or adapt to, life's adversities.*

(Werner, 1984)

Other interesting research articles on positive/negative emotions include: Fredrickson (1998) and Fredrickson *et al.* (2000).
People with a strong negative style NEED to be negative in order to protect themselves against the pain of failure or rejection. If they don't dream of success or happiness, they can't feel hurt when these experiences don't materialise. There can be a need to wallow and brood, to display obvious signs of unhappiness, in order that other people can support, sympathise and empathise (collude) with them. When someone does empathise or collude with them, it only validates how they are feeling and allows them to feel worse!

I was recently working with Ronnie, who I mentioned earlier. Ronnie is a really nice twenty-two year old lad, who recently tried to kill himself by overdosing on painkillers. He lost his job and got dumped by his girlfriend in the same week (poor chap). He ended up spending a couple of days in our local psychiatric hospital. Once discharged, he went back home to his parents' house, where his depression got worse. A week or so later, I saw him for a single session which not only taught him how to stop 'doing' depression but made him feel more positive than he ever had done before. Anyway, the point of mentioning Ronnie is that he told me that there was no way he was going to get better whilst staying at home because *'although my family were incredibly loving and supporting, this only validated my belief that my life was in fact, total shit, so I got worse'.*

Those of you reading this who are parents or teachers will have, no doubt, witnessed this phenomenon on many occasions. Remember a time when your child (or a child in your care) fell over and hurt, say, their knee. They know it's sore and they are pulling their 'sore' face as they inspect their knee for damage. If there is no mark or blood, their 'sore' face turns into a 'disappointed' face for a few moments, and then they run off to play with the other children again, happy as Larry. If, however, upon inspection their knee starts to bleed, then their soreness is validated and they start to cry.

Another reason why people can NEED to feel negative is because they believe that they don't DESERVE or even WANT a positive outcome, this primarily stems from their belief systems and the fact that they cannot IMAGINE a positive outcome.

It can be a 'chicken and egg' situation. Sometimes a person NEEDS to be very negative in order to justify their misery (rather than feeling miserable BECAUSE you have a lot to be negative about). A simple example of this could be when you are feeling tired after a busy week and consequently a little bit stressed or emotional. Rather than thinking 'right I'm just a bit tired, I'll feel better tomorrow after a sleep/ if I get myself a cup of tea and watch a comedy/ if I have a long bath and read a good book', the negative person looks for evidence to support his/her negative emotions. 'I'm unlovable, I'll never get a partner, my life is awful, etc.' Of course once you have thought along these lines then your emotions feel completely justified and you are far less likely to get over them quickly.

Finally, and perhaps most importantly, exercising a strong negative thinking style allows the person, through the fact that they can negate the possibility of gaining any success or happiness, to avoid taking any responsibility for anything. What a lovely, safe, comfortable feeling that must be.

## ACTION! Changing negatives into positives

The opposite of negative is, obviously, positive. So start to recognise when you are thinking or feeling in a negative way and realise that you are choosing to do this. Ask yourself, 'How can I express what I am thinking/feeling in a positive way?' Just because things might not be great for you at the moment, doesn't mean that you have to validate these negatives by expressing them. Why not 'play them down', or minimise them instead? Better still, why not look for the silver lining.

Start looking for positives in every situation, no matter how negative the situation is. Even when an experience is unpleasant, upsetting or even traumatic, finding some positives helps to ensure that you are not making the experience worse by the way in which you are thinking about it.
Research has suggested that even in some very traumatic and unpleasant situations people are often able to find positives and that this helps them to recover and Thrive. Parry and Chesler (2005), for example, interviewed childhood cancer survivors and found that a majority found positives in their experience of having had cancer. Carver and Antoni (2004) found that women with breast cancer who found positives during the year after diagnosis had better psychological outcomes 5-8 years later. A study of US soldiers (Wood *et al.*, 2011) found that those who found positives from their combat experiences were less likely to suffer from PTSD and depression afterwards.

Some studies have suggested that finding positives is linked to physical as well as psychological health. For example, a review by Bower *et al.* (2008) described how finding positives in relation to a range of illnesses, including heart attacks, HIV/AIDS and cancer, has been linked to better health and survival rates.

## The brooding style

Those with a strong brooding side tend to worry and think about every experience in intricate detail. Everything is thought about and gone over at least a hundred times! Brooding is about control. The more you think and brood and worry about something, looking at it from every angle, the more you feel you are likely to understand it, get it right, figure it out, bring it to a conclusion and make the right decision.

Someone with a brooding thinking style is very often rigid, methodical, power-seeking, thinks in black and white, loves routine, order and discipline. An obsessive person is like a hungry dog with a juicy bone!

Imagine for a moment, a non-obsessional person who gets rejected by someone. Rejection hurts but, in a 'healthy-thinking' person, it doesn't tend to last long. The emotional charge is soon discharged, especially once the person has had their self-esteem validated by someone else they care for. Now imagine the same thing happening to someone with a strong obsessional thinking style - they could brood and worry and ruminate about it for weeks and weeks. Every time they think about it, they feel rejected all over again. So this one time of being rejected can become many times (in their mind at least). They could start to feel paranoid or worthless, they might not eat because they are so stressed, their immune system may become depressed, all because they wouldn't let it go and move on.

The ability to brood and ruminate over something for a long period of time is a superb thinking style to have, IF you also have a positive outlook, good self-esteem and an internal sense of power and control. Everything, ever invented, was invented by somebody with an obsessional side to their nature. The Mac computer that I am typing this book on was developed by an obsessive person, as is the watch I am wearing, the jeans I am wearing, the chair I am sitting on, the clock that is ticking in the background, the light bulb providing light, EVERYTHING was designed, developed and built by obsessive people. Speaking of light bulbs, Thomas Edison, the man who first made a mass-producible electric (filament) bulb, made several hundred attempts at designing the long-lasting light bulb until he got it just right. When asked by a newspaper reporter 'how does it feel to have failed seven hundred times?' the great inventor responded, 'I have not failed seven hundred times. I have not failed once. I have succeeded in proving that those seven hundred ways will not work. When I have eliminated the ways that will not work, I will find the way that will work.' He is also the owner of the quote: 'genius is one percent inspiration and ninety-nine percent perspiration'.

Only people with an obsessive side to their nature will focus their attention for so long on one subject, regardless of what other people may think about the subject.

If, however, you have a strong brooding thinking style and social anxiety, you might find yourself suffering from one of the symptoms that, based on my clinical experience, ONLY obsessive/socially anxious people suffer from, like: OCD (obsessive-compulsive-disorder), anorexia, hypochondria, body dysmorphic disorder, IBS (irritable bowel syndrome), ME/PVFS/CF (myalgic encephalomyelitis, post-viral fatigue syndrome, chronic fatigue), clinical depression and Tourette's syndrome. Based on my twenty years of clinical experience and ten years of supervising hundreds of other therapists, many of them with many years of clinical experience themselves, I have never known a non-obsessive person to suffer from any of the aforementioned symptoms. It is the obsessional thinking that keeps replaying stressful experiences (creating more stress), keeps over-analysing situations (creating more confusion and powerlessness) and keeps focusing on unhelpful thoughts (creating a huge lack of perspective) that both precipitates and maintains these symptoms.

Research has also shown that obsessing and ruminating about problems can have very negative effects on mood and can reduce the ability to recover from difficulties. Lyubomirsky and Tkach (2004) found that:

> *Many people believe that when they become depressed or dysphoric they should try to focus inwardly and evaluate their feelings and their situation in order to gain self-insight and find solutions that might ultimately resolve their problems and relieve their depressive symptoms (Lyubomirsky and Nolen-Hoeksema, 1993; Papageorgiou and Wells, 2001a,b; Watkins and Baracaia, 2001).*

The above really encapsulates perfectly the nature of and problem with obsessive thinking: obsessive people believe they NEED to focus inwardly and analyse their feelings - they really believe that they HAVE to obsess, to problem-solve, to try and figure things out and to make sense of their symptoms and their life. Problem is, they are wrong in their assumptions! I've never yet met an obsessive person who actually DID resolve their problem/symptoms after obsessing about them. In fact, they usually made them seem much worse. Lyubomirsky and Tkach (2004) went on to say:

> *Challenging this assumption, numerous studies over the past two decades have shown that repetitive rumination about the implications of one's depressive symptoms actually maintains those symptoms, impairs one's ability to solve problems and ushers in a host of negative consequences.*

So brooding and obsessing actually MAINTAINS the very symptoms that obsessive thinkers were attempting to resolve. Worse than that, what happens when you keep trying to problem-solve (by brooding and analysing) a problem that is not actually solvable? You develop a more external locus:

> *In addition to enhancing negatively biased thinking, rumination in the context of a depressed mood has been shown to impair people's problem-solving skills. . .studies have provided evidence that ruminative focusing leads dysphoric individuals to appraise their problems as* ***overwhelming and unsolvable****.*
> . . (my bolding)

Those with the obsessive style tend to become so caught up in brooding and dwelling that they do not take the correct action to solve their problems. They may think that by obsessing they are gaining control and helping themselves to figure out a problem. In fact, they are far less likely to use active coping skills to deal with problems or stressful life events than those who do not tend to brood. Obsessing about a problem tends to focus all attention on this problem, reinforcing all the negatives, keeping people absorbed in their worries. So rather than increasing your sense of control as intended, obsessing actually decreases it!

## ACTION! Stop brooding - it doesn't help!

You don't HAVE to brood about things! You choose to do it, so choose to stop it. Whenever you become aware that you are starting to brood about something, challenge yourself about why you are doing it and, if necessary, remind yourself of the research above. Ask yourself, 'Do I need to brood about this?' Or, 'Is it helpful for me to do this?' If necessary, stop what you are doing at the time and leave the room or get up from your desk. In other words, ESCAPE from whatever situation you are in and focus your mind upon something else. Put effort into escaping and you'll stop obsessing. Do you brood and obsess when you are out with friends/having dinner/playing golf/having sex? No. Why not? Because when you are doing things like this, you are fully engaged in something else other than your thoughts.

Remember: you only create stress, worry or panic around situations where you feel external and not in control. Brooding and obsessing is an unhelpful attempt by you to gain some control and feel more internal. Complete the ACTIONs in the sense of power and control chapter and you WILL develop greater internality, and you won't need to obsess anymore.

## The paranoid style

If you have the paranoid thinking style you are likely to frequently worry that other people are out to criticise, reject, exploit or harm you. People with a paranoid style tend to have a strong sense of public self-consciousness (social anxiety) and a sense of self-importance. Publicly, self-conscious people tend to worry constantly about how they appear to others. They tend to be very aware that people could be judging them, because they are judging themselves. They are, consequently, very alert to the attention of other people. People with a sense of self-importance believe that others are always interested in and thinking about them. They assume that they are at the forefront of other people's thoughts.

A number of studies have suggested that self-consciousness increases the tendency towards paranoid thoughts. Fenigstein (1984) found that people who were high in public self-consciousness were more likely to perceive hypothetical social situations as being relevant to or targeted toward themselves than those low in public self-consciousness. A study by Fenigstein and Vanable (1992) revealed that people who were high in public self-consciousness were more likely than those low in public self-consciousness to assume that they were being watched when seated in a room with a two-way mirror.

People with a paranoid thinking style are trying to make sense of their world through their distorted belief systems (their version of shit-tinted spectacles). As we know, people tend to develop belief systems over time and these are based on how they perceive their experiences, so it is likely that paranoid people believe they have been subjected to highly critical, abusive or hostile experiences sometime in the past.

> *Typically, individuals who exhibit paranoid thinking are trying to make sense of their internal unusual experiences, often by drawing in negative, discrepant or ambiguous external information (e.g. others' facial expressions). For example, a person may go outside feeling in an unusual state and rather than thinking 'I'm feeling a little odd and anxious, probably because I've not been sleeping well', interpret their feelings, together with the facial expressions of strangers in the street, as evidence of a threat (e.g.*

> *'People don't like me and may harm me'). But why a persecutory interpretation? We interpret internal and external events in line with our previous experiences, knowledge, emotional state, memories, personality and decision-making processes and therefore the origin of persecutory explanations lies in such psychological processes.*
>
> (Freeman and Garety, 2006)

Trust is a huge issue to people with a paranoid side to their nature. Their hyper-sensitivity to criticism and the catastrophic way in which they process events (see The Catastrophic Style) means that they find it incredibly hard to trust people and perceive untrustworthiness in everyone they meet - including their own family, spouse and friends.

> *. . .those with paranoid personality disorders are extremely mistrustful. Convinced that others are out to exploit them, their suspicion is manifested by a marked propensity to misinterpret seemingly innocuous events as personally threatening. . . there is an exaggerated and unwarranted tendency to regard the behavior of others as if it were related to or targeted toward the self, so that, for example, innocent comments from others are taken as malevolent putdowns, or the continual appearance of a stranger on the street means that one is being watched or plotted against.*
>
> (Fenigstein and Vanable, 1992)

Finally, as with anyone having a strong external sense of power and control, a sense of powerlessness further propagates the paranoia:

> *Powerlessness leads to the belief that important outcomes in one's life are controlled by external forces and other persons, rather than by one's own choice and effort. This belief in external control interacts with the threat of victimization or exploitation to produce mistrust, which may then develop into paranoia.*
>
> (Mirowsky and Ross, 1983)

Freeman *et al.* (2005), proposed the following 'Paranoia Hierarchy' (below). The more severe the paranoid thoughts are (the higher the number) the less frequent they are; i.e. your average paranoid person may be consumed by social-anxiety fears (number 1) but may only occasionally worry that people were really out to do them significant physical harm (number 5).

1. Social evaluative concerns (e.g. fears of rejection, feelings of vulnerability, thoughts that the world is potentially dangerous).
2. Ideas of reference (e.g. people talking about you, being watched).
3. Mild threat (e.g. people trying to cause minor distress such as irritation).
4. Moderate threat (e.g. people going out of their way to get at you).
5. Severe threat (e.g. people trying to cause significant physical, psychological, or social harm, conspiracies, known to wider public).

## ACTION! Maintain perspective

Most paranoid thoughts are simply projections of your own judgement of yourself, your social anxiety. Start to challenge your paranoid thoughts. What evidence do you have for them? E.g. when you think someone is 'giving you the eye', instead consider that you are flirting with you or like your outfit. If someone makes a comment about your appearance or your work that isn't incredibly flattering, it's OK, not everyone has to give you top marks for everything and not everyone has to like you. Tolerate the uncomfortable feelings and don't obsess about them and make them seem bigger. Most people who have the paranoid thinking style also have a strong brooding thinking style and 'live' in their thoughts a lot of the time. So also use the ACTIONs for the brooding thinking style to overcome your brooding and obsessing. To think a paranoid thought you must, at least temporarily, have lost your perspective, which means your stress-o-meter needle must be in the red (see Chapter 10 'Anxiety and Stress'). Challenge every unhelpful thought or belief you have and this will help you keep perspective.

## The black and white style

Black and white thinking (also known as 'all-or-nothing', or dichotomous thinking) is a style characterised by people thinking, feeling and reacting to experiences in an 'all-or-nothing way', where there is no grey area or middle ground. For example, if you have a black and white thinking style you may see yourself as either: a success or failure; right or wrong; good or bad. You may think of your life as: fantastic or rubbish; exciting or completely dull. You may think of your relationship as: perfect or terrible; loving or loveless - you are getting the picture I'm sure. From my own experience, this thinking style is often seen in people who have anxiety, fears and sexual problems but it is also associated with a number of other psychological problems, including eating disorders, depression and anxiety (Byrne, Allen, Dove, Watt and Nathan, 2008).
Black and white thinking is often found in people who also have one or more of the obsessional, catastrophic or perfectionist thinking styles.
Obsessive people tend to have very rigid thinking, which goes hand in hand with their desire for control and order. Black and white thinkers find ambiguity and uncertainty hard to tolerate. They dislike shades of grey or anything that is not clear-cut, due to their strong desire for control, which results from underlying feelings of powerlessness (external locus). Their black and white thinking is just a reflection of this.

I'll give you an example. Many of the 'phobias' that my colleagues and I are asked to help with on a day-to-day basis, aren't really phobias as such. They are just situations where the 'sufferer' feels out of control (because they have a strong desire for control and cannot control this particular situation) and has some black and white thinking. These situations include: flying, dogs, water, dying, cancer, spiders, snakes, wasps, hospitals, boats, tunnels, lifts, being burgled. As you can see, all of these 'phobias' appear to be of external, uncontrollable and unpredictable situations. When a client presents for help with one of these 'phobias', they will always regale us with the story of how their 'phobia' was first created. The terrible time when the dog/wasp/snake/spider bit them or when the aeroplane/lift/boat broke down. The reality is though, that these types of 'phobias' are almost entirely cognitive: the sufferer has created them because of their external locus, their fear of being out of control, their strong desire for control and their black and white thinking.

If you are one of these 'sufferers' and you are now thinking to yourself 'That's not what happened to me, I remember that huge spider my brother put down my back,' it may be useful to think again. Take Eric, for example, who suddenly, aged 27, develops a fear of driving on motorways. Eric could have chosen to react to this fear by just thinking 'Ok, I don't like motorways, so I'll go fairly slowly until I regain confidence, no big deal, life goes on.' However, Eric has a fear of being out of control, a strong desire for control and black and white thinking. He NEEDS to understand where his 'phobia' has come from, he must CONTROL how much he is exposed to this situation, he is DRIVEN to brood and ruminate about this situation until he can make some sense of it and thus feels a bit more in control. So Eric has an external locus - what do people with an external locus do when they are searching for a reason for something? They look EXTERNALLY: 'what has happened to me to cause this problem?' They scan their mind back through time until they come across what they believe to be a fitting cause (usually some sort of emotional trauma) that would explain their current symptom and allow them to feel more in control again.

In Eric's case, it almost doesn't matter that he believes his 'phobia' was caused by a near accident he had eight years ago, or that he chooses to brood about it. It's when his black and white thinking kicks in and he thinks: 'right, I'm never going to allow myself to get into that situation again,' and starts to avoid motorways. Actually, the very best course of action that Eric could take would be to immediately get back on a motorway and EXPOSE himself to the uncomfortable feelings (feelings that he is creating but that he believes stem from his near accident many years ago) TOLERATE the discomfort for a short while and the fear would undoubtedly disappear. This is the nature of 'exposure therapy'.

Gordon was a recent client of mine in Cambridge. Gordon is a VERY fit (he's a runner, mountain climber and skier) man in his thirties who had three big phobias (his words) on entering adulthood: a fear of flying, a fear of water and a fear of doctors. On first meeting him I asked, 'How can I help?' He stated that he had got over two of his fears - he just needed help to get over his fear of doctors. I asked him what happened to his other fears. He replied, 'Well, three years ago I got married to a French girl and once a month she flies back home to Bordeaux to see her parents. If I wanted to see her that weekend I had to go with her, so I went with her, had some difficult flights but gradually got over my fear.' I asked about his fear of water and he replied, 'Well, I had always wanted to go surfing, so last summer I took a month off work and stayed in Newquay (Cornwall) for a week. I went in the water three times a day and by the end of the week my fear of water had gone!' 'OK', I said, 'so when's the last time you went to see a doctor?' He replied, 'I've not been to see a doctor since I was a baby.' For more than twenty-five years he had avoided doctors and hospitals and, every time he avoided one, he had made his fear bigger and bigger. Because he had never TOLERATED his fear and EXPOSED himself to going to a doctor, he had never challenged his black and white thinking. After working through this book with me, Gordon visited his doctor easily within a couple of weeks.

Black and white thinking leaves little room for any perspective over a situation which can then, in the right person, trigger an overdramatic emotional response - which we call catastrophising (see next thinking style). If you tend to view things in absolute terms you will probably find it difficult to recognise the more complex reality of an experience. When a person with a black and white thinking style is looking at a situation positively, then, they don't tend to suffer any negative effects, as they see things in a firmly positive manner (although they may still not have true perspective on the situation!). If, however, this thinking style is present in someone who has some self-esteem issues and social anxiety (which it usually is, due to its link to an external sense of power and control) then they are likely to view many experiences as rigidly 'bad'. For example, a person with this unhelpful thinking style, who experiences some criticism from their boss at work about a recent assignment, is likely to think along the lines of 'my boss doesn't like me and I can't do these assignments' rather than the probably more realistic 'I made some errors in this assignment and my boss isn't happy with it but my work is generally good and I now know what I can do to improve next time'.

The black and white thinking style is a significant contributor to the perfectionist thinking style (discussed in a moment). Egan, Piek, Dyck and Rees (2007) found that dichotomous thinking was related to negative perfectionism in all groups tested and to a particularly large extent in the group that had been clinically diagnosed as having an anxiety or depressive disorder.

This unhelpful thinking style is often expressed in a person's approach to life, which also tends to be black and white, or all or nothing - they either do something with 100% commitment or they completely avoid doing it. Again, this is often related to the black and white thinker's strong desire for control. For example, when faced with a fear or anxiety, the person who tends to think in a black and white way will frequently completely avoid the anxiety-provoking situation. Although this temporarily increases feelings of control, it only further reinforces the fear of the situation, which ultimately leads to increased feelings of powerlessness. The positive side of black and white thinking and behaviour is that when a person with this thinking style does decide to overcome an anxiety or problem they tend to commit fully and follow things through. All-or-nothing behaviour is particularly common amongst black and white thinkers who also have the perfectionist thinking style, in an attempt to avoid failure. Black and white thinking has been found to correlate with weight regain (Byrne, Cooper and Fairburn, 2004). Those who thought in a black and white way were more likely to regain weight after one year post-slimming. These weight re-gainers are likely to have believed that falling short of any weight loss targets was evidence of complete failure and thus completely gave up any further efforts to lose weight (Byrne *et al.*, 2008).

## ACTION! Learn to tolerate uncomfortable feelings

Black and white thinkers tend to think that way in order to exercise more control and make their lives more predictable, e.g. 'If I know the party is going to be 'horrible' I won't go, I'll avoid the 'horrible' experience and am therefore more in control'. This unhelpful thinking style, like many of the others, stems from a strong desire for control. The easiest way to change it then is to create a more internal locus - see the **ACTIONs** at the end of the sense of power and control chapter. On a day-to-day basis, whenever you are aware that you are thinking in a black and white way, tell yourself to 'tolerate the experience'. If you are at the dentist/on a plane/in a meeting/on a date/in a lift/on the phone etc. and you are feeling anxious and want to get away, slow your breathing down and tell yourself you can tolerate the situation, e.g. 'this is OK, I can tolerate this situation', or 'it will be alright at the meeting, I don't have to feel panic, nothing bad is going to happen, I can tolerate it'. If you have a fear or phobia, tell yourself the fear you are experiencing isn't being caused by a spider/plane/height/situation but by your black and white thinking about the situation - 'this fear is coming from inside me, not outside of me and I can tolerate it'.

## The catastrophic style

Catastrophising is the process where a person emotionally magnifies, exaggerates or blows out of proportion a perceived threat or worry. The 'catastrophiser' is the person who uses very strong (exaggerated) language and who thinks and feels in a dramatic fashion.

If you are a catastrophiser, instead of saying, 'I've got a headache', you might say, 'My head is killing me.' Instead of saying, 'I feel I'm stuck at home all the time,' you might say, 'I'm stuck in this prison cell and I don't know where the key is to get out.' When you have a sore leg, you might think, 'Oh my god, I've got a deep vein thrombosis.' When you have a spot on your arm, you worry it's cancer. When you have hiccups, it's a heart attack. When the phone rings, it's your mum to say someone has died. . .

Common catastrophic words include: all, never, always, totally, completely, forever, terrible, awful, hideous, starving, nightmare, calamity, devastated, havoc, chaos, fiasco, tragedy, depressed, shock, terror, disgusting, appalling, atrocious, dangerous, disastrous, dread, extreme, hate, repulsive, revolting, serious, severe, shocking, vile, terrifying, evil, horrible, ridiculous.

The main problem with catastrophising is that it very often goes hand in hand with having a highly suggestible nature and you can see where that might lead. With the catastrophiser, as soon as the 'suggestion' has been thought or given, the perspective that would normally give some sense of rational control disappears, due to the ensuing panic. Then there is nothing stopping the person from acting out whatever the suggestion was. For example, someone who catastrophises: 'Oh my god, I'm going to be so terrified at the dentist this afternoon, it's going to be so awful,' is very likely to indeed feel anxious and panicky.

Catastrophising builds up small things into big ones. Minor problems become unbelievable disasters very quickly. This can lead to your limiting belief systems being reinforced by many seemingly 'hugely significant' experiences that were in fact fairly minor before you built them up by catastrophising.

There is a great deal of scientific evidence to support the fact that magnifying and exaggerating problems can have negative effects on both psychological and physical well being. Catastrophising is positively correlated with depression, anxiety and stress (Martin and Dahlen, 2005). A large number of studies have shown that catastrophising about pain is linked to pain intensity:

> *The relation between catastrophising and pain has been observed across measures and in diverse patient groups, including mixed chronic pain, low back pain, rheumatoid arthritis, aversive diagnostic procedures, surgery, dental procedures, burn dressing changes, whiplash injuries, and survey samples of young adults, asymptomatic individuals participating in experimental pain procedures and varsity athletes.*
>
> (Sullivan *et al.*, 2001)

One study with children (Vervoort *et al.*, 2005) investigated the effects of catastrophising in both a group of schoolchildren and a group of children with chronic pain. In both cases, catastrophising about pain was positively related to somatic symptoms, pain severity and disability. Another study (Vervoort *et al.*, 2010) looked at the future effects of pain catastrophising in children. Incredibly, children's levels of catastrophising about their current pain uniquely contributed to pain and disability experienced six months later.

Catastrophising is more common in people whose parents tended to catastrophise. If, as a child, your parents usually responded to you in an 'over the top' catastrophic manner, you are likely to pick up on this and learn to catastrophise yourself. Let's say a young child forgets to pick up her school bag from the bottom of the stairs. If her father responds very emotionally by yelling and screaming, saying that he could have tripped over and broken his neck, the child is likely to also respond with a disproportionate emotional reaction. Alternatively, imagine the child who falls over and bumps his head. The child initially seems ok, but his mother panics and fusses over the child, envisaging concussion, almost hysterical herself. As a result the child bursts into floods of frightened tears. Obviously all parents shout unnecessarily at, or worry overly, about their kids from time to time. It is when the child is consistently presented with extreme emotional reactions to perceived mistakes or dangers that he or she is likely to learn to respond in the same way.

> *Specifically, it is possible that parents who tend to catastrophise are visibly anxious and demonstrate anxious behaviors in the presence of their child. It is also possible that child learning of anxiety develops, at least in part, from parents modeling anxious interpretation of situations. Thus, children may also come to interpret situations in an overly anxious or catastrophising manner, further contributing to their experience of anxiety symptoms.*
>
> Fisak and Grills-Taquechel (2007)

## ACTION! Mind your language

Catastrophising is, perhaps, one of the most damaging thinking styles to exhibit but one of the easiest and simplest to change. Pay attention to the words you use - either in your head or out loud - and change any catastrophic words for more appropriate ones. 'I'm starving' becomes 'I'm hungry'; 'it's terrifying at the dentist' becomes 'it's unpleasant at the dentist'; 'you're an idiot for breaking that plate' becomes 'it's no big drama - we can get another plate'. Have a little laugh with yourself (or whoever you are with at the time) when you use catastrophic words, as this helps to remind you that you are grossly exaggerating your reality.

## The impulsive style

The impulsive thinking style (sometimes referred to as 'instant gratification') is where a person wants to feel happy/good/safe/relaxed/loved/satisfied RIGHT NOW and feels that they need to perform a particular behaviour or action in order to achieve that. They, without much consideration, decide that they NEED: chocolate, sex, a new car, to go shopping, a cigarette, to self-harm, to buy something, to go on holiday (you get the idea). The fact that they are overweight already, had sex yesterday, already own a nice car, don't need to go shopping, are trying to quit smoking, feel bad after cutting their arms, haven't got any money to spend, and recently returned from holiday, doesn't really enter their mind. They want to feel better/happier/calmer/more relaxed, right now.

This unhelpful thinking style often occurs spontaneously, or even out of the blue, with a person deciding very rapidly that they must to do a particular thing to feel good. They may, for example, see something expensive that they like in a shop and think that they have to buy it right away! The impulsive desire to feel better can also often be a response to a particular event that has been interpreted as stressful. The person with this thinking style then promptly feels that they must go shopping, eat something nice, smoke, self-harm etc. in order to feel better. Of course everyone wants instant gratification some of the time, but some people are able to get a good balance between sometimes satisfying themselves right away and other times waiting. They take other factors into account. A person with the impulsive thinking style tends to find it hard to defer long-term gains - they 'can't' think or worry about what might happen in ten years, ten months, ten weeks, or even sometimes ten minutes time - they just want to feel good/better now! Recognise the thinking from the last sentence? If so, you may have this unhelpful thinking style!

A contributing factor to this style of thinking is the black and white thinking we have looked at a moment ago. In the impulsive thinking style there is the thought that, 'I can't deal with these feelings I am having right now, I must do something to get rid of them.' Add in a big external locus and you have a recipe for disaster. The impulsive thinker believes he or she needs external help in order to feel good; he or she has no belief in his/her own ability to feel positive.

An obvious example of which is people who are chronically overweight due to excessive eating. Everyone knows that if you eat less and exercise more, you will lose weight, right? Then why, at the time of updating this book (February 2015) are British doctors saying that about half of all British adults will be obese by 2020? If it's that easy to lose weight, why are millions of people eating themselves into diabetes, coronary heart disease and an early grave?

It IS true that everyone knows that if you eat less and exercise more you will lose weight BUT, people with the combination of unhelpful thinking styles above 'can't' wait six months to see some change/feel fitter/feel happier/feel thinner - they find it hard to think that far ahead, it's almost as if it doesn't exist. However, build an internal locus, keep some perspective, tolerate the uncomfortable feelings and everything is different. Am I suggesting that this is all these millions of obese Britons need to do? Yes.

I'm sure you see that there is probably quite a lot of 'present moment-ness' going on here also, as well as a little learned helplessness and, I'm sure, some catastrophising.

## ACTION! Tolerate the desire

When you think impulsively, it's very likely that your stress-o-meter needle is quite high (see Chapter 10 'Anxiety and Stress'), which means you are quite stressed and probably lacking perspective (the more stressed or emotional you are, the less perspective you have). Recognise this fact and take action! Tell yourself you can have the cigarette/drink/sandwich/gamble/phone call in 30 minutes time, if you still feel you want it. There is some black and white thinking involved with impulsive thinking, so tell yourself to 'tolerate the desire and not give in to it'. Anticipate the regret you will experience if you do give in to your desire for instant gratification: what is your partner going to say if you gamble away all the money? How will you feel tomorrow if you skip the gym today? How will it affect your weight loss if you have that extra sandwich? You've been sober now for three months, do you really want to blow it all by having a drink? There is plenty of evidence to suggest that 'anticipating regret' is a good way of staying focused and not giving in to instant gratification (see for example: Abraham and Sheeran, 2004).

## The perfectionist style

'I'm a bit of a perfectionist', is something that I quite often hear coming from my brooder/social phobic/obsessive/catastrophic/black and white thinking style clients during our initial consultation/assessment session. It sounds quite nice if you think about it - 'I'm a bit of a perfectionist'. It's a little bit like saying 'yes, I am a little bit special'.

Difficulty is, due to the intense social anxiety these people suffer from (although they often don't know it) there is a lot of 'spin' going on with a phrase like this. I say this, because actually a 'perfectionist' is really a person running away from feeling like shit. Deep down, they usually feel worthless, unloveable and a failure. They are continually fighting to get away from these unbearable deep-down feelings. As a result, they set themselves very high standards. They cannot tolerate failure, because failure puts them back in touch with some very uncomfortable feelings.

The trouble is, if you set yourself ridiculously high standards you inevitably do not meet them a lot of the time. This means that you frequently see yourself as failing - which is exactly what you were trying to avoid! You then tend to give yourself a really hard time for failing to reach your standards, often berating yourself for days after a perceived poor performance. This only increases your desire to be 'perfect' so that you can get away from these feelings of worthlessness and 'not being good enough'. You, therefore, work even harder at being faultless, setting further high standards for yourself. As perfectionists have low self-esteem and quite often a very negative underlying attitude towards themselves, they do tend to focus on their failings rather than their successes. So, even if they do meet most of their very high targets, they tend to brood about the ones they didn't meet.

A typical perfectionist cycle of thinking is as follows:

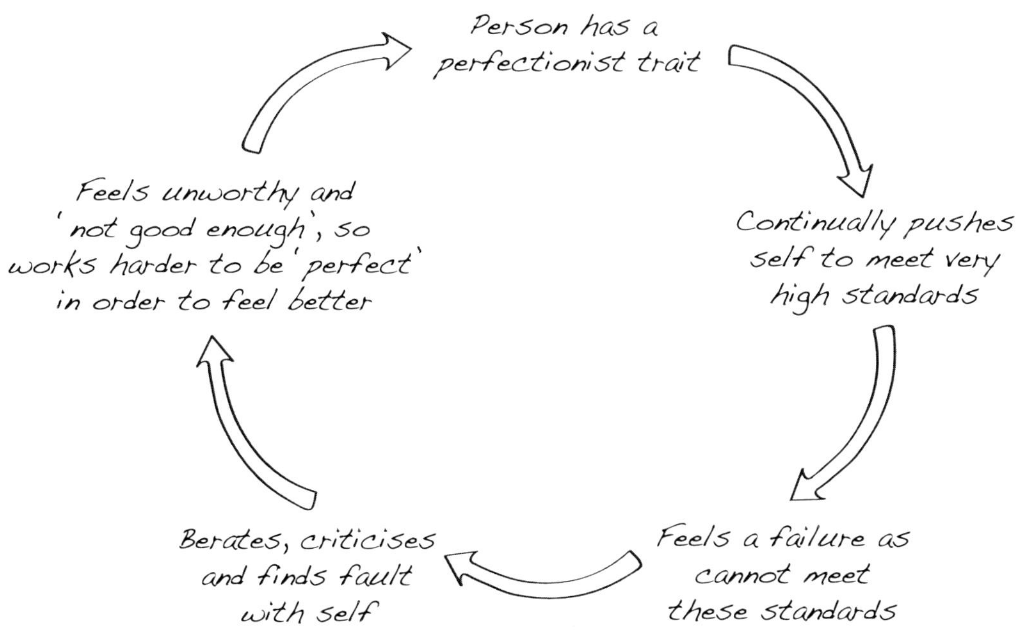


Due to the very high standards they have set themselves, perfectionists tend not to 'see', or process their achievements. When you are striving to be perfect, 'normal' accomplishments tend not to be seen as noteworthy! Perfectionists often do not process the things that many people would be really pleased and proud to have achieved (e.g. managing to achieve and maintain a good level of fitness). They dismiss or explain away their many successes. This explaining away of achievements can also be partly due to social anxiety and a desire not to appear big-headed or arrogant to others.

Even when perfectionists do achieve a difficult goal they have set themselves, they tend to move the goalposts and the success is yet again mitigated: 'well I only achieved that because I was lucky' or 'it wasn't really that difficult to achieve' or 'I should have pushed myself harder and done such and such as well' or 'so-and-so achieved a lot more than I did so I didn't really do that well'.

Perfectionists do tend to be highly achieving people as they spend so much time working to improve upon everything they do! Yet (deep down) you do not see yourself as successful if you are a perfectionist. All your achievements are set aside, as you strive to improve yourself and become faultless. Sooner or later you are inevitably going to be disappointed in your inability to meet the high standards you have set.

So, as a perfectionist, your thinking is likely to be quite distorted and you see yourself through those 'shit-tinted spectacles' I mentioned earlier. An example of this is a recent client of mine, Liz, who was always striving to excel at whatever she did, but she really didn't see herself as having achieved anything much at all. Instead she was focused in on the fact that a number of years ago she had, unfairly, been sacked from her job. Yet many other people would love to be as successful as she is: she is very fit and healthy, has a great figure, studied at Harvard University, has won several university rowing races and now has a high-flying career.

By default, the perfectionist also tends to have the negative, obsessive and catastrophic styles that I have just discussed and ALWAYS has the black and white thinking style. If you are a perfectionist, you are likely to display this thinking in relation to overcoming your symptoms. You probably want to **quickly** and **completely** rid yourself of them, thinking that you would be a failure otherwise. It is important to recognise how unhelpful this is. You do not want to pressure yourself in this way. Instead, allow yourself to slowly build up the knowledge and skills you need to make permanent changes. It is also really common for perfectionists to overreact to minor blips whilst working through this book. As soon as they have a wobble they tend to think something along the lines of 'I've ruined everything, I'm so stupid, I'm never going to get better'. 'Beating yourself up' in this way is enough in itself to maintain your symptoms, because it drags in all your other thinking styles and beliefs. So stop it. Stop beating yourself up, it serves no purpose at all, other than helping to maintain your symptoms. Give yourself a break, be nice to yourself and tolerate the blips.

You want to realise that you are going to create good days and not-so-good days in the forthcoming weeks. You are going to feel that you are getting somewhere but then create a bad day. Tolerate it. Put up with it. It's par for the course. Early on, when putting this programme into action, you aren't going to be able to find and challenge every single unhelpful thought or belief that you have. Some - probably many in fact - are going to slip through your net. This means, that in the near future at least, you are still going to have some of your symptoms. If you have a difficult day, calm yourself down, reassure yourself, and move on. Most often, all you'll need to do is remind yourself that there are always going to be 'blips' along the way. Every time you create a blip (remember: they don't happen 'to' you) remind yourself that you are learning something else about your thinking and beliefs that will ultimately help you to overcome your fear. Everybody has blips. Even people who are completely thriving have blips every so often. It is the way in which you react to them that is important. The following drawing demonstrates the two main responses you can have to a blip: you either manage your thinking and emotions well and get over it, or you 'tear the arse out of it' and create a three day catastrophe.

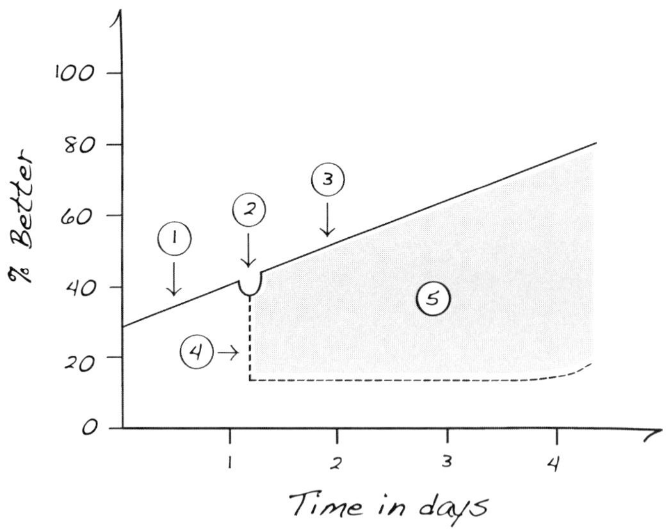


So, the drawing shows four days in the life of someone going through this programme. Position (1) shows them steadily improving up to position (2) where they have a bit of a blip. Here they have two choices: they either, put in lots of helpful effort and overcome the blip, or they over-react with the perfectionist thinking style, beating themselves up and catastrophising their 'stupidity' or 'complete lack of control'. If they prevent themselves from over-reacting at position (2) (by using whichever ACTION is appropriate at the time) they get out of their blip, usually within 10-30 minutes, and don't lose any forward momentum (3).

If the person does over react to their blip, the emotional reaction they create can be huge. They can make themselves go from being happy, feeling positive, feeling in control and really beginning to change their limiting beliefs, to feeling totally worthless, hopeless and stupid. In fact they can make themselves so low, that they might even temporarily become worse than they have been for a long time. Position (4) shows them really beating themselves up, thinking things like 'I've fucked this up', 'this isn't working', 'I'm never going to get over this bloody thing' and 'I'm so stupid'. They hit rock bottom and make themselves feel completely useless and really low. Sooner or later (the maximum is usually about three days!) they run out of energy to keep on berating themselves and stop it. As they stop, their mood starts to improve, they start to put effort in again, and start to get better. In fact, it's completely inevitable that they will start to get better and get back on track again. The shaded area (5) shows the three days of feeling like an abject failure - three days that could have been limited to three minutes. In order to minimise any blips you want to really work on your perfectionist thinking.

## ACTION! Maintain perspective

Recognise that you have the perfectionist thinking style and challenge thoughts you have and decisions that you make. Ask yourself: 'am I REALLY a failure if I haven't handed my essay/report in by Saturday?' or 'is it REALLY that bad if I only score 90% on my test, when the pass mark is 70%?' or 'do I really have to get everyone at work to like me?' Get some perspective, see the bigger picture, and realise that the pressure you feel under to be perfect comes from within you and not from outside of you. Recognise and challenge your black and white thinking: get used to TOLERATING the uncomfortable feelings of not being perfect.

### Remember: Thriving is not about being perfect

You want to remember not to put too much pressure on yourself. Many readers of this book are perfectionists and are likely to worry about whether or not they are making enough progress. Don't berate yourself if you get two thirds of the way through the book and you still have some, or even all, of your symptoms. Don't panic if, after making progress, you have a wobble and take a step backwards. Think about the jigsaw metaphor (page 11) and realise that working through this book is a learning process and that you will be gradually acquiring all the knowledge and skills that you need. Blips are not failures – they are learning opportunities, where you can gain insights and develop your resources.

## The hypervigilant style

Being in a state of constant over-alertness and sensitivity can cause significant problems for some people. This hypervigilant style may result from a combination of the other unhelpful thinking styles mentioned previously. Hypervigilant people tend to be bright and very observant, taking in everything around them. They are, also, likely to be fairly socially phobic or paranoid, and thus very attentive to the signals given off by others. If you are hypervigilant you may find that you pick up on very small negative cues (either external or internal) that other people do not even notice. You may also tend to obsess and brood about negative experiences, replaying them in your head. You are likely to then catastrophise and blow these situations out of proportion.

This results in you being in a pretty much constant state of stress arousal. The body responds to stressors in a number of physiological and psychological ways, in order to allow the person to react effectively to danger. One of the most significant responses, from our point of view, is that the mind becomes very focused on the stressful situation. You develop 'tunnel vision' with respect to the situation you are in. If you have ever been in a traumatic incident such as a car crash you may remember being very highly focused on the incident. Perhaps you felt as though time was moving more slowly and that all your senses were amplified?

This focused attention is obviously very useful in a situation in which there is true danger as it allows you to be highly alert to your surroundings, giving you the best possible chance of survival. For people who are hypervigilant and constantly responding to even very small cues, however, it causes even more problems. Firstly it means that you pay even more attention to the situation in question, amplifying it even further. It also means that you will find it very difficult to concentrate on anything else. You tend to live very much in the present moment as you are in this almost constant state of over-arousal, which focuses your attention very much on whatever situation you are in.

This 'present moment-ness' (for want of a better term!) means that it is very hard for a person to connect to past positive experiences when they are feeling negative. If you are in a state of over-arousal, and thus always intensely focused on the present situation, it can be very difficult to think about anything else. When most people feel a bit upset or negative, they are able to conjure up positive feelings associated with other experiences, gaining some perspective and enabling them to feel better. The hyper-alert person finds it very difficult to do this.

Imagine yourself in a situation where you have asked a friend out for a drink and at the last minute he/she cancels on you, saying he/she has too much work to do. If you are a bit insecure you are likely to worry that maybe your friend didn't actually want to see you and that perhaps he/she doesn't really like you. Most people would then, however, be able to connect emotionally with previous positive experiences, gaining some perspective on this negative thought. For example, you may think about the fact that last week you and your friend went out and had a great time or that your friend held you a surprise birthday party last month or that your friend has always helped you out when you've needed it.

The hypervigilant person would instead be so focused on the negative thought, blowing it up bigger and bigger, that he/she is unable to hold onto past experiences. In some cases these past experiences are forgotten about, in a similar way to dissociation (where a person can be disconnected from their experiences) although this is a different process occurring. In other cases you may be consciously aware of these experiences, but disconnected from them emotionally - you may be able to see the true perspective BUT you CANNOT feel it.

If you are hypervigilant you are likely to get yourself caught in a cycle of negative behaviour. Your over-sensitivity and alertness means that every single negative cue, whether external or internal, is picked up on. You then tend to catastrophise and magnify everything, in the process creating a lot of anxiety. Your body responds to the perceived threat and you find yourself in a state of stress arousal. Consequently your attention becomes even more focused on the negative situation and you build it up even further. Being in this state of arousal also means that you are even more alert to negative cues, maintaining this hypervigilance.

Hypervigilance means that your belief system is continually reinforced as you pick up and notice every negative cue around you. It also prevents you from gaining any real perspective on your problem as you become so focused on, and alert to the present moment. Some people live their entire life in this hypervigilant state, so they don't even know that they are in it! The state has become 'normalised' and they don't know anything else. Their anxiety levels never really calm down and their brain never really relaxes, so there are no 'wake-up calls' as to the fact that they are hypervigilant.

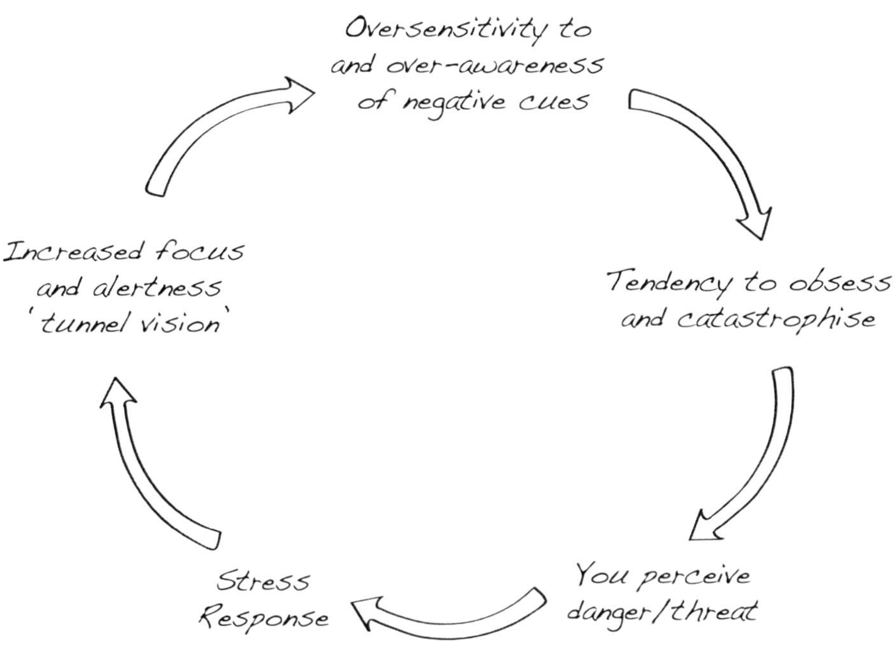


A number of different models (explanations) of anxiety disorders suggest that anxious people are hypervigilant to threat. Eysenck (1992) proposes that anxious individuals may selectively focus on threatening rather than neutral stimuli. They may display a broadening of attention before detecting a threatening stimulus and then a narrowing of attention once a threat has been detected. Consistent with the proposal that anxious people are hypervigilant, Bradley *et al.* (1999) found that compared to controls (people without anxiety problems), patients with a general anxiety disorder were more attentive to emotional faces (if there were a number of people in the room, the anxious person would focus on the people whose faces were displaying more emotion - as these were thought to be more threatening).

Hypervigilance is key in hypochondria. Hypochondriacs tend to catastrophise about physical symptoms, and often end up in a state of over-awareness and scrutiny with respect to their bodies.

> *Clinical observation and research findings suggest that many hypochondriacal patients perceive their*

> *bodies as threatening. This leads to hypervigilance about their bodies, greater attention paid to every bodily sensation and symptom, tendency to misinterpret these sensations and symptoms as loss of control over body and/or as a sign that patients have succumbed to a serious disease that leads to death.*
>
> (Starcevic, 2005)

Distorted beliefs and hypervigilance are also significant features of Borderline Personality Disorder (BPD) where the sufferer has unstable moods and self-image problems, along with an intense fear of abandonment.

> *The model hypothesizes that BPD patients process information through a specific set of three core beliefs or schemas of themselves and others, i.e., 'I am powerless and vulnerable', 'I am inherently unacceptable', and 'Others are dangerous and malevolent'. Needing support in a dangerous world but not trusting others brings BPD patients in a state of hypervigilance.*
>
> (Sieswerda *et al.*, 2006)

A review by Crombez, Van Damme and Eccleston (2005) suggested a very close link between chronic pain and hypervigilance.

## ACTION! Manage your thinking better

Hypervigilance is created by the constant worrying, negative thinking, brooding and catastrophic thinking you exhibit - so stop it! The many small worries that you have continuously throughout your day 'snowball' into bigger, more significant anxieties, so that you are constantly on the alert for danger. Nip the small worries in the bud and you won't create the big ones. Complete the **ACTIONs** for the other unhelpful thinking styles and 'manage your thinking' better - it doesn't mean you are going to be burgled just because you heard a noise at night; it doesn't mean you are going to get cancer just because you have a mole; it doesn't mean your new boyfriend doesn't love you just because he wants to stay home tonight.

## The learned helplessness style

Learned helplessness is an unhelpful thinking style in which a person believes that they are helpless and behaves in a helpless manner, even when they have the power to alter their damaging situation. Learned helplessness theory is the idea that clinical depression and similar mental illnesses arise from the perception that you have no control over the outcome of a situation (Seligman, 1975). I've mentioned resilience in this book a couple of times, and resilience is the opposite of learned helplessness.

The learned helplessness thinking style is one that is learned in childhood (and sometimes early adulthood) and develops from the way in which the child learns to cope and react to a stressful, abusive, neglectful or an otherwise threatening environment. Some children learn (or are taught) coping mechanisms and ways of defeating anxiety - they build an internal sense of power and control and they stick two fingers up and say 'get lost' (metaphorically at least) back to whoever or whatever is causing them stress. Think about the children with leukemia I mentioned earlier in the book, the ones with the internal sense of power and control. Other children don't develop useful defence mechanisms, or gain some power by fighting their anxiety, or learn to cope with stress, pressure or neglect. These children don't go on to develop an internal sense of power and control, quite the opposite in fact. They learn to surrender very quickly, feel helpless very easily and give in to feelings, doubts and worries without putting up much of a fight.

Learned helplessness was first detailed in the 1960s. A famous experiment was conducted using dogs and electric shocks (Seligman and Maier, 1967). If you were in the first group of dogs, you were fortunate enough not to be shocked at all. Another, rather less fortunate, group was restrained and shocked repeatedly. These dogs, however, were able to stop the shocks by pressing a lever with their heads. The final particularly unfortunate group of dogs was repeatedly subjected to uncontrollable electric shocks. These dogs could do nothing to prevent the shocks; they were confined and unable to escape. These group three dogs did have a lever to press but doing so did nothing. In fact, when these group three dogs were paired with dogs in the second group their shocks stopped when their group two partners pressed their own levers. This ensured that the two groups were shocked for the same amount of time so that the results were down to difference in control rather than anything else.

This was not the end of the experiment though, the dogs had yet another ordeal in store. Twenty-four hours later all the dogs were placed in a box. This box had a low barrier separating it into two halves over which the dogs could jump. Once the test began, the dogs were given 10 seconds to jump the barrier before they were given electric shocks through the floor. Jumping over the barrier then stopped the shock, otherwise the shock continued for one minute. This was repeated ten times for each dog (poor things).

The dogs from the previous 'no shock' and 'controllable shock' groups easily learnt to jump the barrier to prevent or stop the shocks. The time taken to jump decreased with the number of test attempts as they learnt how to escape. The majority of those in the 'uncontrollable shock' group, however, simply lay down and endured the shocks, despite the fact that they now had the ability to avoid or stop the pain. These dogs had learnt to be helpless. They believed that they could do nothing to stop the shocks, so didn't even bother trying. Even when some of these dogs managed to jump the barrier unintentionally, thus stopping the shock, on the following attempts they reverted to helpless behaviour. Seventy five percent of dogs in the 'uncontrollable shock' group failed to escape the shock on nine or more of the ten attempts.

Many similar experiments involving animals, electric shocks and other punishing behaviours have been conducted with the same results (see Seligman, 1972). Interestingly, Seligman found that in his experiments, some dogs, despite being in the uncontrollable shock group, still learnt to escape from shocks normally when they were able to do so. These resilient dogs did not become helpless. Seligman suggested that perhaps these dogs had prior experience of controlling trauma in their lives, and other experiments have supported this. Significantly, exposing animals to controllable events before the uncontrollable ones prevents the animals from becoming helpless.

Experiments have also shown that it is possible to reverse learned helplessness. Forcing animals that had learned to be helpless to show an appropriate response to subsequent controllable events reversed the learned helplessness. For example, with the helpless dogs in the box, repeatedly dragging the poor things over the barrier eventually enabled them to learn to escape the shocks on their own. These animals were able to 're-learn' that they could control what occurred to them.

Learned helplessness experiments have also been conducted with people (although not involving electric shocks!). One interesting study investigated learned helplessness in children (Dweck and Repucci, 1973). Initially the children were given solvable problems by one experimenter. Another experimenter then presented the children with problems that could not be solved. After a time these unsolvable problems were switched to solvable ones, almost identical to those the children had already solved. Some children were then able to solve these problems and indeed improved their performances compared to before. Other children showed significant performance decreases compared to the initial solvable problems and some completely failed to solve the problems at all even though they had previously completed very similar ones.

> *The Ss* [students] *who showed the largest performance decrements were those who took less personal responsibility for the outcomes of their actions (as measured by pre-experimental Intellectual*

> *Achievement Responsibility Scale scores) and who, when they did accept responsibility, attributed success and failure to presence or absence of ability rather than to expenditure of effort. Those Ss who persisted in the face of prolonged failure placed more emphasis on the role of effort in determining the outcome of their behavior*
>
> (Dweck and Repucci, 1973)

So the children who felt that they could not affect an outcome, because success or failure was due to external forces or innate ability, were most susceptible to learned helplessness.

Learned helplessness is something that can be applied to any area of a person's life. As an example, people who become unemployed may become susceptible to learned helplessness as unemployment time increases, particularly if they are not very resilient and have a strong external sense of power and control. If initial attempts to find a new job are unsuccessful, the person may become disheartened and feel powerless to influence future employment. Efforts to gain a new job may then decrease (see research by Baum *et al.*, 1986).

As you may already have noticed, one big problem with learned helplessness is that it is somewhat self-propagating. You believe that you are powerless to alter your situation, so you do nothing to try to change things. As you are doing nothing, your situation doesn't change, which then further backs up your belief that things are hopeless.

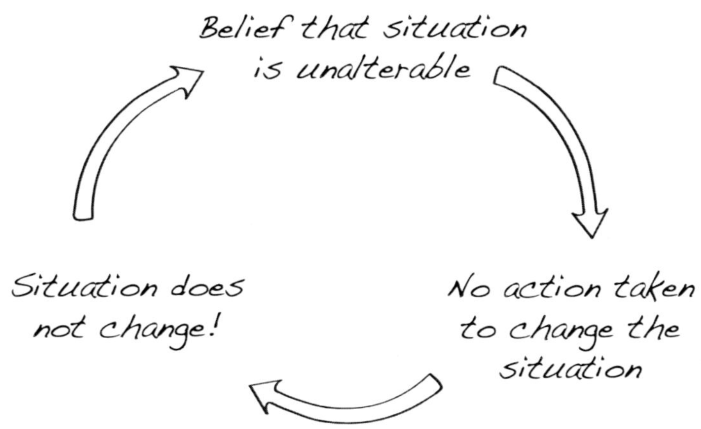


A simple example of this could be the child (or adult) who believes that he is stupid and will never do well in all his exams no matter how hard he tries. So he doesn't put any effort in to studying and consequently does do badly, which reinforces his belief that he cannot ever do well. This type of self-fulfilling prophecy is, unfortunately, very common.

## ACTION! Challenge your limiting beliefs

As with any of the unhelpful thinking styles, recognising that you have one (or more) of them is the first step in doing something about it. Learned helplessness ISN'T REAL! It's NOT that you CAN'T say 'no' to that bar of chocolate, it's not that you WILL get rejected if you get into a relationship, it's not that you ARE powerless, it's just that you BELIEVE these things. Recognise when you do experience these feelings that they are coming from within you, not from reality. Tolerate the possibility that you might not get something quite right, or might not get a high score, or that you might feel rejected, and realise that these things are not the end of the world. Build an internal locus, start setting some small but achievable goals and build your self-esteem. There are currently around fifteen million obese adults in the UK - it's not that they can't lose weight, or that diets don't work, it's that they have lost all their belief in their ability to stick to a diet and keep the weight off. You don't need to believe, just do it! (As the man from Nike says.)

# Unhelpful Thinking Styles - Recap

- ✓ Unhelpful thinking styles are basically just habitual styles of thinking. They are exaggerations of normal thinking that people start to exhibit when they don't have strong foundations, and are creating stress or anxiety as a consequence.
- ✓ Thinking styles can be helpful or unhelpful depending on the situation.
- ✓ People with a **negative thinking style** always look at the bad things in a situation or experience. They assume that things will fail, will go wrong, won't work etc.
- ✓ People with an **obsessive thinking style** worry, brood and think about every experience in intricate detail.
- ✓ People with a **impulsive thinking style** want to feel happy/good/safe/ relaxed/loved/satisfied RIGHT NOW and feel that they need to perform a particular behaviour or action in order to achieve that.
- ✓ Those with a **paranoid thinking style** worry that other people are out to criticise, reject, exploit or harm them.
- ✓ The **black and white thinking style** involves seeing situations in a very rigid and inflexible, 'either/or', manner.
- ✓ People with a **catastrophic thinking style** magnify, exaggerate or blow out of proportion a perceived threat or worry.
- ✓ The **perfectionist thinking style** involves setting oneself ridiculously high standards. The perfectionist is constantly striving to avoid failure because failure puts them in touch with some very uncomfortable feelings.
- ✓ People with a **hypervigilant thinking style** are over-alert and sensitive to negative cues, focusing completely in on these, resulting in a loss of perspective.
- ✓ Those with the **learned helplessness thinking style** believe that they are helpless and behave in a helpless manner, even when they have the power to alter their damaging situation.
- ✓ By recognising and then modifying any unhelpful thinking styles you have, you are helping to: reduce stress and anxiety, build a more internal sense of power and control, create higher self-esteem and lower your social anxiety.

## What should I be working on from now on?

1. Keep working on the **ACTION**s described in chapters 3 to 5. In particular, remember to process your positives **every day**.

2. Complete the **ACTION**s that relate to any of your unhelpful thinking styles. If you scored highly on lots of the thinking styles, then start working on just a couple of these and then, once you have made progress in addressing these, move on to tackling the others in turn.

**Notes** - The blank area below is for you to make any notes.

# Chapter 7

# Mind Your Language!

# Mind Your Language!

So we have already taken a brief look at some of the language that you think and speak in when we explored your 'inner voice' or the way in which you talk to yourself (chapter 1). Now that you have a good insight into your psychological foundations and understand your different unhelpful thinking styles we are going to explore language further throughout this chapter. This is because the language we use is so important!

Our language is a window through which we can easily recognise our thoughts and beliefs. The language that we speak, and the language we use in our thoughts are an expression of what we think, feel and believe. Right now, I am writing this in a Microsoft Word document. I'm making very simple changes to this document by hitting different keys two or three times a second. By typing away, I am changing the look of the page, but I am not seeing the other effects my key hitting is having. The actual hidden 'computer language code' that I am changing looks nothing like the very clean, clear white page that my typing appears on. I am changing the underlying code through this Word document. You are going to change your underlying code, your thoughts and beliefs, through your language. When I say 'language', I'm not just talking about the words and statements that you actually speak, but also the ones that you think (your inner voice).

Just in the same way that our '*body reacts upon our mind, and our mind reacts upon our body*', our '*thoughts and beliefs affect our language, and our language affects our thoughts and beliefs*'.

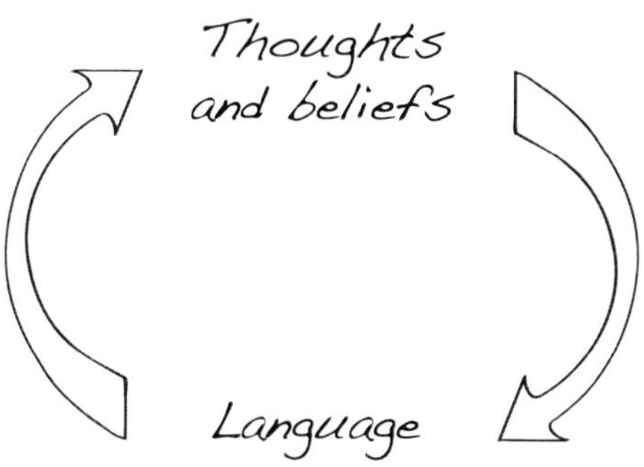


If you speak and think negative words, you will lower your mood, anticipate negative outcomes, make yourself stressed, feel powerless and contribute to an external sense of power and control. If you use positive words, you will feel positive, feel powerful, anticipate positive outcomes, create less stress and contribute to an internal sense of power and control.

***Even if you are feeling 'like shit', never say it!***

Perhaps the most amazing study I came across whilst researching this book is about nuns and their dirty habits. Well, bad habits rather than dirty ones. I could go on to describe it as an un-**convent**-ional study, but that would be a childish joke to make, especially as the study was about life and death.

On the 22nd of September 1930, the Mother Superior of the North American Sisters, who were from Milwaukee, Wisconsin, sent a letter to her fellow nuns requesting that they all write an autobiographical essay. Sixty years later, 678 of those nuns, who had been born before 1917, agreed that their earlier autobiography could form part of a modern research study, and 180 of these essays were selected for inclusion. The following comes from the research by Danner *et al.* (2001).

At an average age of 22, each nun was asked to:

> . . . *write a short sketch of [her] life. This account should not contain more than two to three hundred*

> *words and should be written on a single sheet of paper . . . include place of birth, parentage, interesting and edifying events of childhood, schools attended, influences that led to the convent, religious life, and outstanding events.*

In the later study, each of these 180 essays was coded for certain expressions of emotion, in a very simple fashion. Basically each text was analysed for the positive emotions of accomplishment, amusement, contentment, gratitude, happiness, hope, interest, love, and relief; the negative emotions of anger, contempt, disgust, disinterest, fear, sadness, and shame, and the neutral emotion of surprise.

Effectively, each nun's paper was scored on the amount of positive, negative and neutral emotional content. Here are two examples from the study:

> *Sister 1 (low positive emotion): I was born on September 26, 1909, the eldest of seven children, five girls and two boys . . . My candidate year was spent in the Motherhouse, teaching Chemistry and Second Year Latin at Notre Dame Institute. With God's grace, I intend to do my best for our Order, for the spread of religion and for my personal sanctification.*

> *Sister 2 (high positive emotion): God started my life off well by bestowing upon me a grace of inestimable value . . . The past year which I have spent as a candidate studying at Notre Dame College has been a very happy one. Now I look forward with eager joy to receiving the Holy Habit of Our Lady and to a life of union with Love Divine.*

(I just want to point out, that it would be easy to assume that young women entering the Catholic Church during this period in America might not have been very well educated, and that their decision to take holy orders may have been made partly because there weren't many other options open to them. This would be a mistake as these were bright, intelligent women. By the time the nun study was initiated in 1991, 91% of the nuns had earned, at the very least, a university degree.)

When all the information had been gathered and placed into a table, it was split into four sections, depending on how many positive emotional statements were in each. The bottom section contained the least positivity and the top section contained the most positivity.

When all the 'scoring' was complete, the tables were finalised and the data correlated, the amazing and frightening evidence was clear to see.

Around 50% of nuns in the lowest (not very positive) section had died, but only 20% of nuns in the 'most positive' section. If you have a positive outlook on life, and feel positive emotions about life, you are - according to this study - two and a half times more likely to survive to your nineties.

I'm not trying to suggest that just by thinking and feeling positively about your life that you will live into your nineties, like the nuns did, but it's a start! It's not just that the nuns thought and felt positively, it was more about the fact that they thought and felt positively about EVERYTHING - about their health, about their happiness, about their fulfillment, about their love, about their friends and their spiritual beliefs. They CHOSE to think and feel positively about everything in their lives, and because of this they were happy, contented, could deal with stressful situations, were fit and in good health, had good coping mechanisms, felt resilient and were grateful. Their positive attitude permeated every area of their lives.

There is plenty of other research surrounding language suggesting that what you think and say is important. For example, those with depression and those who are suicidal tend to use a greater number of first person singular pronouns, mostly 'I', and a lack of second and third person pronouns, such as 'we' and 'he' (Pennebaker, Mehl and Niederhoffer, 2003). This might suggest a lack of connection with others and a focus on the self. Pennebaker and King (1999) found that linguistic style and personality traits were linked. For example, results suggested that 'neurotic' people use more negative and fewer positive words than those who are not neurotic. A higher ratio of positive to negative words has been found to be associated with better health (Pennebaker, Mayne and Francis, 1997). Wolf, Sedway, Bulik, Kordy (2007) found that language use of inpatients with eating disorders contained high numbers of negative emotion words and low numbers of positive emotion words, along with high rates of anxiety words. They stated that:

> *Overall, the cognitive style of individuals in our sample is best described as ruminative, past-oriented, negativistic, self-focused, and avoidant.*

Gill and Oberlander (2002) studied the language differences between introverts and extroverts. They found that introverts tended to use more quantifiers, such as 'a lot', 'a few', 'all the', 'one of', 'lots of' and 'loads of'. Extroverts showed a preference for 'a bit' and 'couple of'. This suggested that introverts were more prone to exaggeration than extroverts. Additionally, differences in language use between extroverts and introverts suggested a difference in their self-belief and views on capability. They stated that:

> *For Extroverts, their ability to do something should they choose is confidently and assertively relayed using want-, need-, and able- (to); which they use uniquely. Introverts more timidly and tentatively state that they are [trying to] or possibly- and at some point in the future- they are [going to].*

As I said in chapter 2, you need to pay attention to your thinking for a few weeks, and this is going to take effort. I'm not going to lie to you: although this process is VERY EASY, it is going to take effort, MASSIVE DETERMINED EFFORT in fact.

What you want to notice in your language are clues that give away how you think or what you believe about something. Once you recognise what the thinking behind the language is, you can change the thinking by changing the language.

A phrase I would like you to get used to saying to yourself is **'what does that say about what I think, feel or believe?'**

Have a look at the following statements/thoughts:

'I <u>couldn't</u> do that'
'I <u>wouldn't</u> be able to make it'
'I'm <u>not</u> good enough'
'She's out of <u>my league</u>'
'I <u>haven't</u> got the qualifications'
'I <u>should</u> have gone to see granny today'
'I'm <u>not</u> strong enough'
'I <u>should</u> be able to do this by now'
'I'd <u>never</u> be able to afford one of those'
'I <u>must</u> get better at sending Xmas cards'
'This is <u>too</u> much for me to deal with'

The statements are all very negative, and I have underlined the key word or words that make them negative.

People with low self-esteem and social anxiety, because they are forever scrutinising themselves and comparing themselves to others, are often very self-critical and judgemental. They judge and compare themselves continuously to what they think they SHOULD have done, OUGHT to do, and MUST do. A well-known psychologist, Albert Ellis, called this 'Musterbation', as in 'I must do this' (actually, he went on to say: 'Masturbation is good and delicious, but musterbation is evil and pernicious'. I'll leave you to make your own mind up about that!).

In a 'musterbation statement', you are stating what you think you SHOULD be doing, rather than what you are doing. For example: you might be out clothes shopping and thinking 'I should really have gone to see grandma today'. In other words, you are making yourself feel bad and guilty because you are out shopping and enjoying yourself. You don't feel that you DESERVE to be out enjoying yourself, so you berate yourself (give yourself a hard time) by stating something nice that you could be doing for someone else instead. The actual message behind the statement could be 'who do I think I am, wandering around these shops and spending money without a care in the world, when my poor granny is at home ill, what sort of person am I?' So, in effect, this statement is a real (though self-inflicted) put-down. It's not surprising that people who speak to themselves like this, have low self-esteem and judge themselves very harshly.

See the same statements below, now with a more positive, kind and 'internal' version beneath:

'I couldn't do that'
'I can do anything that I put my mind to'

'I wouldn't be able to make it'
'I can make anything I want to'

'I'm not good enough'
'I'm a great guy who can do whatever he sets his mind to'

'She's out of my league'
'I am a lovely guy, who anyone would love to be with'

'I haven't got the qualifications'
'I can go back to college and gain whatever qualifications I want'

'I should have gone to see granny today'
'I am a lovely person who deserves some new clothes, I'll go and see granny soon'

'I'm not strong enough'
'I have the inner strength to do whatever I want to do'

'I should be able to do this by now'
'I'm getting better at this every day'

'I'd never be able to afford one of those'
'I can achieve anything I want to in life'

'I must get better at sending Xmas cards'
'I'm a lovely person and it is alright to be a bit scatty sometimes'

'This is too much for me to deal with'
'I have the strength to deal with anything that life throws at me'

Here are some more, this time can you spot any social anxiety or self-esteem issues that might also be in there?

'I always get that wrong'
'I hope I don't make a mistake'

'I don't know what to do'
'I'm probably wrong, but . . . '
'What if people can see I'm nervous?'
'People don't like me'
'I bet he didn't mean that compliment'
'Everyone is looking at me'
'I hope I didn't make an idiot out of myself'
'What if I look silly?'
'That would be really embarrassing'

Remember: it doesn't matter whether these are statements you have said out loud, or just thought in your mind.

If you are one of those people (like most who read this book) who doesn't tend to think and speak in a very positive, internal and active way, then *Minding Your Language* might seem a little daunting at the moment. However, don't despair, as it is actually incredibly simple, as the only thought you EVER really need to worry about, is the one that is in your mind right now. Thoughts from the past are now ancient history, and you can worry about your future thoughts when you have them.

Please memorise this phrase:

**'The thought that is in my mind right now: is it helpful?**
**If not, then either change it for one that is, or bin it'!**

A 'helpful' thought is one that is helping you to achieve the life that you want, one that is making you feel happier, more in control, stronger, more full of joy and life, helping to strengthen your immune system, helping to raise your self-esteem, helping to build an internal sense of power and control, helping to overcome social anxiety, helping you to take responsibility for your life, helping you to achieve all the health, happiness and success you really want.

I hope by now you have realised that every single thought you have has a direct affect upon your life. Some thoughts might only affect your life a little bit, some, a lot more, but they all affect it to a greater or lesser extent.

Have a glance back to the previous chapter and remind yourself how much of each of the individual thinking styles you (currently) exhibit. If you scored more than two or three on any of the unhelpful thinking style questionnaires, then you will probably start to be aware of when you are thinking in that particular style. Here are some examples:

'I'm starving, when is dinner?' (catastrophic)

'There's no way I could run a marathon - I'm not fit enough' (learned helplessness, black and white, negative)

'Did I lock the front door before I left for work today?' (obsessive)

'I'm hungry - I'll have another chocolate' (impulsive)

'I'm not going into school today - all the kids are going to be talking about me, after we lost the match on Saturday' (paranoid, learned helplessness)

'I can't move to the country, because I can't stand spiders' (black and white, negative, catastrophic)

'If I stay in tonight I'm going to be bored - who can I go and see?' (impulsive, negative, black and white)

'I cannot hand in this assignment as it is - it's not good enough' (perfectionist, negative, black and white)

'What's that noise - is it a burglar?' (hypervigilant, catastrophic)

'I need a drink - it will help me relax' (impulsive, black and white, catastrophic)

So, if you are saying one of the statements above, you ask yourself the question: 'The thought I am having right now - is it helpful?' When you recognise that the thought isn't helpful, then either stop thinking it (by doing something else), or change/modify the thought.

Here are the same examples again, modified to make them 'helpful':

'I'm getting a little hungry, when is dinner?'

'I'm not very fit at the moment, so I would have to train hard for a marathon'

'Did I lock the front door before I left for work today? Yes, I locked it, I'm just being obsessive.'

'I'm hungry - but I can wait until dinner'

'I feel a little 'on the spot' going into school today after we lost the match on Saturday. It's no big deal though - everyone has a busy life, and nobody worries that much about school football'

'I can move to the country, and get rid of my anxiety about spiders - it's all in my head anyway!'

'I'm going to stay in tonight and have a bit of 'me' time - it will be nice'

'I cannot hand in this assignment as it is - it's not good enough. Wait a minute, that's just my perfectionism talking, I don't need to bust a gut over this, I've done a good piece of work here - I'll send it in'

'What's that noise - is it a burglar? What am I saying? I often think noises are burglars, but they never are - it's just me being a bit over-aware. Just go back to sleep now. . .'

'I'm going to take a few minutes just to clear my mind and relax a little'

## Exercise: Positive Language

And some more - can you spot any of the foundations, social anxiety and unhelpful thinking styles in the sentences below?

'Life is just shit'
'Why are they staring at me?'
'I think those people are laughing at me'
'Did she mean something negative about me when she said that?'
'This illness is going to kill me'
'I'm such an idiot, this is never going to work'
'He didn't call me because he doesn't care'
'We didn't laugh at the same time - we're not right together'
'I'm sure he was trying to tell me something'
'I'll never get myself out of this depression'
'What's that noise - could it be a burglar?'
'It's cloudy and dark outside - today is going to be shit'
'It would be devastating if I lost my job'
'What if absolutely nobody likes me?'
'What if I'm really ill and die?'
'I should be married and have kids by now'
'This is the worst day ever'
'I'm so fat there's no point in trying to lose weight'
'Without my girlfriend, life isn't worth living'

'I'm never going to feel any better'
'There's nothing I can do'
'I may as well give up'

Now go through the last list again (see below), but this time, write underneath the statement a more positive, friendly and hopeful version. Recognise any catastrophising or other unhelpful thinking styles hidden within the statements, and remove them. I have completed the first one for you:

'Life is just shit'
*'I am making my life better every day'*

'Why are they staring at me?'

'I think those people are laughing at me'

'What did she mean when she said that?'

'This illness is going to kill me'

'I'm such an idiot, this is never going to work'

'He didn't call me because he doesn't care'

'We didn't laugh at the same time - we're not right together'

'I'm sure he was trying to tell me something'

'I'll never get myself out of this depression'

'What's that noise - could it be a burglar?'

'It's cloudy and dark outside - today is going to be awful'

'It would be devastating if I lost my job'

'What if absolutely nobody likes me?'

'What if I'm really ill and die?'

'I should be married and have kids by now'

'This is the worst day ever'

'I'm so fat, there's no point in trying to lose weight'

'Without my girlfriend, life isn't worth living'

'I'm never going to feel any better'

'There's nothing I can do'

'I may as well give up'

Excellent, well done!

## Active versus passive language

Another very important factor in the language that you use, is whether it is 'Active' or 'Passive'.

Active language is positive, empowering and is all about you taking control. It helps you build an internal sense of power and control by taking responsibility for your actions and thinking. Active language helps to create perspective, is solution-orientated and encourages you to make changes.

Active language is different to 'positive language' in that it sometimes DOES still need you to focus on a negative thought, feeling or belief, with the SOLE INTENTION of making the thought, feeling or belief more INTERNAL.

Have a read of the following statement:

**'I'm really depressed'**

Now ask yourself: **'What does that say about what I think, feel or believe?'**

The person saying it believes that their depression is being 'done to them', or, at the very least, that it is 'just happening'. This is why we call it 'passive language'.

An active version of the statement would be: 'I'm making myself depressed today'. If we were just interested in positive language at the moment, we would never say 'I'm making myself depressed today', we would say something like 'I'm going to have a wonderful, happy day today'. BUT, we want to make ourselves realise that WE are creating the depression, because, once we accept that WE are creating it, then WE can choose not to.

Here are some more passive statements, with an active version beneath:

Passive: 'Life is shit'
Active: 'I am **making** my life shit'

Passive: 'This illness has got a hold on me'
Active: 'I am **keeping** myself ill'

Passive: 'I'm addicted to smoking'
Active: 'I smoke because I **want** to'

Passive: 'I've always been like this'
Active: 'I've always **allowed** myself to be like this'

Passive: 'The other kids at school keep bullying me'
Active: 'I **allow** the other kids at school to bully me'

Passive: 'Mum always has a go at me'
Active: 'I **choose** to react when my mum is telling me off'
Passive: 'I've been ill for 20 years'
Active: 'I've been **making** myself ill for 20 years'

Passive: 'I get angry when people look down on me'

Active: 'I **<u>choose</u>** to get angry in certain situations'

Passive: 'It was shit at the weekend - it rained the whole time'
Active: 'I **<u>chose</u>** to let the weather affect my weekend'

Passive: 'I'm just having one of those days'
Active: 'I am **<u>doing</u>** one of those days'

Let's look at that first statement again, now in more detail:

We know from research that people become depressed because they brood and ruminate about negative thoughts and feelings and feel powerless to do anything about it. 'I'm really depressed' is a very powerless and negative statement to make, even if it is true! It is also a very powerful suggestion, which can then further impact upon the person.

Let's look at both of the statements in detail and see what actually is being suggested/stated/inferred:

Passive: 'I'm really depressed':

- There is something really 'final' inferred in this sort of statement, as if the sufferer is at the end of the line and can't go any further
- Though not specifically stated, the statement suggests that this state of depression is happening TO the person, they are a victim of the depression, which means they are helpless and powerless to do anything about it
- They are not just depressed, they are REALLY depressed - this is a bold, emotional statement, and just a tad catastrophic
- The statement is 100% negative - there is nothing positive about it at all, it is suggesting an on-going depressive feeling with no end in sight
- It is a very 'loaded' and controlling statement (although not necessarily consciously and deliberately manipulative) that gives a listener (the person who the statement is being made to, if there is one) no other option than to feel really sorry and sad for the depressed person. This statement is like a magnet pulling the listener in so that they collude with the sufferer's belief system. This is the sort of statement that draws people in so that they become colluding 'significant others' (more later). Think about it, how could you reply to a friend or loved-one, who has said this to you? 'Don't worry, it will be alright tomorrow' would likely meet with 'are you mad, I'm clinically depressed'. 'You need to think more positively' would likely meet with 'you think this is just me being negative, do you?'. 'Come on, let's go for a walk' would likely meet with 'yeah, a walk is going to make my life better and stop me from wanting to die'. In other words, the listener has been completely backed into a corner, where ANY reply they make is likely to attract a negative response. It's as if the person making the statement is saying: 'I'm really depressed - please do something to help', whilst at the same time not enabling anyone to do or say anything that might actually help. This just further reinforces the sufferer's sense of powerlessness and hopelessness.

Active: 'I'm making myself depressed today':

- Although negative in as much as they are stating something negative, (they are depressed) the statement is more positive because of the word 'today'. The sufferer is ONLY stating that they are depressed TODAY. This suggests and infers that tomorrow is a whole different ball game
- 'Making myself' is an internal statement, meaning that it helps to create an internal sense of power and control. If my leg is sore because I keep jabbing my fork into it, I can always stop it. If the person is MAKING him/herself depressed, all is not lost, because he/she can choose to

STOP making him/herself depressed

- It is a very honest, open and non-manipulative statement, this person isn't trying to emotionally blackmail a listener into colluding with their (distorted) belief system (more later)
- It is minimising the situation. It's as if the person is saying 'minor hitch everyone, just making myself depressed for a couple of hours, normal me will be returning shortly'. This person is seeing their temporary depressed state as an annoying fly buzzing around them, they know it's there, but they are not going to let it ruin their whole day or week
- The person making this active statement won't feel anywhere near as powerless and helpless as the person who made the passive statement, because they are taking responsibility for their current condition.

It's incredibly easy to change a Passive statement into an Active one. All it takes is a little practice. See some more examples below:

Passive: 'I was ok, then the feelings just swamped me'
Active: 'I felt bad when **I started** brooding about things'

Passive: 'My marriage is in a terrible mess'
Active: 'I'm **making** my marriage suffer'

Passive: 'These bloody headaches are ruining my life'
Active: 'I'm **causing** myself to suffer these headaches'

Passive: 'This cancer is killing me - I'm going to die'
Active: 'I **own this** cancer, I'm going to fight this thing'

Now, what if I not only wanted to make the four statements above ACTIVE, but also POSITIVE:

Passive: 'I was ok, then the feelings just swamped me'
Active/Positive: 'I felt bad when **I started** brooding about things, so I'm going to stop brooding, and focus on feeling much better'

Passive: 'My marriage is in a terrible mess'
Active/Positive: 'I'm **making** my marriage suffer, so I'm going to pull my finger out and get it working properly again'

Passive: 'These bloody headaches are ruining my life'
Active/Positive: 'I'm **causing** myself to suffer these headaches, so I'm going to deal much better with stress and pressure from now on, and get rid of them'

Passive: 'This cancer is killing me - I'm going to die'
Active/Positive: 'I **own this** cancer, I'm going to fight this thing and put 100% effort into getting better'

The above Active/Positive statements would be made even more powerful, if you visualised or rehearsed the successful outcome in your mind, as you said them. This would create the anticipation of success and power, which would, in turn, help to make you feel even more powerful and hopeful. We learnt earlier in the book that the more powerful you feel, the more effort you put in.

## ACTION! Making your language active and positive

Your turn now: think of four negative and/or passive statements that you often say or think, and write them in the four Passive sections below. Then for each one write an Active version, then an Active and Positive version, in the spaces provided:

(1) Passive:

Active:

Active/Positive:

(2) Passive:

Active:

Active/Positive:

(3) Passive:

Active:

Active/Positive:

(4) Passive:

Active:

Active/Positive:

## Language in the media

In his book: 'Creating fear: News and the construction of a crisis' (2002) Professor David Altheide describes a process he calls 'the exploitation of fear', by which governments and large organisations - mainly through the media - exert pressure and control over people by creating fear through the use of dramatic and catastrophic language. For many years now he has studied the use of language in the media (television, radio, newspapers and magazines) and noted how it has changed whenever those in power wanted to exert more control over their subjects.

There was a major shift during the autumn of 1989. Before that time the media generally did not make major use of terms such as 'cataclysm', 'plague', 'crisis', 'catastrophe' or 'disaster'. For example, during the 1980s the word 'crisis' would appear in news reports about as often as the word 'budget'. Prior to 1989 it wasn't often that you would see or hear adjectives such as 'dire', 'dreaded' and 'unprecedented', but that was all about to change.

The word 'catastrophe' was used 500% more in 1995 than in 1985, and its use had doubled again by the end of the millennium. General news reports and stories started to emphasise more the fear, risk, panic, danger and uncertainty that was going on all around us. Cast your mind back to the autumn of 1989 - what could have happened to cause this major shift?

Altheide suggested that it was the tearing-down of the Berlin wall, which signalled an end to the thirty-year long 'Cold War', that led to this language change. Until that point, fear and unpredictability (external locus - reliant on others to 'look after us') kept people behaving as good citizens. Countries spent trillions of pounds/dollars on their armed forces, and the threat of nuclear war was never far away. On the 9th of November 1989 the world saw those amazing images of East and West Germans climbing over the wall - without being shot - for the first time, to visit family and friends on 'the other side'.

What is perhaps also interesting - and possibly just a tad paranoid - (I just re-took the paranoid thinking style quiz, and scored '0' though. Mind you, I did write the quiz) is that literally within weeks of the Berlin wall coming down, a brand new terrifying threat had emerged that suggested a huge global disaster was just around the corner (cue 'Jaws' music). The environmental crisis was hardly reported upon before late 1989, but suddenly it was in every newspaper, discussed on every chat show, several out-of-vogue pop stars were suddenly experts on it, and everyone was talking about 'global warming', 'greenhouse gasses', and the depleting ozone layer. It is true that Nature hates a void, but maybe the 'environmental crisis' - or at least the catastrophic reporting of it - was orchestrated to keep us scared, and in need of someone to look after us? Funnier still, perhaps, but since 'global terrorism' has been on the news everyday, I haven't heard so much about the 'environmental crisis'. Paranoid, me? Now where did I put those WMD?

What Altheide suggested in his book though is actually backed up by other research. Twenge, Zhang and Im (2004) studied the increasing externality in society between 1960 and 2002. They stated:

> *These larger social trends have been accompanied by increased media coverage of negative, uncontrollable events on 24-hour cable news. In contrast, news broadcasts in the early 1960s were confined to a 15-min evening segment (Stark, 1997). The news events these media outlets cover are almost all negative and uncontrollable, especially to the average viewer (a partial list: wars, natural disasters, plane crashes, murders, child abductions, stock market crashes, and the events of September 11, 2001). Sitting in their living rooms, modern citizens may increasingly feel that they belong to a huge, complex, confusing, and terrible world that is utterly beyond their control to change*

I'm not discussing the media's use of language to make you external or paranoid, but just to bring it to your attention. Next time you are listening to or watching the news, pay attention to the language the reporter is using, think what effect that language might be having on you.

## Language and medicalisation and labelling of symptoms

The way in which you describe and name your symptoms and problems is important as a label can carry a lot of meaning with it. Medicalisation is the process where symptoms and problems are classified as medical conditions or disorders, often requiring medical interventions. This can be helpful, enabling effective treatment of the problem. But for symptoms that are minor and likely to resolve themselves, or that are mostly psychological or stress-related, then medicalisation can be very detrimental. For example, if you have rabies, it's useful to know that you have rabies, so that you can obtain the correct treatment and be cured. If, however, you sometimes get depressed during winter - because you have an external sense of power and control and aren't managing your thinking very well - the last thing you need is to be diagnosed as suffering from 'Seasonal Affective Disorder' (or just 'SAD'). Being diagnosed with a 'recognised psychological disorder' ('SAD'), isn't going to help a person, who already feels quite powerless, to overcome their depression. If anything, it's going to make the sufferer feel even worse!

Often people 'want' a medical diagnosis for their symptoms. Such a diagnosis may make things seem a bit more understandable. Social anxiety often means that people do not want their problems to be psychological or stress-related because they perceive that this will bring judgement from others (and themselves). People may sometimes even 'want' a diagnosis of a 'proper psychological disorder' (such as depression or obsessive compulsive disorder, rather than feeling miserable or being obsessive) because that might signify to them that they have a 'proper' problem that isn't their fault. But labels tend to carry a lot of meaning. Medicalisation often renders a person powerless to do anything about their symptoms as they are more likely to believe that they need medical treatment and there is nothing that they can do to help themselves. Labelling symptoms as a medical condition may represent them as being more severe and outside the sufferer's control.

Regardless of the causes of symptoms and problems, the label you give them is important and impacts upon the way you subsequently view those symptoms. For example, detecting and labelling hypertension (high blood pressure) in people after a work-based screening led to an increase of over 80% in the number of days that they had off work, regardless of whether or not their hypertension was treated (Haynes, Sackett, Taylor, Gibson and Johnson, 1978). Just having that label affected the way in which individuals saw themselves. Perhaps even more interestingly, having a 'medical label' attached to one kind of symptom may affect how you see symptoms in unrelated areas. Mold, Hamm and Jafri (2000) looked at two groups of people. Those in one group had been diagnosed with hypertension and the other group hadn't. The hypertensive group believed that it would take them almost twice as long to recover from a cold as the other group did (11.7 vs 6.0 days). Another study compared how a condition was perceived when it was given its established common name or a newer medicalised label (Young, Norman, Humphreys, 2008). People rated the conditions as more serious, more representative of a disease, and less common when they had the medical label attached. Labels are not neutral.

One of the more ridiculous medicalised terms to appear in recent years (in my humble opinion!) is 'an addictive personality'. I hear this quite a lot these days, and it's used as an excuse for just about everything. I often hear comments such as 'I'm going to find it difficult to come off the fags/booze/drugs/glue/coffee/chocolate - because my doctor said I have an addictive personality'. The sufferer is repeating the (ridiculous) term by way of explaining just how difficult they believe the process is going to be!

Don't even get me started on the term 'addiction'. I've now helped about 8,000 smokers to quit, who only smoked because they thought it would be too difficult to quit, because they were told they were addicted to it!

## ACTION! Amending medicalised terms

Have a think about the kind of language you use to describe your symptoms - do you tend to use more 'medical' or catastrophic terms to describe your problems? For example:

| | | |
|---|---|---|
| Depression | vs | Feeling miserable |
| Phobia | vs | Fear |
| Insomnia | vs | Difficulty sleeping |
| Migraine | vs | Headache |
| Flu | vs | Cold |
| PMS | vs | Feeling moody |
| Addiction | vs | Habit/desire/want |

Please write some examples of terms that you used to describe your symptoms, problems or difficulties that may be medicalised, catastrophic or just unhelpful! Then make sure you go about changing these in your day-to-day speech and thoughts.

## Mean what you say

As a general rule, when it comes to your use of language, mean what you say. Are you starving, or just hungry? Are you tormented by your partner's snoring, or just pissed off? Are you really fine, or are you sad/happy/bored/annoyed?

There are a couple of phrases that I tend to hear regularly in the consulting room, and I always challenge the person saying them. The first one is 'not too bad', and I was recently told this three times in one week, in reply to my question 'how are you'? The first time I received the reply, I overlooked it because I thought of it as just one of those statements people make like: 'fine thanks', 'ok' or even 'not bad'. When I heard it for the second time though, from a client with similar issues to the first, I thought 'hang on a minute,' not too bad,' what does that actually mean?'

Firstly, it's quite a negative and catastrophic statement. Secondly, there is a context issue: 'not too bad', in relation to what? In relation to a normal week? In relation to their worst week ever? In relation to their illness, their symptoms, their holiday, to dying? I was just asking how they were that day, I wasn't asking them to compare and contrast their experiences to anything else! It's as if they were actually answering: 'not too bad - nobody died or got struck down with a major illness, none of my friends let me down really badly, my girlfriend didn't leave me, I didn't get food poisoning, I didn't have a hang-over, I wasn't the victim of road-rage, and no-one caught me masturbating - so, not too bad really! In the context of how bad my week COULD have been, it really wasn't too bad!'

The point here is that when people are managing their thinking well, they don't relate or compare their everyday experiences to how bad they could have been, how ill they could have felt, or what trauma could have occurred. Instead, they just relate their thoughts and experiences to what ACTUALLY happened that week, not what COULD have happened. The use of this type of statement usually stems from the person having both the hypervigilant and obsessive thinking styles (see previous chapter).

To demonstrate just how unhelpful and misleading this type of statement is, I replied to the third person who said it to me that week: 'Oh I'm sorry, I didn't realise you were having a bad day', to which he replied 'Oh I'm not, I feel better than I've felt for six years, **and** I've just played my best round of golf **ever'.** I asked him to think about why he replied 'oh, not too bad' to my question, when a more appropriate response would have been something like 'I am having a fantastic day Rob, life couldn't get much better and I am seeing improvements all the time'. To his credit, he realised that he was both protecting himself by saying 'not too bad', and also being a little churlish. He didn't want to recognise that in fact, far from being 'not too bad' he was 'really bloody good', because this meant he was getting better and this put a lot of pressure on him to stay better. Far better to see his progress as 'not getting any worse'. As for being churlish, he didn't want to tell me - or even recognise himself - that he was clearly getting better because that would mean I had been right in what I was saying all along and, because of his social anxiety, he found that difficult.

The other misleading comment I hear quite often is the phrase 'open-minded'. Why do people tend to use this phrase when they are being as far from open-minded as humanly possible?

Question: *Do you believe in ghosts?*
Answer: *I like to be open-minded about these things*

If you search through any dictionary or thesaurus for the term, you will come across definitions of 'open-minded' such as fair, impartial, unprejudiced, balanced, as well as the standard meaning of 'open to new ideas'. It's one of those phrases that is often used out of context to infer something else. 'Open-minded' suggests that the person has a very balanced view on something; that maybe they have looked at both sides of an argument and come to some sort of weighted and balanced opinion on the issue, perhaps deciding that evidence is inconclusive. This is usually not true when people actually use the phrase 'open-minded'. It's spin. It's like the phrase 'I'm a perfectionist' mentioned in the previous chapter. The person is using it as a self-compliment that allows them to maintain their usually dogmatic, unrealistic and unhelpful belief system, e.g. 'I know no one has ever photographed an angel, but that doesn't mean they don't exist, I like to be open-minded about these things'.

A far more honest and realistic statement for this type of belief could be: 'I know it is extremely unlikely, and that there is not one shred of evidence to back up my belief, but I would really **like** to believe that angels actually exist.'

Am I being a bit tough here? I don't think so. Many people that I have helped with this programme who were consulted on how much I should put into this book, how honest I should be, how tough they thought I should be, all said: 'spell it out in black and white Rob, we just want you to be clear with us.'

If you are working this programme just to help yourself overcome a few minor anxieties in life, then you could probably go on using the phrase 'open-minded' without it having much negative impact upon your life. However, if you are using this programme to help overcome significant symptoms and many unhelpful belief systems you NEED to drop it. Just like the phrase 'I'm a perfectionist', 'I'm open-minded' puts a positive spin on something that prevents us from looking further into what we are actually saying. I've treated lots of perfectionists with this programme, and not one of them was aware of the negative connotations of being a perfectionist - they only saw the spin, the positive character trait implied. None of them was aware of the hugely negative impact being a perfectionist had upon their self-esteem, and hence also their social anxiety and sense of power and control.

Maybe a better way to tackle this kind of comment would be to simply ask, 'Do you really want to be open-minded at the moment? Maybe you would do better right now to look for hard evidence of how you could actually resolve your problems and symptoms'?

Meaning what you say is also important in relation to not making empty positive statements. You don't want to think or say anything that you can't back up with evidence. Although an empty positive affirmation may help to temporarily boost mood, sense of control and self-esteem, sooner or later you will only end up feeling really disheartened and powerless, as you realise that there is no substance behind your statement.

So, telling yourself something along the lines of 'I love flying' would be unhelpful if you were still creating anxiety about flying at that moment. You would almost certainly think 'Well hang on a minute, that's not true' and you would feel disheartened that this 'positive thinking' wasn't working. Instead a statement of 'I'm gradually overcoming my dislike of flying by challenging my unhelpful beliefs and thinking and building my skills and resources' would be much more realistic and empowering.

How about saying to yourself:

*'Every day I am making my life better and better by challenging my limiting beliefs and thinking styles. I am gradually building the skills and resources I need to overcome my symptoms and thrive.'*

## ACTION! Setting a daily focus

When I talk with clients who are undertaking this programme, they often say things like 'I didn't realise until lunchtime that I was thinking negatively', 'I didn't know I was wearing my shit-tinted spectacles until you pointed it out to me' and 'I wasn't aware that I was in a bad mood'. My reply is always the same: 'why wait to find out that your thinking hasn't been helpful today'?

It's a bit of a waste – when you are trying so hard to get yourself thriving – to discover at three o clock in the afternoon that you have been having lots of unhelpful thoughts all day. Wouldn't it be better to spot these thoughts earlier? Better still, wouldn't it be great to not have them at all?

As I've said elsewhere, looking out for negative or unhelpful thoughts is in itself a negative thing to do, and actually therefore creates more negativity. Effectively you are looking out for what you are doing wrong. Much better to invest your time and energy into looking out for what you are doing right…

So, why wait – and react with disappointment – to discover you have been having unhelpful thoughts, and have effectively 'blown the whole morning'? This can be avoided quite simply by setting yourself a daily focus.

A daily focus is much like a goal, but more general, and relates to how you want to manage your thinking today, and what you want to get out of today. So ask yourself a question:

**What do you want to get out of today?**

Let me make it easier: do you want a shitty day today? Do you want to feel miserable today? Bored? Negative? Sad? Angry? Do you want to dwell on the past? Do you want to feel bad about being overweight? Still smoking? Not been going to the gym? Going bald? Bad breath?

I imagine (hope?) that your answers to all these questions is 'no'. Then what? What DO you want out of today? Wherever you are right now, whatever time of day – or night – it is, what do you want to get out of the rest of the day? Maybe you just want to feel positive? Perhaps you want to get out and do some exercise? Maybe just stay calm during a busy work meeting…

So, make that choice. If you want to feel positive for the rest of the day, make that choice, visualise it, set your focus for the rest of the day: 'For the rest of the day I'm going to put lots of effort into being positive and happy'. Write this statement down, maybe put it on your phone, write it on a post-it note and stick it next to your desk/in the loo/by your bed/on the fridge/in the front of your car/all of these places! Every twenty minutes or so, glance at the note and repeat your intention, say it out loud if you can. By doing this you are helping yourself to stay focused on your 'goal for the day'.

Right, now let's think about tomorrow. Write yourself another note - and this one could do with being on really good quality card, if you are an obsessive/perfectionist you could even laminate it! – and this one you are going to stick next to your bed, so it's the first thing you see every morning. The message is a clear question to yourself:

**'What sort of day do you want today'?**

Before you have even got out of your bed tomorrow morning, I want you to have already realised that you can choose what sort of day you are going to have. So lie there in your bed and spend just two minutes mulling over what sort of day you want, then write it down. Set yourself up for the day BEFORE the day actually starts. For me, this morning (a lovely spring morning in Cambridge) I set my focus as 'today I'm going to stay calm and relaxed and write another chapter for my next book'. This has helped me to: stay focused on what I wanted to achieve today, not lose perspective and go off-topic, not get distracted by other things going on around me, stay calm and relaxed and write another chapter.

If you currently have emetophobia (a fear of being sick), your focus for today might be 'to stay positive and confident in knowing that I will soon be feeling much better'. If you are currently battling with cancer or any other significant, painful or debilitating condition, your focus might be 'to stay calm, positive and happy'. If you're attempting to lose weight it could be 'I'm going to stay positive today and stick to my healthy eating plan. As someone who has just quit smoking 'today I'm going to feel proud and happy being a non smoker'. Just going through a break-up 'I know I'm a worthwhile loveable person, and that I'm going to make my life better every day'. You get the gist?

Your daily focus is therefore a combination of a goal, a focus, an affirmation, a self-suggestion, a visualisation exercise, a statement of intention.

So, set yourself a focus for the rest of today, and write a 'what sort of day do you want today' card to go by the side of your bed.

Every morning you want to wake up and make the following positive and active affirmation: *'Today I am going to put effort into overcoming my symptoms. I have the skills and resources to do this. I am going to challenge any limiting beliefs, manage my unhelpful thinking styles and process my positives. Today I am another step closer to thriving!'*

You want to add this affirmation to your list of positives (in your phone or notebook), so that you can continue to remind yourself of it throughout the day. Setting your context will have a hugely positive impact on you.

# Mind Your Language - Recap

- ✓ Our thoughts and beliefs are apparent in our language.
- ✓ The words we use (both in speaking to others and to ourselves) show us what we believe - this is particularly important when our thoughts and beliefs have become almost implicit.
- ✓ Additionally our language can impact upon our beliefs.
- ✓ If you speak and think negative words you will lower your mood, anticipate negative outcomes, make yourself stressed, reduce self-esteem, increase social anxiety, feel powerless and contribute to an external sense of power and control.
- ✓ If you use positive words you will feel powerful, anticipate positive outcomes, create less stress, increase self-esteem, reduce social anxiety and contribute to an internal sense of power and control.
- ✓ As well as positive language, active language is really important as it empowers you and suggests that you are able to take control of your situation.
- ✓ It is important to avoid unnecessary medicalisation of symptoms and problems because this can increase perceptions of severity and powerlessness.
- ✓ Every time you use a dramatic, catastrophic or medicalised term to describe how you are feeling, or the state of your symptoms, you are creating anxiety and stress which could then make your symptoms (or your ability to fight your symptoms) worse.
- ✓ Minimise your symptoms and the effects of your symptoms. 'Play them down' instead. Better still, use humour to describe them: 'Yeah, got a little cancer thing going on at the moment' or 'Who needs a left arm anyway?'
- ✓ Mean what you say: try not to use words and phrases that don't really express how you genuinely feel or what you genuinely believe.
- ✓ Set yourself a positive and empowering focus for the day every single morning.

## What should I be working on from now on?

1. Keep working on the **ACTION**s described in chapters 3 to 5. In particular, make sure that you process your positives **every day**.

2. Keep challenging and changing your unhelpful thinking.

3. Put effort into using POSITIVE and ACTIVE language.

4. Amend any unhelpful medicalised language.

5. Set the context every day, by starting with a positive and active affirmation: '*Today I am going to put effort in to overcoming my symptoms. I have the skills and resources to do this. I am going to challenge any limiting beliefs, manage my unhelpful thinking styles and process my positives. Today I am another step closer to thriving!*'

## Notes - The blank area below is for you to make any notes.

# Chapter

# 8

# Anxiety and Stress

# Anxiety and Stress

'Anxiety' and 'stress' are two of those medical terms that have become weakened to the point of almost being meaningless by their over-use in the general press and on television. Though often the words 'anxiety' and 'stress' are frequently used interchangeably, as they mean similar things and often overlap, there are some subtle differences. For the purposes of this book, I will clarify the terms.

Generally speaking, the term 'anxiety' is used to describe a fearful state of apprehension, worry and doubt. Anxiety encompasses the thoughts, worries and feelings either behind or resulting from, a physical response or symptom.

The word 'stress' is more often used to describe the physiological response that occurs within your body in response to a perceived difficulty, threat or danger. This response could occur due to anxiety, or other pressures and situations in life.

So, anxiety can cause stress, and stress can cause anxiety. Simply creating anxiety and worrying about something can easily cause your body to make physiological changes, in order to deal with the perceived threat. For example, brooding about the fact that you have to go to the dentist next Thursday is likely to make you quite stressed. Alternatively, imagine you are happily walking down a country lane in the sun, when suddenly a farmer's dog starts barking and chasing you. Your body instinctively initiates a 'fight or flight' stress response allowing you to run away. This stress response will quite probably also result in anxiety. You may find that even when you have escaped the dog, you keep worrying and looking round to check you are safe. An anxious, apprehensive mood has replaced your happy relaxed one. You can have a situation where a person creates anxiety about something, leading to a stress response, which then increases anxiety.

One thing to bear in mind is that the causes of anxiety and stress don't need to be real - they can be perceived or imagined.

Let's look at anxiety in more detail.

## Anxiety

Anxiety encompasses the thoughts, worries and feelings a person creates in relation to a perceived threat. Holding the three primary limiting beliefs and engaging in any of the unhelpful thinking styles can lead to anxiety. In particular, people's perceptions of control are key factors in determining whether or not they will create anxiety about a scenario. Bandura (1988) stated:

> *People who believe they can exercise control over potential threats do not conjure up apprehensive cognitions and, hence, are not perturbed by them. But those who believe they cannot manage potential threats experience high levels of anxiety arousal. They tend to dwell on their coping deficiencies and view many aspects of their environment as fraught with danger.*

There are two ways in which people can feel in control of potential challenges. Firstly, they can have a high sense of **direct influence**, believing that they can prevent a potential threat from occurring. They could, for example, be certain that they have the skills to complete an important work assignment on time. As a result, they do not worry about the possibility of not getting the work done, as they are sure that this will not occur.

People can also have a strong belief in their **coping sills**, believing that even when a potential threat is outside their direct influence, they have the resources to respond positively, cope and bounce back. They could, for example, be confident that if they didn't finish their assignment on time they would be able to manage the consequences. So, again, they do not create anxiety about the assignment.

In relation to anxiety, a person's beliefs about their coping skills is particularly significant since, although many outcomes are within people's direct influence, there are events that are not always controllable. People who create a lot of anxiety, or have specific fears or phobias, always have little belief in their coping skills. They do not believe that they have the resources to deal with certain situations, so they worry about them! When actually faced with a challenging situation these individuals can feel very panicky and powerless and they may turn to external sources for help, because they have no faith in their internal coping skills.

Anxiety is best broken down into two component parts:

1. Real-Time Anxiety
2. Anticipatory Anxiety

**Real-Time Anxiety** is just as it sounds. It's the anxiety experienced in real-time, when you are physically in an anxiety-causing situation for example: on an aeroplane, driving on the motorway, near a frightening barking dog, in court for speeding or walking home late at night. These can all be Real-Time anxiety-causing situations for many people. Real-Time anxiety means that the event is actually happening NOW and that you are experiencing some anxiety during the event. It may be that there is some genuine inherent danger during the event so it is entirely appropriate to feel anxious (driving on an icy road, the dog has its teeth bared and is growling menacingly) or that the event is symbolically significant, as in a phobia (spiders, darkness, cancer, germs etc.). The essential point about Real-Time anxiety is that it occurs in the moment - there is no build-up to it and you weren't necessarily expecting it.

**Anticipatory Anxiety** is also quite self-explanatory. It is the anxiety experienced when 'anticipating' (thinking, worrying or brooding about) a stressful, dangerous, frightening or challenging experience. For example, when you are: worrying about a dentist appointment next week, thinking about an aeroplane flight that you are taking soon, imagining what the magistrate is going to say to you when you appear in court for speeding next month.

Basically, the sufferer is thinking and worrying about a future event, imagining that the event is going to be stressful, unpleasant, frightening or otherwise challenging, and that they are going to either die, feel very panicky, be in great pain, feel out of control, or look stupid. By focusing on this feared event (and catastrophising about it), the sufferer magnifies the sense of anticipation and the fear and the dread get stronger.

The more anxiety (either Real-Time or Anticipatory) or stress a person suffers, the more focused they become on it. This has the effect of 'zooming in' on it. When you zoom in on something, you lose focus on what else is happening around it: you get 'tunnel vision'. Therefore, the more anxious or stressed a person becomes about something, the less they are able to think logically, clearly and practically about it and, therefore, actually DO anything about it.

Some people experience more anticipatory anxiety than others. Those with brooding and catastrophising thinking styles tend to do so. People with social anxiety are also prone to suffering greatly from this type of anxiety. The bottom line is this: for some reason you brood/worry/anticipate what you imagine might happen 'on the day', and this creates intense amounts of anxiety.

As if this isn't bad enough, this anticipatory anxiety makes you feel more apprehensive of the real event. You begin to really expect that the whole event is going to be terrible. You experience a heightened state of awareness and agitation, your heart beats fifteen to the dozen and there is a sense of impending doom. Then you get to the airport (or walk into court or lie down in the dentist's chair) and the event happens and, surprise, surprise, it is indeed incredibly anxiety-causing. Were it not for the build-up of tension due to the huge sense of anticipation, the event would have been much less significant, much smaller, much less frightening and much easier to deal with.

So, it is the prior build-up of this **anticipatory anxiety**, which often makes events particularly frightening and unpleasant. Many people do not particularly enjoy flying, but for most of them it does not cause significant problems. If, however, you spend the three weeks before a flight worrying and brooding about it, creating lots of anxiety and apprehension, imagining everything that can go wrong (like the wheels falling off, having to crash-land in the sea, suffering incredible turbulence or being hijacked by terrorists) you will find your flight terrifying! If you have been imagining the plane crashing and are in a heightened state of awareness, when the plane jolts slightly on take-off you immediately think, 'Oh my God, I'm going to die!' When the seatbelt sign is switched on mid-flight you assume it is because something has gone wrong with the plane or you are about to encounter terrible turbulence, but actually it is just that the captain wants to leave the cabin to go to the loo! You think you detect the smell of burning, 'Shit the plane is on fire!', when really it is just the smell of the in-flight meals being reheated! You have built up a huge amount of anticipation that something will go wrong, and so normal flying experiences are instinctively interpreted as being frightening and threatening, just like wearing the belief-tinted spectacles I mentioned in chapter 1.

The very best way to fully understand the impact of anticipatory anxiety, is to watch the film Jaws.

Most people have seen one of the Jaws films but I think that everyone has probably heard of them. When the film came out (in 1975) it was one of the most terrifying films ever, and some (just ever-so-slightly-hysterical) people haven't swum in the sea ever since! Ask someone if they have seen the film, and the first thing they will remember is the scary music: dum-dum, dum-dum, dum-dum (getting faster and faster). They remember the music because it was the music that created the anticipatory anxiety which, in turn, made the film so scary.

Try this out: rent the DVD, or find a clip of the film on YouTube. Find a scary bit, then watch it with the sound turned up loud. As the music gets louder and quicker, you will probably notice that your heart is beating stronger and faster and that you are sitting on the edge of your seat. As the music reaches a crescendo the shark appears and you nearly jump out of your skin as it savages a poor, powerless, swimmer or water-skier. The blue sea turns black as the victim's blood flows into it.

Now, go and have a nice cup of tea, and calm down for ten minutes.

Right, now go back and watch exactly the same frightening clip all over again BUT, this time, watch it with the sound turned completely off, no sound at all. This time, you'll almost certainly find that the clip wasn't really scary at all - you weren't on the edge of your seat, your heart wasn't beating hard and fast, and you didn't have a near panic-attack when the shark gobbled up the unsuspecting victim. In fact, this time around, because you weren't anxiously anticipating something terrible happening, the shark didn't look at all frightening. All you see is a big plastic fish flapping around, 'chomp, chomp, chomp', and some food colouring!

The vast majority of the overall scariness of the film is created by the director skilfully manipulating the viewer's sense of anticipation.

Lots of anticipation = very scary
Little anticipation = not very scary at all

The more anticipatory anxiety the film director can arouse in you, the more focused you become on the film, and the more 'tunnel vision' you will have. You start to lose your sense of perspective and you are now living 'in the moment': your ability to think calmly, logically and rationally has disappeared, and your emotions are heightened, you are now just waiting for something terrible to happen.

At any time you could have turned the music off, and the sense of fear and anticipation would have very quickly disappeared, your emotions would have come back under your control and you would have regained your sense of clarity and perspective.

Many, many everyday fears, phobias, anxieties and other symptoms (including some illnesses) are created and maintained by this anticipatory anxiety process. Wouldn't it be good if you could simply 'turn the music off' in these situations as well? You can. I'll show you later in this chapter, when I talk about 'The DREAM Technique'™.

One important thing to realise is that anticipatory anxiety is strongly underpinned by desire for control. The person has little belief in their coping skills in relation to the situation and, because of their related desire for control, then spends a lot of time thinking and worrying about the event, trying to figure out how to avoid or control it. This brooding then results in a great deal of anticipatory anxiety, further increasing the person's desire for control.

Whether a person is suffering from real-time, or anticipatory anxiety, the psychological and physiological effects are much the same.

## Stress

The word 'stress' originally derived from the Latin term *stringere* which means to 'draw tight', (a good explanation for it). People use phrases such as 'work is really stressful at the moment', but, technically, work isn't stressful. Neither is flying, going to the dentist, having an argument, driving during the rush hour or any other experience we believe to be stressful. **Stress doesn't happen to us, stress is what we create when we don't manage our thinking very well.**

The word **'stress'** is used to describe the physiological response that occurs within your body in response to a stimulus known as a stressor. Stress is commonly seen as a bad thing but this is not always the case. A small degree of stress arousal can be positive and motivating. One example of this is that many athletes will produce personal best performances during competitions due to the stress associated with competing and the resulting ability to become 'psyched up'. Prolonged or high levels of stress, however, often have negative or damaging effects on a person.

Many things can be classed as stressors. Some things directly cause stress. For example stimulants, such as amphetamines or caffeine, cause stress by the biochemical effects they have on the body. Exercise also causes a stress response. In the context of this book, we are more interested in the events or experiences, either real or imaginary, which can cause stress. Many potentially stressful events or experiences occur around us every day of our lives. You may be running late, you may have a deadline at work, you may have an interview, or you may have a large bill to pay. Whether or not you experience excessive stress depends upon how you interpret an event or experience. When stuck in a traffic jam on the way to work, one person could stay calm and relaxed thinking, 'Well never mind, I'll just give work a ring and let them know I'm going to be delayed. I can always work a bit later this evening if this traffic doesn't clear soon.' Another person may think, 'Oh my god, I'm going to be late for work! I'm really busy at the moment! What if my boss is angry and I get sacked? What if I'm stuck here for hours?' Obviously the first person avoids a stress response, whereas the second becomes really quite stressed.

If you interpret an event or circumstance as being in some way challenging, threatening or aversive (i.e. creating anxiety about an event) this leads to an emotional arousal. A stress response is then initiated and various hormones are released in the body. These hormones cause your body to make changes which are intended to help you to deal with a threat. For example, your heart and breathing rate may rise and you may become very focused on the 'threat'. These changes are useful in aiding a person to deal with a physical threat, the kind that we had to face hundreds, or even thousands, of years ago. Nowadays, however, many of the things that people become anxious about are not physically threatening and the stress response may be very unhelpful.

Additionally, the stress response has effects on various systems and organs within our body, as well as our psychological functioning. If the stress response is particularly intense or prolonged this can cause stress-related symptoms and illnesses.

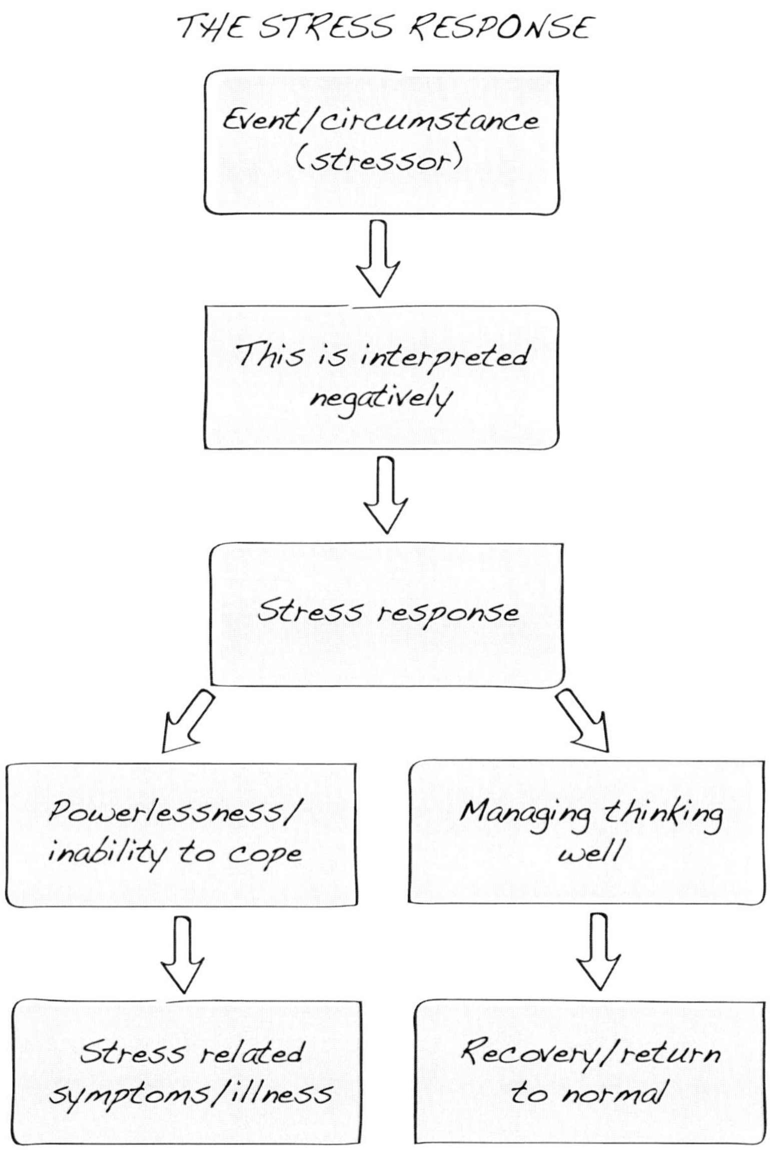


The effects of stress include:

- **Thinking -** confusion, difficulty making decisions, poorer concentration, problems with memory and recall, anxiety
- **Emotional** - feeling overwhelmed, agitated, shock, anger, depression, grief
- **Physical -** sweating, dizzy spells, increased heart rate, higher blood pressure, rapid breathing, lowered libido, changes in immune system

- **Behavioural -** changes in normal behaviour, changes in eating, changes in sleeping, poorer personal hygiene, withdrawal from other people, prolonged silences.

Basically, the more anxiety or stress a person is experiencing, the more their thinking, feelings and symptoms and health will be affected, almost certainly for the worse. A good example of this, in the research I came across, looked at the effects of a hurricane on the symptoms of chronic fatigue sufferers. People with CFS exposed to the hurricane and its after effects were more likely to suffer a relapse and reported greater symptoms of chronic fatigue syndrome. Even more interesting, however, was the fact that:

> *Although extent of disruption due to the storm was a significant factor in predicting relapse, the patient's post hurricane distress response was the single strongest predictor of the likelihood and severity of relapse and functional impairment. Additionally, optimism and social support were significantly associated with lower illness burden after the hurricane, above and beyond storm-related disruption and distress responses.*
>
> (Lutgendorf *et al.*, 1995)

So, those who interpreted their situation as being more distressing, independent of actual disruption and material loss, suffered more symptoms and were more likely to relapse.

I was talking to a client one day, and thinking that I really wanted to come up with some kind of diagram, or visual metaphor, to help explain how stress, and the poor management of our thinking, affects us. I liked the idea of linking stress to the 'rev counter' in a car - the more you put your foot down, the more the needle heads towards the red 'no go' zone. So, I came up with the idea of The Stress-o-meter.

## The Stress-o-meter

Stress and the general pressures of life make your symptoms, worries, habits and anxieties worse. So basically, the less stressed (anxious, and not managing your thinking very well) you are, the happier, more positive, more powerful, more energetic, more healthy, more in control you are likely to be.

When you get in your car in the morning and start it up, the engine just ticks over, and the needle hovers just below the number one. This means that your engine is hardly doing any work at all. This is the desired 'setting' for your mental rev-counter, your Stress-o-meter, in the morning. You want to wake up and start your day and have your brain just ticking over. This way you will almost certainly have just had a good night's sleep and now be starting your day feeling calm, relaxed, anxiety and stress free and in full control.

As you go through your day and experience the pressures of work, family life, kids, the school run etc., your needle will rise up and, hopefully, fall back down again. If you are managing your thinking well, your needle should never go anywhere near the red danger-zone (around 8, 9 or 10 on the Stress-o-meter). You will be thinking clearly, feeling calm, in control and great!

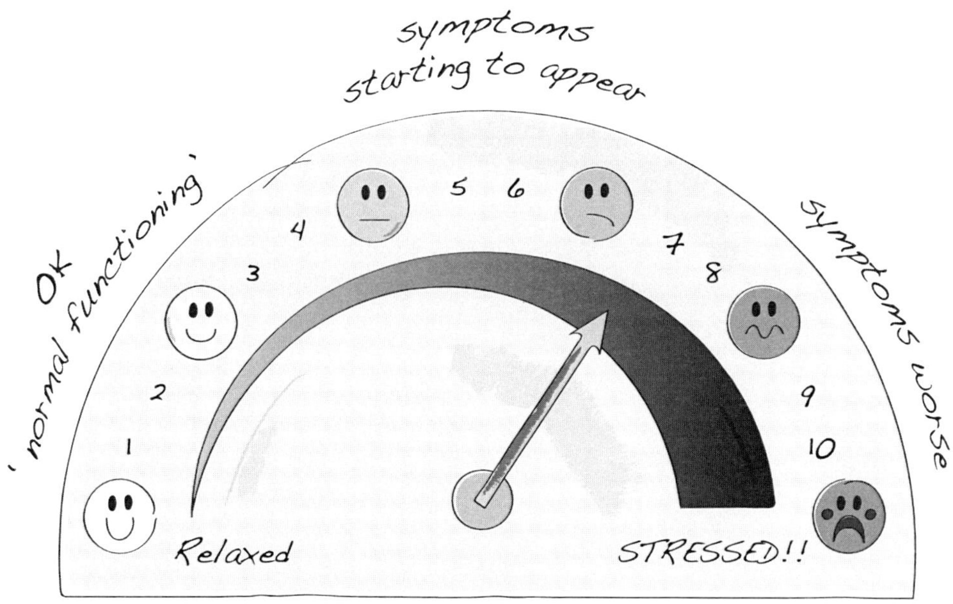


Let's look at what happens if you are not managing your thinking very well.

As an example, let's look at an insomniac:

The people least likely to have had a good night's sleep, the people most likely to suffer from insomnia, are those people who have a strong obsessional (brooding and ruminating) thinking style. Almost always, when an insomniac consults for help with their sleeping, we find that they have a strong obsessional thinking style and are stressed. They report that their work or life was becoming very stressful, possibly triggered off by some sort of work, or relationship-related setback. Even though they may be very tired when they go to bed at night, 'their mind' seemed to be working overtime, and they were plagued with thoughts and worries about their (perceived) stress that wouldn't leave them alone. They usually report only having a few hours of sleep each night. When this person rises in the morning, their Stress-o-meter needle is already hovering perilously close to the red danger zone. It's not going to be far into the day before this person starts to experience stress and anxiety-related symptoms.

Most people experience some type of symptom, for example: an eating disorder, migraine, insomnia, anxiety or depression, that seems to come and go throughout their lives. They may suffer with their symptom for weeks and months and then it disappears for weeks or even years.

Why?

The vast majority of symptoms and problems that people want help in either (a) totally resolving, or (b) minimising to make their life easier, are either created, or brought on, by stress. The more stressed a person is, the worse the symptoms get.

The higher the numbers on your dial, the less relaxed and calm you are, and the greater your stress levels. Your dial can move in response to any situation depending on how you react. As we have already explored, having any of the unhelpful thinking styles mentioned in the previous chapter means that you often create a lot of stress and anxiety in response to a challenging situation.

Managing your thinking effectively so that your Stress-o-meter dial remains low is very important. As you become more stressed, your poorly managed thinking and symptoms mentioned previously increase in intensity and the more stressed you then become, i.e. as your anxiety levels increase you tend to feel more powerless, catastrophise more, obsess more, become more negative, more socially phobic, less confident and more hypervigilant. This in turn increases your stress levels even more.

It can, therefore, be very difficult to escape from a highly stressed state as all your unhelpful thinking styles, which contribute towards creating such a state, become heightened further when you are stressed. Everyone has a stress level 'threshold' (around about 5-6 on the scale where your anxiety symptoms start to appear) after which point it becomes much more tricky to reduce your stress levels as your negativity, catastrophising, obsessing, paranoia, perfectionism, hypervigilance, helplessness are increased to such an extent that any perspective on your problem is completely lost.

## Maintaining perspective

I remember reading an account by someone who was able to maintain perspective - even under the most anxiety-causing conditions. He was a warship captain during the battle for the Falklands, back in 1982. The captain was talking to an on-board news reporter, describing what happened when they had three missiles heading towards their 'boat'. I say 'what happened', but actually it was 'what didn't happen'. The newsman was surprised to find that, on seeing three Exocet missiles racing towards them on their radar, neither the captain nor the crew panicked. Instead, the captain stood back and thought about his situation for a moment (not too long though, he had about 90 seconds I think!) and said, something like, 'Well, in a situation like this it's very important to maintain perspective. We have three French-made, Argentinian-operated Exocet missiles heading straight towards us, chances are, one of them won't even reach us.' Almost as he said this, one of the missile's blips on the radar disappeared. He continued, 'Chances are that both the remaining missiles will hit us. One probably won't explode though; this one will make a hole in our boat, there will be a small loss of life, but it won't sink us. The final missile probably will go off, there will be loss of life, but it probably won't sink us either.' I remember the reporter being flabbergasted at how calmly the captain was describing the situation.

A bit of an extreme example I know, but something that has always stuck in my mind very clearly and examples that stick in our minds are very useful.

If the captain had panicked and started running around like a headless chicken (unlikely I know, since British Naval training is the best in the world; we don't rule the world anymore, but we still have the best navy!), he would have lost control of his thought processes, ended up with 'tunnel vision' and, probably, died as a result. He didn't though. Due to his training and experience he was able to stand back, see the bigger picture, keep functioning normally, and do his job. He was able to maintain a clear perspective, despite the stress and pressure around him.

When you have perspective, you have a complete and unobstructed view (or understanding) of a situation, you have clarity and you see the full picture. You understand all the different factors involved. When you see the full picture, you can make informed opinions and decisions, and you know what your full options are.

When you don't have perspective, you are unable to have any objectivity over your sense of symptoms, your personal relationships, or your progress (in changing your life). When looking at your belief systems and breaking them down so that you can see the component parts (distorted thinking, powerlessness, secondary gains etc.), you are gaining some perspective on your 'problem'. You get to view it from a different angle and thereby gain power, and shift your sense of power and control.

Gaining perspective is particularly important for someone learning not to catastrophise. Imagine your boss asks you in for a meeting next week, and you create loads of anxiety worrying that he is going to sack you because he thinks you are no good at your job. Before you send your Stress-o-meter needle into the 'very stressed' zone and you totally lose the plot, you want to just take a step backwards and get some perspective. Ask yourself 'Is it likely my boss wants to sack me?' and 'Have I been performing badly at work recently?' and maybe 'Is my company making any redundancies at the moment?' If the answer to all these questions is 'no', then you were probably just over-reacting, and you can now calm down and relax again. The key lies in getting perspective as early as possible in the catastrophising/worry process. The earlier you do it, the more stress and grief you can save yourself. The exercises I will discuss later in the book will help you to achieve this.

Imagine you are looking at a painting hung on a wall, but that your face is right up close to it so that all you can see is the middle of the painting - can you describe the painting to me? No you can't, because you can't see the whole picture. You have to take a step or two backwards, and as you do, more and more of the picture comes into view, until you have a clear view of the whole thing. Now you can see exactly what is going on.

## Phobias and fears

In my clinic I have helped about two thousand people to overcome their fears and phobias, from the very common ones like: flying, dying, cancer, spiders, lifts, dogs, driving on the motorway, to the slightly strange: fear of the number 13, fear of jam, fear of killing your parents, fear of double-decker buses, and a fear that the earth will stop spinning and that we will all fall off!

The difference between a fear and a phobia is usually just about severity and how much 'it' impacts upon the sufferer's life. For the purposes of this book, we can discuss fears and phobias in the same section because they are identical in how they are formed and maintained; it's just the strength that is different. In the rest of this section then when I refer to phobias, I am referring to both phobias and fears.

Who develops phobias? Anyone can. It would be easy to say that all phobia sufferers have a huge external sense of power and control, but this is not true. What IS true, is that all phobia sufferers have an external locus in relation to their phobia.

There are many myths about phobias, most of which are nonsense. Over the years I have been told by various people that their phobia: was the result of a trauma in their previous life, was because of their poor diet, was passed down from their mother, was because of a dream, was because of a story they heard... The list goes on and on. Let me put the record straight: for the couple of thousand phobics I have treated, and the hundreds of thousands my colleagues have treated, the cause was never one of the reasons mentioned above. Not once.

Phobias are all very similar – whether they are about dogs, dying, being sick, frogs, getting old or train carriages, they are all alike. A phobia is created when a person experiences a situation as frightening/guilty/challenging/stressful, and reacts in a powerless and sometimes catastrophic way to it. Now sometimes phobias are triggered by real traumatic experiences and other times they are completely created by the sufferer's thinking. Even when real experiences are at the root of the phobia, it is still the sufferer's thinking that maintains and determines the severity of it. As we have already discussed, how a person responds to any sort of emotional or traumatic experience depends very much upon their sense of power and control, belief systems, and unhelpful thinking styles. So, internal children will show resilience and thrive despite hardship, trauma or neglect, whilst the more external and less-powerful ones will respond with anxiety, stress, phobias, and other symptoms.

If you think back to the chapter on cognition, you'll remember that people don't actually experience reality. They experience reality through the filters or lenses of their belief systems and unhelpful thinking styles. So, much like two people sitting in my office and experiencing it in different ways (one person thinking its big, warm and airy, the other thinking it is cold, dark and gloomy), people experience EVERYTHING in different ways.

Two people have a minor car crash that caused a couple of bruises but no broken bones. One jumps straight back into their car and drives off, but the other never drives again. Why? As outside observers we can see that this was a minor car crash and that everything is going to be OK. If you ask the driver who drove away from the accident what it was like, they might say: 'it was a bit scary, but no real harm done'. Ask the other driver though, and they may reply 'it was absolutely terrifying. I saw my life flash before me. I was sure I was going to die, it's so dangerous on the roads these days'.

In other words, though both drivers suffered the same accident, their experience of it was totally different. The driver who was fairly internal, managed his/her thinking well, didn't catastrophise and managed to maintain perspective, recovered from the crash within a few minutes or hours. The driver who perceived the crash as terrifying, out of control, panicky, black and white, life and death, had a totally different experience to the other driver. It's as if one of the drivers had a minor car crash, whilst the other had been to hell.

The internal driver is going to process the experience internally: 'Due to my driving skills and quick reflexes I avoided a major accident. Well done me – it's great to be alive.' The external driver is going to process it externally: 'God that was close, it really is a lottery driving on the roads these days, the cars go so fast and there are so many of them, I'm not surprised more Americans die in car crashes each year than died in the whole of the Vietnam war.' The next day, the internal driver feels BETTER about their driving skills, they feel better behind the wheel because they have tested their driving skills to the limit, and come out a winner. The next day, the external driver starts to catastrophise their route to work, thinking about all the things that could go wrong, where the worst accident spots are, and they start to create anticipatory anxiety.

In short: the person experiences some sort of emotion/idea/trauma/fright – let's call it a 'trigger', and then processes the experience (in relation to their foundations and unhelpful thinking styles). If they have a fairly internal sense of power and control, and generally manage their thinking quite well, they will probably get over the experience quite quickly. If they have an external sense of power and control and badly managed thinking, they will in all probability, unintentionally, turn the experience into a full-blown phobia.

My estimate is that about 90% of all phobias are almost entirely driven and maintained by the sufferer's poorly managed thinking, rather than being triggered by a specific traumatic event. Yet most sufferers actually believe the cause of their phobia to be something external due to their external sense of power and control. The vast majority of phobias that we are asked to help people with symbolise being out of control. For example, heights, water, darkness, spiders, dogs, flying, dying, being sick, getting cancer or other illnesses, wasps or bees, lifts, bridges, motorways, knives, contamination, tunnels, underground trains, panic attacks, pain etc. These phobias essentially stem from the sufferer's external sense of power and control and their strong desire for control. How can they best avoid feeling out of control? By avoiding any situation that might make them feel a little out of control. Yet this only increases their fear.

Going back to the car crash example above, a fear of driving (a car) is actually one of the least common phobias therapists like me are consulted for, and yet most adults have had some sort of crash/scrape/near-miss whilst driving. So why don't we all have a fear of driving? Well most people NEED to drive so are very motivated to get over their crash/scrape/near-miss. They get back in the saddle within a few days and EXPOSE themselves to what they fear, and as a result quickly get over their trauma. Hence few people have a phobia of driving.

Another good example of a phobia is a fear of flying...

How many people have a phobia or fear of flying? What do you think? Well, according to Van Gerwen, Spinhoven, Diekstra and Van Dyck (1997), in industrialised countries, between 10 and 40% of the population are estimated to have a fear of flying. In Britain, that means there are somewhere between six and twenty-four million people with a fear of flying (based on a current population estimate of sixty-one million). In the U.S.A. the figures are between thirty-one, and one hundred and twenty four million (based on a current population estimate of three hundred and eight million). That's a lot of people. What percentage of these phobics have been involved in a plane crash do you think? I would estimate less than 0.00001% (loosely based on the fact that there were 4.8 billion worldwide air travellers in 2009-2010, with only 817 fatalities). So where do all these millions of people get their phobia from?

It's probably safe to say that most people who have a fear of flying DON'T have it because they have suffered some huge trauma in an aeroplane. So for the vast majority of flying-phobics, it's entirely about their thinking. As you'll read below, a fear of flying is the single most common phobia people consult people like me for and yet it is entirely down to their badly-managed thinking. Do they know this? No.

I have scoured my memory banks to think of a single flying-phobic, or any other phobic client come to mention it, who didn't 100% absolutely believe that their phobia was caused by some sort of trauma, emotional experience, or just suddenly happened 'to them'. Why would they do that? Well, it's really simple: a person with an external sense of power and control looks externally (outside of themselves) for reasons why things happen (Just as an aside for a moment, think about the catastrophic use of language used in air travel: with words like 'terminal', 'turbulence', 'departed' and 'final destination', it's surprising more people don't create anxiety about it!).

Imagine if you suddenly developed a fear of heights. You're standing on top of a tall building and you suddenly feel very panicky, so you step back from the edge and calm down. What goes through your mind is probably something like this: 'Wow, where did that come from?' You then start to look back through time to find an experience that fits, and you suddenly remember the time that your brother pushed you off the top of the climbing frame at school and it all fits! 'Oh my God, I knew that would come back to haunt me'. Now the person is defining their new fear in terms of the school accident forty years before, which has the effect of validating it, legitimising it. 'Well you'd have a bloody fear of heights if your brother pushed you off a climbing frame!!' Now you believe you have a cause for your problem, which goes back forty years, how are you going to resolve it? Every time you now define your fear in terms of the schoolyard prank you are making it BIGGER and STRONGER. You now start to worry about heights, try to avoid heights, create anticipatory anxiety about heights and think in black and white terms about heights.

What do you think would have happened on top of that building if, instead, you thought: 'I'm creating this anxiety, calm yourself down, I'm in charge of my emotions, this isn't scary, I can manage this?'

Let's look at the other common phobias people ask for help for...

In a recent survey of around one hundred of my colleagues, we found that the four most common phobias we are asked to help with were: flying (17.3%), fear of having a panic attack (15.5%), fear of being sick - emetophobia (14.5%), and a fear of being judged - severe social anxiety (13.7%). This means that of all the thousands of people who approach us for help with a phobia, the vast majority of them (more than 60%) are asking for help with just one of the four mentioned above: flying, being sick, panic attacks, being judged (social anxiety).

Flying we've just talked about. There is a separate section (in this chapter) on a fear of being sick, social anxiety is one of the primary limiting beliefs we have already discussed, so let's look at the panic attacks.

During a panic attack a person may suffer many physical symptoms, including rapid heart beat, chest pains and tightness, shortness of breath, sweating, shaking, lightheadedness and tension. Many sufferers feel as though they are completely losing control or going 'mad'. A panic attack often includes a feeling that something awful is about to happen and many people initially fear that they are having a heart attack. Experiencing a panic attack/s and having a fear or phobia of having one tend to come hand in hand. In our terminology, panic attacks are created when a person's anxiety levels go into the red on their Stress-o-meter. Basically, panic attack sufferers are creating more and more anxiety, not managing their thinking, and instead winding themselves up to 'boiling point'. They don't know this though. They tend to believe that their panicky feelings are caused by some external force, and whilst they continue to process their experience externally, they will get worse and worse. They begin to fear having panic attacks, creating more anxiety and hypervigilance, and only increasing the likelihood that they will have another attack. Unsurprisingly, panic attacks and the fear of having them are essentially about an external sense of power and control.

According to Cloitre, Heimberg, Liebowitz & Gitow (1992) it was found that those with panic disorder tended to see events as occurring in a random and uncontrollable way. They went on to say:

*For individuals with panic disorder, the experience of an attack as occurring "out of the blue" and the sudden onset of symptoms and change in state may be experienced as random or reinforce a belief in the random and unpredictable nature of events.*

So, as we've seen before, when someone interprets an event as external and unpredictable, they feel even more powerless, and try even harder to gain some control. The trouble is, those who have panic attacks tend to do this in a way that only reinforces their powerlessness. For example, being hypervigilant to the possibility of having a panic attack, avoiding situations that might cause attacks, taking medication.

The following illustrates just how important a sense of powerlessness is in panic attacks. In an interesting, but perhaps slightly cruel experiment, Sanderson, Rapee and Barlow (1988) had participants with panic disorder breathe in carbon dioxide enriched air, which is known to often induce panic attack symptoms. One half of the participants believed that the amount of carbon dioxide they were inhaling could be adjusted with a dial if needed. The other participants believed that they could not control the carbon dioxide levels. Yet, in reality, in both groups the level of carbon dioxide was held constant, so the only difference was the amount of control each group felt. The participants who felt that they had no control over the situation reported a greater number of panic attack symptoms; rated the symptoms as more intense; reported greater anxiety; reported a greater number of catastrophic thoughts; reported a greater similarity between the experience and a naturally occurring panic attack and were significantly more likely to report full-blown panic attacks.

Fears and phobias are really quite simple to understand: they represent an external sense of power and control, and black and white thinking; 'I'm frightened/feel out of control in that situation, there is nothing I can do to stop it, and I therefore must avoid it'.

## Psychoneuroimmunology (PNI)

I first started to think about the links between our psychological health and our physical health when I first met Sarah. Sarah was not a client of mine, but a friend who I met at a party. She was telling me about her job as a physicist in an Oncology department in a well-known hospital. Basically, her responsibility was to decide how much radiotherapy to give cancer patients, specifically, children with leukaemia. She would study their medical histories, speak to their consultants and surgeon, and agree a specific course of radiotherapy. Anyway, she was telling me (over a very large gin and tonic) how '*it didn't really matter much anyway*' because '*in lots of cases she could tell which kids were going to live or die - regardless of their treatment - just by observing their behaviour in the waiting room*'.
I have to tell you, I was absolutely floored by this statement.
Just read that last line again: '*just by observing their behaviour in the waiting room*'.

At first I thought 'Oh here we go again, another weirdo who thinks they can predict the future' (apologies here to any readers who can, actually, predict the future!) but then she went on to qualify her statement by saying, '*yes, basically, the helpless, needy children die, and the determined, independent ones tend to live*'.

I still wasn't incredibly comfortable with her assertions, so I pressed her for more information, and what she went on to describe to me was the differences between the children who were 'thriving' and those who were not. The children with an internal sense of power and control, high self-esteem and the skills to manage anxiety and stress were more likely to survive their leukaemia and thrive than those who did not.

I know. It's a horrible, horrible thought. In fact it's such a horrible thought, I debated long and hard whether to even mention it in this book. However, research has also demonstrated that there is a significant link between psychological factors and illness. Over the last few decades the field of psychoneuroimmunology, or PNI, has arisen. This field studies the interaction between people's psychological processes, their endocrine and nervous systems and their immune system. It provides the scientific basis and evidence behind what is commonly known as the 'mind-body' connection. Robert Ader and Nicolas Cohen coined the term 'psychoneuroimmunology' in the 1970s.

So what exactly is the scientific basis behind the mind-body connection? How do our psychological processes impact upon our physical health?

### A very basic guide to stress and the immune system

Our immune system consists of the biological systems and processes that protect our body from disease and infection. It can tell the difference between the body's own cells and invading ones. The immune system's many different cells, tissues and organs work together to find and destroy foreign (for example bacteria or virus) or tumour cells within the body.

When the body activates a stress response, various hormones are released and the sympathetic nervous system is activated. This causes changes in the body such as increased heart and breathing rate, allowing us to respond to the stressor. If the stress response is maintained, however, there will be an impact on the immune system.

The various hormones released during the stress response can affect the cells of the immune system. In order to work efficiently, these immune system cells require 'normal' or equilibrium concentrations of these hormones. Temporary, infrequent changes do not tend to cause any significant problems as the hormone levels soon return to normal. If the stress response is either prolonged or very frequent however, the immune system may suffer.

The exact scientific explanation of how the immune system is affected by all the different stress hormones is somewhat complicated so I am not going to bore you with such details! Generally, however, chronic or very intense stress tends to lead to immuno-suppression (your immune system is less active) and increases your likelihood of catching a cold, flu, and other infectious diseases. You may have found that when you have been particularly stressed for a long time that you are more likely to catch any and every bug that is going around.

Less intense, shorter-term stress is associated with an over-active immune system and inflammatory conditions, such as asthma or hay fever. If you have one of these conditions you may have noticed that having a particularly stressful day increases your symptoms.

Some people can become caught in a cycle of stress and illness. If, for example, an anxious person falls ill and then creates a great deal of anxiety about being unwell, this can result in a sustained stress response. This can then lead to the immune system becoming suppressed, prolonging the person's recovery or making him or her very susceptible to catching whatever other illnesses are going round.

As soon as the person starts to recover from the first virus or illness, he or she catches another one.

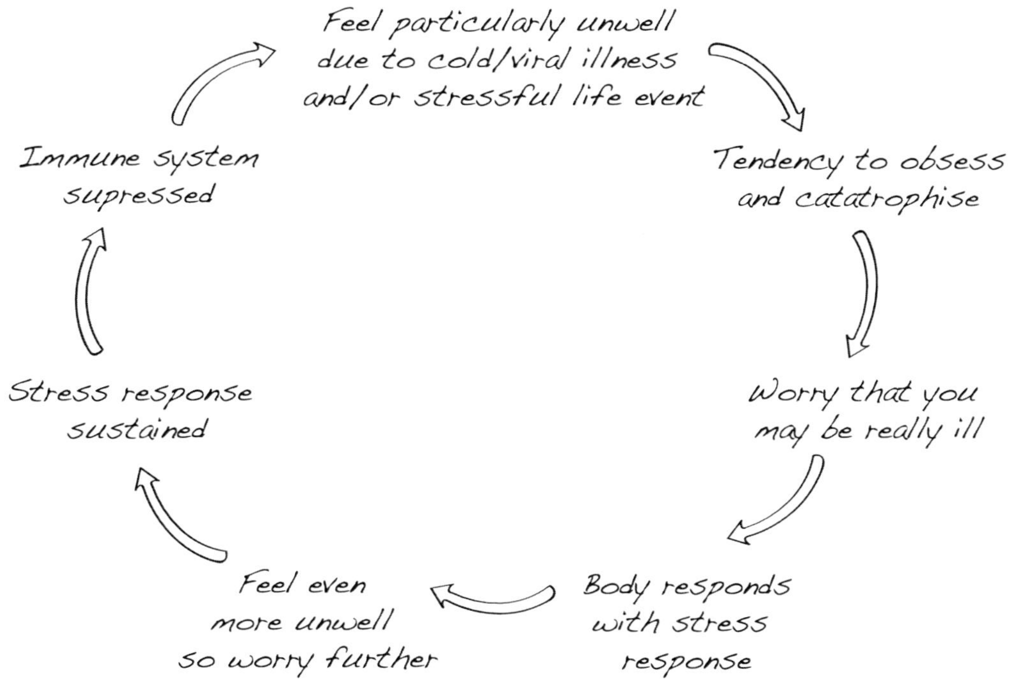


Of course, a person who is frequently highly stressed will not just be more susceptible to minor illnesses, but also more serious and debilitating ones. Indeed, I've already mentioned many pieces of research that back up the fact that psychological factors such as sense of power and control, poorly managed thinking and the resulting high levels of stress can increase a person's susceptibility to a wide range of illnesses, diseases and conditions.

Other research includes work by Shekelle *et al.* (1981) who found that men who were depressed were twice as likely as those who were not depressed to die from cancer in the following seventeen years, independently of other factors such as smoking, age and alcohol consumption. Kato *et al.* (2006) found that self-reported stress conferred a 64-65% greater risk for the development of chronic fatigue syndrome in the subsequent twenty-five years.

So not managing your thinking well and creating lots of stress is going to impact upon your immune system, increasing your susceptibility to a wide range of illnesses and diseases. Additionally, if you are diagnosed with an illness or disease, then the way in which you respond psychologically is going to affect your ability to recover. It is very understandable that when diagnosed with a potentially serious illness, many people become anxious, upset and stressed. Finding ways to minimise stress and take back control (by, for example, managing your thinking, minimising negatives, focusing on positives, engaging in relaxing activities - more about this later) is, however, going to benefit your immune system and ability to recover.

Lengacher *et al.* (2008) found that patients with breast cancer who underwent a relaxation and guided imagery intervention had higher natural killer cell (immune cells which kill infected and tumour cells) activity compared to a control group.

A great deal of PNI research has occurred with HIV/AIDS. Leserman *et al.* (1999) followed initially symptom free, HIV-infected men for five and a half years. Those who had stress levels above the median were two to three times more likely to have progressed to AIDS after the 5.5 years than those who had stress below the median. Reed *et al.* (1999) found that symptomless HIV positive men, who were recently bereaved and additionally had negative HIV related beliefs, were more likely to develop AIDS related symptoms in the next 2.5 to 3.5 years compared to those who were positive and/or not bereaved.

Being stressed doesn't necessarily mean that you are going to become really ill or that you won't recover from an illness. There are lots of factors involved in susceptibility to, and recovery from, illness such as whether you smoke, your diet and your exercise levels, to name a few. Additionally, everyone becomes stressed from time to time and, as I mentioned earlier, small amounts of stress are not necessarily bad. Prolonged or intense stress can, however, impact negatively upon your immune system, increasing your susceptibility to becoming unwell or reducing your ability to fight disease.

Remember, it is possible to control your stress levels, and keep them to a minimum, by simply developing better psychological foundations and managing your thinking better.

# The DREAM Technique

So, you are working hard to build your deep, solid foundations, and you are starting to create a thriving mindset. What though of those naughty little 'blips' and of those thoughts, doubts or physical aches and pains - which you are still creating - that slip through your net and run the risk of affecting your day?

Don't worry, for those you have The DREAM Technique.

The DREAM Technique is a quick, simple and yet incredibly powerful intervention that you can put into practice at any time, which – with a little practice – will allow you to stop any unwanted thoughts, feelings or behaviours in their tracks AND get yourself back into a thriving mindset.

Think of The DREAM Technique as a fire extinguisher, a really good fire extinguisher, in fact the very best fire extinguisher on the market. You can use this fire extinguisher to easily and quickly put out any fires that you have inadvertently built. This fire extinguisher is well made, very powerful, and can put out any fire… you'll have a lot of confidence in it. Because of your confidence in your ability to put out fires, you'll stop worrying about fires. If you stop worrying about fires, what do you think will happen? Yes, you're right, if you stop worrying about fires, you'll stop building fires! You want to feel calm and relaxed, safe in the knowledge that if you did build yourself a little fire, you could easily put it out – probably even with one eye closed – with your brilliant fire extinguisher. It's a bit like having the very best burglar alarm: you want one, but you never want to hear it go off! Just having it makes you feel more secure, and you sleep soundly at night.

In an ideal world you'll never need to use The DREAM Technique – once your foundations are strong and deep, you won't be creating scary/unhelpful/anxious/stressy thoughts or responses – but it's still useful to practice the technique so that it is in good working order should need to use it. You can use this technique on any unhelpful thoughts, beliefs or feelings that won't disappear easily or quickly by normal means.

This technique is particularly useful for people overcoming symptoms and problems such as ME, post viral fatigue, chronic fatigue, fibromyalgia, chronic pain, or when experiencing a big blip, but can be used to tackle any situation, thought, problem or experience. Once you get to the point where you are thriving, you won't need to use this technique - except on the rarest of occasions. However the technique is also very useful for you in helping to build better coping skills, and better foundations generally.

Ok, so here we go...

DREAM is an acronym for a simple five-step process that brings together a number of **ACTION!**s already discussed in earlier chapters. It stands for:

**Detect, Reward, Escape, Amend and Magnify.**

The process has been developed so that wherever you are, and whatever you are doing, you can perform it, easily and quickly.

These are the actions each word refers to:

1. **Detect:** detect that you are having a unhelpful or limiting thought or feeling
2. **Reward:** reward yourself for 'detecting' the unhelpful thought or feeling
3. **Escape:** escape from the situation that brought on the unhelpful thought or feeling
4. **Amend:** amend the thought or feeling to create a positive and empowering one
5. **Magnify:** magnify this new thought and image: make it bigger, stronger and brighter.

In more detail:

1. **Detect:** this is when you become aware ('detect') that you have just created an unhelpful or limiting belief, thought or physical experience. It may have been an actual thought you had, for example, 'I can't go for that job, I'm not good enough' or 'I'm never going to get over this illness' or 'this therapy is not going to work'. It may have been a response to an environmental cue, like when it starts to rain, or your car breaks down, or your date stands you up. So 'detect' is that moment when you realise 'Shit, that's a really unhelpful thought!' If you REALLY want to make the moment significant and you are on your own, you could shout 'NO' or 'STOP' at the moment you recognise the unhelpful thought. Or if you are driving along the road, you could slam your hand down on the dashboard. Feel free to be as theatrical as you like with this part of the process - the more effort you make, the quicker the technique will start to work for you.

2. **Reward:** this is one of the most important parts of this process, and the part that people tend to have most difficulty with, primarily because most people who aren't thriving, also have low self esteem. Rewarding yourself, giving yourself praise, or patting yourself on the back, is about saying 'well done mate, you spotted that unhelpful thought and avoided it'. That unhelpful thought/feeling/belief could have negatively affected you day, or even your week! You've done really well to spot that sneaky little thought and stop it in its tracks. You've just taken a major step in the right direction, so pat yourself on your back, tell yourself 'well done', praise yourself, be really pleased with yourself. You want to process this positive. See the 'Processing your positives' Action! on page 76. Imagine every unhelpful thought, feeling or belief as a *pothole on your road to thriving*. What would you do if, while walking down the street one day, your friend grabs your arm and steers you clear of a huge pothole? You would be really grateful. You'd say 'thank you so much'. So, thank yourself, praise yourself (you are changing your life after all!) and mean it.

(You should still be regularly practising the 'processing your positives' Action! from page 76 on a daily basis. If you aren't, and this Reward part of the DREAM Technique feels strange or difficult for you, then you probably still have low self esteem. If so, go back and re-read the processing your positives Action! then put it into regular daily practise.

3. **Escape**: interrupting a pattern of behaviour helps a person to unassociate a thought or impulse from another experience. For example, if you always want a cigarette when you have a coffee, don't have a coffee. Drive a different way to work one day, and see how differently you feel about work

when you arrive. If you are sitting at your desk feeling depressed, move away from your desk whilst you change how you feel about it. It's easier to change how you feel when you (temporarily) change your situation. If watching telly at home, move to a different chair. If busy at your desk at work, and unable to move away temporarily, then cross your arms whilst you 'avoid the pothole' and re-phrase the unhelpful thought, belief or feeling. If you can't cross your arms, cross your fingers and close one eye - just do SOMETHING to ESCAPE the familiar pattern, even if it's just for a few seconds.

The 'escape' allows you to feel powerful and in control. You are making the choice to take action, and say 'I don't have to put up with this!' By getting away from the unhelpful, painful or limiting thoughts or feelings, you feel empowered, you're not a victim or slave to these experiences anymore because there is now something you CAN do about them. Every time you escape, you are building a more internal locus, you are creating a sense of resilience, making yourself feel more powerful, and when you feel more powerful you put in more effort.

4. **Amend:** this is where you take a few moments to simply re-phrase and amend the unhelpful or limiting suggestion/thought into a more helpful one. For example, 'I'm never going to get a decent job' could be changed to 'I'm feeling much more confident and I am improving my life on a daily basis, I CAN get a new job', or 'It's just typical that I have got this bloody illness' could be changed to 'I'm feeling better and better every day, I'm in charge of my life and I'm getting fitter and healthier by the minute!' If the negative thought was an image or a fantasy, again change the image/fantasy into one that you do want. If you imagine having a horrible time at the dentist later in the day, now imagine having a very relaxing and calm time at the dentist. See the 'Use your imagination' Action! on page 63.

Perhaps the very best all-round Amend you can do is just to say to yourself: 'I am learning to thrive, I can tolerate this, I am getting stronger and better every day'.

5. **Magnify:** this is where you magnify the newly created positive suggestion/fantasy, and actually imagine the outcome happening. To magnify it, make the colours brighter, make the sounds louder, make the feelings stronger, make the sensations more specific etc. The stronger the emotions and feelings attached to the new thought/image, the more powerful it is. Really take a few moments to visualise/imagine/rehearse this new suggestion/idea/belief as strongly as possible. Imagine looking at the experience through a magnifying glass, on a huge cinema screen, or listening to the experience through amplifiers at a rock concert! To use the example above (in Amend), now visualise yourself in absolute peace and tranquillity in the dentist's chair - feeling completely relaxed. Imagine yourself feeling more contented and happy than you have ever felt before in your life. The room is dazzling white, and the dentist (and his assistant) both have dazzling white teeth!

If you want to **Magnify** my suggested best all-round **Amend** from above, remind yourself what you have learned about yourself over the last few weeks, remember the changes you have made in your life already: how much better you are feeling, how much more positive and powerful you feel. Visualise getting stronger and stronger, more and more capable, happier and happier…

Some examples of The DREAM Technique in action:

### Tackling specific behaviours - A smoker who has recently given up

The ex-smoker may find himself sitting at home after a hard day's work and settling down with a nice cup of tea. He used to smoke whilst drinking tea, so the thought of a cigarette comes into his mind, and he starts to crave one. Immediately, on noticing the craving (an unhelpful thought, 'you need a cigarette, you are addicted to them'), the man tells himself, 'Well done Dave, you nearly fell for that one'. He gets up, moves to another chair, and settles down again (if he is REALLY determined, he may even tip his cup of tea down the sink). Once settled, he closes his eyes and visualises himself as a happy, confident and proud non-smoker. He really focuses in on this feeling, visualising and magnifying it. Perhaps he imagines that he is feeling fitter, healthier, slimmer, richer, more confident etc. He can feel himself become 'taller'. He feels his chest puffing out as if he were a sergeant major on parade. He imagines his breathing being easier and lighter. He imagines people at work offering him a cigarette, and replying, 'No thanks, I'm a non-smoker', and feeling fantastic. He may imagine his next visit to his GP and his GP patting him on the back.

### Reducing anxiety and stress - Learning to fly

Six or seven years ago now, I was being taught how to fly something called a paramotor. A paramotor is basically a big petrol-engined fan that sits on your back in a harness. As well as this motor on your back you also need a paraglider, which is like a big kite, to act as your 'wing'. So, you can imagine it: a big bloke with a huge petrol-fan on his back and a giant kite above his head. Why would that possibly cause anyone anxiety? Anyway, I would create intense anxiety at the idea of me actually leaving the ground and flying up into the air, so much so, that I was rapidly losing my confidence to complete the training course. Don't tell anyone, but on more than one occasion I created so much anxiety that I had to self-medicate with a can of beer before I even arrived at the aerodrome!

One day I decided to make a stand, and when I first started to think anxious thoughts I told them 'NO', in no uncertain terms. I imagined it was the 'school bully' who was telling me things like: 'you'll never be a pilot, don't be daft', and 'you'll die if you go up in the air', to which I replied 'I can be whatever I want to be' and 'this form of flying is very safe', and 'I've got a great instructor'. I then thanked myself for helping myself (rather than berating myself for being an idiot). I then really imagined launching, leaving the ground and flying, feeling really good, really safe, really comfortable and really relaxed. This process took just two weeks to completely kill off ANY and all anxiety I had about flying. Six months later I was entering flying competitions, a year later I was in the British Team in the World Championships, two years later I was one of the British Team leaders when we won silver medals in Beijing for doing things like flying over the Great Wall of China!

Honestly, in twenty five years of being a therapist I have not come across any techniques anywhere near as powerful as my DREAM technique, for stopping and changing unhelpful thoughts, feelings and beliefs.

Once you start to effectively use the technique, why not add a note about each occasion to your positives list? For example: 'used DREAM to feel better about school', or 'used DREAM to overcome urge to smoke', or 'used DREAM to stop my panic attack'. By adding these successful actions to your positives list, you are not only creating more positives to process (enhancing your self esteem and creating a more internal sense of power and control) but also recording the fact that you are becoming more successful at overcoming unhelpful thoughts.

# Anxiety and Stress - Recap

- ✓ 'Anxiety' is used to describe a state of apprehension, fear, worry and doubt. It encompasses the thoughts, worries and feelings either behind, or resulting from, a physical stress response or symptom. We create anxiety and stress in, or about, situations where we have an external locus - in particular a poor belief in their coping skills.

- ✓ Anxiety is best broken down into two component parts:

  1. Real-Time Anxiety - the anxiety experienced in real-time, when you are physically in an anxiety-triggering situation.

  2. Anticipatory Anxiety - the anxiety experienced when 'anticipating' (thinking, worrying or brooding about) a stressful, dangerous, frightening or challenging experience.

- ✓ Anticipatory anxiety creates more anxiety during the actual anxiety-provoking event, due to the expectation and tension built up.

- ✓ 'Stress' is used to describe the physiological response that occurs within your body in response to a perceived difficulty, threat or danger. This response could occur due to anxiety, or other pressures and situations in life.

- ✓ A stress response is initiated when an event or circumstance is interpreted as being in some way challenging, threatening or aversive.

- ✓ Not all stress is bad, but if a stress response is maintained, there can be an impact on the immune system.

- ✓ It is possible to control your anxiety and stress levels, and keep them to a minimum, by managing your thinking.

- ✓ Stress isn't something that happens to you. Stress is what you create when you don't manage your thinking very well in response to pressures and situations in life. We tend to create stress when we are in situations where we either feel out of control, or where we don't believe we can influence the outcome: where we have an external sense of power and control.

- ✓ The DREAM Technique can be used to return yourself to a relaxed and calm state if you have created substantial anxiety and stress.

## What should I be working on from now on?

1. Keep working on the **ACTION**s described in chapters 3 to 5. In particular, make sure that you process your positives **every day**.

2. Keep challenging and changing your unhelpful thinking (chapter 6) and mind your language (chapter 7).

3. Set a focus every day, e.g. '*Today I am going to put effort in to overcoming my symptoms. I have the skills and resources to do this. I am going to challenge any limiting beliefs, manage my unhelpful thinking styles and process my positives. Today I am another step closer to thriving!*'

**Notes** - The blank area below is for you to make any notes.

# Chapter 9

# Thriving…

Now it is time to really start thriving!

You have had a go at all of the exercises, and understand what changes each one of them achieves, so now we need to be very specific, in order to ensure that you really understand exactly how to thrive.

As you have read, it takes, on average, about two solid weeks of determined effort to change a habit, especially a thinking habit. Your two weeks start now, because it's only now that you have all the knowledge and insights you need. 'Determined effort', means different things to different people, but essentially what you are after is an attitude: the attitude of 'I don't care what it takes, I am going to thrive!' The moment you have this attitude, everything gets easier.

In a nutshell, this is what you need to do…

For the next few weeks (usually around 6) you want to put in lots of effort EVERY SINGLE DAY. This isn't something you can spend a few minutes here and there, once or twice a week on.

There are a number of areas that you need to target in order to thrive:

### 1. Build solid foundations

This is the most important part of the programme. Without strong foundations, you cannot thrive. So you want to develop a more internal sense of power and control, whilst at the same time increasing your self-esteem.

How do you do this?

a) Complete the **ACTION**s in chapter 3
b) Complete the **ACTION** chapter 4
c) Everyday you want to challenge any external thinking and process the positives to build your self-esteem

### 2. You need to reduce your desire for control

It is your desire for control that drives your unhelpful thinking styles: your obsessing, catastrophising, black and white thinking, hyper-vigilance and perfectionist thinking. You want to aim for a score of 2 or less on the desire for control scale.

How do you do this?

a) Build your internal sense of power and control, so that you don't feel the need to over-control. In particular focus on developing the belief that you do have the skills and resources to deal with challenges.
b) Challenge yourself whenever you are thinking in an 'over controlling way'. Learn to recognise the difference between 'feeling competent and skilful' (internal), and 'needing to control' (external). Think about the Stockdale Paradox, and actively develop a sense of 'I can deal with whatever situation arises, I have the skills to get though this easily'.
c) As you are challenging situations, learn to tolerate them. Keep a mantra going through your head: 'I can tolerate this, this is okay' and 'I've got the skills to deal with this, I can tolerate it'.

**3. You need to reduce your social anxiety and start responding to social pressures in an empowering way**

a) Complete the **ACTION** in chapter 5

**4. You need to calm down/manage your unhelpful thinking styles**

If you look back to the unhelpful thinking styles chapter, you'll remember that they only exist in relation to your sense of power and control, and your desire for control. This means that you will only obsess, catastrophise, be negative, be paranoid, think in very black and white terms etc. when you are in a situation where you feel external, and/or one where you have a strong desire for control.

You want to aim to score 2 or less on all the unhelpful thinking styles quizzes.

How do you do this?

a) Keep working on your foundations
b) Review and practise all of the **ACTION**s in the unhelpful thinking styles chapter (chapter 8).
c) Use the DREAM Technique when you have created anxiety and stress

### The importance of persistent and continuous effort (PACE)

One REALLY IMPORTANT thing to realise is that, as you work through the book, you should not expect yourself to suddenly make huge improvements. You have probably been (inadvertently) creating your symptoms for a long time, so it is going to take sustained effort to change your beliefs, thoughts, emotional responses and behaviours. You need to gain in-depth self-understanding and gently build new beliefs and skills that enable you to thrive instead. You want to spend the next six weeks or so re-training yourself: changing your limiting beliefs and unhelpful thinking styles and developing new skills. You need to put in some work every single day.

You are building up momentum and you want that momentum to become so big and powerful that it becomes habitual. At that point, you can more or less stop putting any effort in. Imagine you are creating a big snowball and you are starting to push that snowball down a hill… it is only when it becomes big enough, and the momentum sufficient, that you can stop pushing it, and it will continue on down the hill under its own steam. Stop pushing too early and the snowball will grind to a halt. Then you have to start pushing all over again.

Another metaphor could be push-starting a car. When you have owned crappy cars, like some of the ones I've owned in the past, you'll get this straight away. When push starting a car, you need to first get the car moving, then keep it moving whilst the driver engages a gear and waits for the engine to splutter into life. Only once the engine has taken over completely, can you stop pushing. Stop too early and you have to start the whole bloody thing over again. In fact, push starting a car is a great metaphor for learning how to thrive for another reason. It needs a really REALLY good push to get moving in the first place. You aren't going to get a car moving without putting all your bodyweight and effort behind it. Once it's moving, you can stop pushing quite so hard, but you MUST keep up the momentum until the engine takes over. This is exactly what you need to do in order to overcome your symptoms and learn how to thrive.

If you throw yourself into this programme and put in loads of (the right) effort for a few days, you will start to feel better. If you stop for a day, or have a big blip (see below) your snowball or car will come to a grinding halt, and you will need to start all over again. This is fine - if you can put up with stop/start, stop/start and you can manage all the emotions that you will create in the process. But you will find the whole process smoother and easier if you apply persistent and continuous effort!

Have a look at the diagram below:

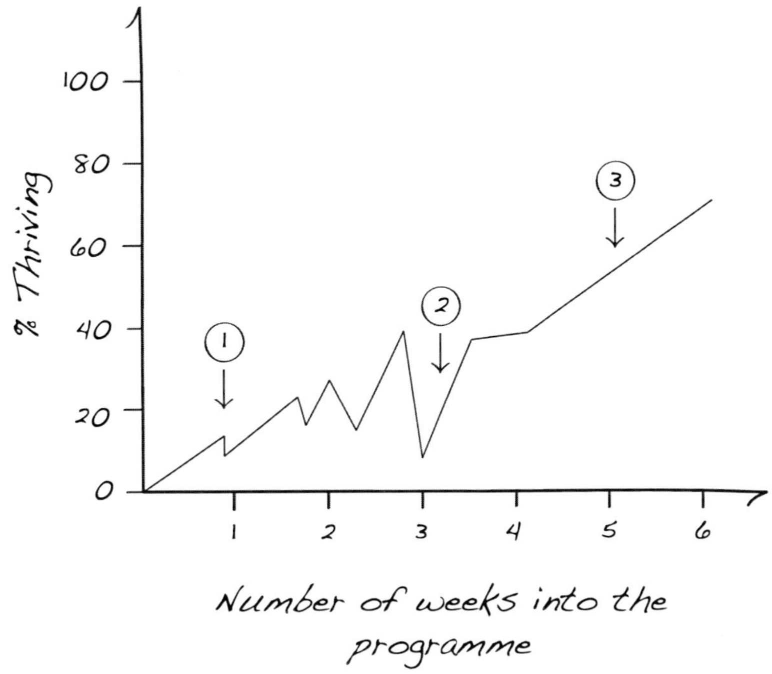


This diagram shows the effects of someone starting then stopping, starting then stopping putting in effort. Position (1) is at the end of the first week. The person has done really well and is starting to feel better, so eases off the effort. They then experience a decline. This goes on for the next couple of weeks. Position (2) - at the end of the third week - shows a big blip. The person went really downhill because they stopped putting in the effort, but manages to pull it back again over a few days. Position (3) is where the person is really putting in persistent and continuous effort. They have finally got control of the whole thing, know how to minimise blips, and are well on the way to thriving - albeit a few weeks later than they could have been.

This diagram shows someone always recovering. Even though this person kept creating setbacks initially, they maintained their belief in the process and kept getting back on track. Though you don't really want any big setbacks at all, this diagram shows why The Thrive Programme is successful where other treatments fail. The person in this diagram kept on 'getting back into the saddle' and not giving up, because they understood WHY the blip had happened, and WHERE they had gone wrong. Because this programme is understandable and predictable, people can recover even though they sometimes go through some shitty times. But applying persistent and continuous effort as you work through the programme will make your journey far smoother! You will minimise your blips and make more consistent progress.

## Blips

By putting in persistent and continuous effort you will minimise blips. It is, however, important to remember that everybody has blips from time to time. Even people who are completely thriving have bad days. It's managing your reaction to them that is important. You want to minimise the impact of a small wobble and not make it into something bigger than it really is.

So, remember that you are going to create good days and not-so-good days in the forthcoming weeks. You are going to feel that you are getting somewhere but then create a bad day. Tolerate it. Put up with it. It's par for the course. Early on, in putting this programme into action, you aren't going to be able to catch and change every single unhelpful thought or belief that you have. Some – probably many in fact – are going to slip through your net. This means, that in the near future at least, you are still going to have some symptoms.

If you have a difficult day, calm yourself down, reassure yourself, and take the actions you deem necessary in order to get over it and move on. Don't focus on that 'bad day', don't wallow, don't think 'it's not working'. Remember, there is no 'it' – YOU are doing this to yourself – and focus upon the fact that you are gradually making progress. Every time you create a blip, remind yourself that you are learning something else about your thinking and beliefs that will ultimately help you to overcome your fear.

The thinking style most often associated with a big blip is the perfectionist style. Perfectionists are hypervigilant about their perceived imperfections, mistakes and flaws. Add in some of the other thinking styles and a 'minor blip' can easily become 'I've ruined everything, I'm so stupid, I'm never going to get better'. 'Beating yourself up' is enough in itself to maintain your symptoms, because it drags in all your limiting beliefs and thinking styles. So stop it. Stop beating yourself up, it serves no purpose at all, other than ensuring you keep your problems. Give yourself a break, be nice to yourself and tolerate the blips. Remember the blip drawing in the perfectionist thinking style section? If not go back and look at it again now. When you create a minor blip, you can go one of two ways… You can either get back on track quickly, or you can blow the whole thing out of proportion, beating yourself up and wallowing in misery for several days.

## Take Action!

Right. You now know everything you need to know in order to thrive. If there is anything you are unsure about, please go back and re-read that chapter. The more you understand how well equipped you now are to beat this thing, the more powerful you will feel, and the more effort you will put in. Follow the instructions I have given you, and in just a few weeks you will have created a new life for yourself.

Get in touch via our Facebook page if you have any questions.

# Well Done!

Well done, you made it! Give yourself a few minutes to really thank and praise yourself for seeing this whole project through. Make sure that you add 'finished the Thrive book' to your on-going list of positives to process.

Don't stop now - keep going - you want to practise your new way of thinking as much as you can, until it becomes habitual. Don't put the book down just because you've completed it - research suggests you'll only take about 30% of it in the first time you go through it. Please go back and start again. If you learn just one more thing that helps you to thrive, it's worth reading it again.

In a couple of weeks' time, go back to the online TQ Thrive Assessment and work through the quiz again so you can see just how much better your TQ now is.

Remember not to view this project as 'resolving my symptom' or 'overcoming my problem', because if you do, you are likely to stop making changes as soon as you feel better. Don't stop at 'feeling better'; why not set your sights higher? Set your sights on thriving? Set your sights on 'having a fantastic life'. It's all a simple question of building your foundations and creating a thriving mindset.

I truly believe that every single thought you have will have impact upon your life. I have a little saying that I use whenever in any doubt: 'The thought that is in my mind right now, is it helpful?' (by helpful I mean: helping to create a wonderful, happy, healthy life). If the answer is 'no', then I either change the thought until it becomes helpful, or I just chuck it straight into the bin.

Creating and maintaining these core psychological strengths won't turn you into a superman or superwoman, but they will make you more powerful, more resilient, and much happier.

You now know everything you need to know about changing your limiting beliefs and really learning to thrive. Thousands of people have successfully used the insights and techniques described in this workbook to make significant changes in their lives, and I hope that includes you too!

I honestly and truly believe the statement above. If the problem/symptom/anxiety/fear/worry etc. that prompted you to buy this book in the first place is not yet resolved, please, please, PLEASE go back through the book again and re-do all the exercises and actions. If there are any parts that you just don't get, or some exercise that you cannot make sense of, or you have an unhelpful thinking style that isn't listed, visit the support section of the Thrive website: www.thriveprogramme.org where you will find more help and guidance. If necessary, you can even arrange a meeting (either face-to-face, online or over the telephone) with one of my consultants, who can work through the book with you.

It may help you to view some of the life-stories, testimonials and feedback from people who have already used this book to make changes in their lives - sometimes it helps to read how other people struggled but then overcame their own issues. Enough people have used this book now that I am sure there is a testimonial or story on the website from someone with a similar background or issue/problem as you. Again, these can be viewed on the Thrive website.

I would love to hear how this workbook has helped you, so please get in touch - either via our website or via Facebook.

As I have self-published this book, and don't have access to millions of pounds worth of advertising and marketing, could you help me to get this book out to more people? Maybe you could leave some feedback on Amazon, or recommend the book to your friends?

I won't say 'good luck' because it is not about luck; it is about you taking control, and making things happen. So get cracking.

All the best . . .

Rob Kelly
May 2010

# References

**Abouserie, R (1994).** 'Sources and levels of stress in relation to locus of control and self-esteem in University students.' *Educational Psychology,* 14 (3) 323-330

**Abraham, C, Sheeran, P (2004).** 'Deciding to exercise: the role of anticipated regret.' *British Journal of Health Psychology,* 9, 269-278

**Abrahamsson, K.H, Berggren, U, Hallberg, L, and Carlsson, S.G (2002).** 'Dental phobic patient's view of dental anxiety and experiences in dental care: a qualitative study.' *Scandinavian Journal of Caring Science,* 16 188-196

**Adolfsson, B, Andersson, I, Elofsson, S, Rössner, S, and Undénc, A.L (2005).** 'Locus of control and weight reduction.' *Patient Education and Counseling,* 56 55-61

**Altheide, D.L (2002).** *Creating Fear: News and the Construction of Crisis.* AldineTransaction

**American Psychiatric Association (1994).** DSM-IV: The Diagnostic and Statistical Manual of Mental Disorders. (4th ed.). American Psychiatric Press Inc.

**Averill, P.M, Diefenbach, G.J, Stanley, M.A, Breckenridge, J.K, and Lusby B.L (2002).** 'Assessment of shame and guilt in a psychiatric sample: a comparison of two measures.' *Personality and Individual Differences,* 32 1365-1376

**Balch, P and Ross, W. (1975)** 'Predicting success in weight reduction as a function of locus of control: A unidimensional and multidimensional approach.' *Journal of Consulting and Clinical Psychology,* 43 (1) 119

**Baum, A, Fleming, R, and Reddy, D.M (1986).** 'Unemployment Stress: Loss of Control and Learned Helplessness.' *Social Science and Medicine,* 22 (5) 509-516

**Blair, A and Leyshon, G (1993).** 'Imagery effects on the performance of skilled and novice soccer players.' *Journal of Sports Sciences,* 11(2) 95-101

**Bower, J.E, Low, C.A, Moskowitz, J.T, Sepah, S, and Epel, E** (2008). 'Benefit Finding and Physical Health: Positive Psychological Changes and Enhanced Allostasis.' *Social and Personality Psychology Compass,* 223-244

**Bradley, B.P, Mogg, K, White, J, Groom, C, and de Bono, J (1999).** 'Attentional bias for emotional faces in generalized anxiety disorder.' *British Journal of Clinical Psychology,* 38, 267-278

**Brooks, C.H (1922).** *The practice of autosuggestion, by the method of Émile Coué,* Gresham Press

**Burger, J.M (1984).** 'Desire for control, locus of control, and proneness to depression.' *Journal of Personality,* 52 (1) 71-89

**Byrne, S.M, Allen, K.L, Dove, E.R, Watt, F.J, and Nathan, P.R (2008).** 'The reliability and validity of the Dichotomous Thinking in the Eating Disorders Scale.' *Eating Behaviors,* 9 154-162

**Byrne, S.M, Cooper, Z, and Fairburn, C.G (2004).** 'Psychological predictors of weight regain in obesity.' *Behaviour Research and Therapy,* 42, 1341-1356

**Carver, C.S and Antoni, M.H (2004)**. 'Finding Benefit in Breast Cancer During the Year After Diagnosis Predicts Better Adjustment 5 to 8 Years After Diagnosis.' *Health Psychology,* 23 (6) 595-598

**Clark, D.M (1999).** 'Anxiety disorders: why they persist and how to treat them.' *Behaviour Research and Therapy,* 37 S5-S27

**Cloitre, M, Heimberg, R.G, Liebowitz, M.R, and Gitow, A (1992).** 'Perceptions of control in panic disorder and social phobia.' *Cognitive Therapy and Research,* 16 (5) 569-577

**Cohen, S, Doyle, W.J, Turner, R.B, Alper, C.M, and Skoner, D.P (2003)**. 'Emotional Style and Susceptibility to the Common Cold.' *Psychosomatic Medicine,* 65 652-657

**Cohen, S, Tyrrell, D, and Smith, A (1993).** 'Negative life events, perceived stress, negative affect, and susceptibility to the common cold.' *Journal of Personality and Social Psychology,* 64 (1) 131-140

**Collins, J (2001).** Good To Great: Why Some Companies Make the Leap… and Others Don't. Random House Business

**Cooper, P.J and Eke, M (1999).** 'Childhood shyness and maternal social phobia: a community study.' *British Journal Of Psychiatry,* 174 439-443

**Crisson, J.E and Keefe, F.J (1988).** 'The relationship of locus of control to pain coping strategies and psychological distress in chronic pain patients.' *Pain,* 35 147-154

**Crombez, G, Van Damme, S, and Eccleston, C (2005).** 'Hypervigilance to pain: An experimental and clinical analysis.' *Pain,* 116 4-7

**Danner, D.D, Snowdon, D.A, and Friesen, W.V (2001).** 'Positive Emotions in Early Life and Longevity: Findings from the Nun Study.' *Journal of Personality and Social Psychology,* 80 (5) 804-813

**Davidson, R.J, Kabat-Zinn, J, Schumacher, J, Rosenkranz, M, Muller, D, Santorelli, S.F, Urbanowski, F, Harrington, A, Bonus, K, and Sheridan, J.F (2003).** 'Alterations in Brain and Immune Function Produced by Mindfulness Meditation.' *Psychosomatic Medicine,* 65 564-570

**Dembroski, T.M, MacDougall, J.M, and Musante, L (1984).** 'Desirability of Control Versus Locus of Control: Relationship to Paralinguistics in the Type A Interview.' *Health Psychology,* 3 (1) 15-26

**Driskell, J.E, Copper, C, and Moran, A (1994).** 'Does mental practice enhance performance?' *Journal of Applied Psychology,* 79 (4) 481-492

**Dunkley, D.M, Zuroff, D.C, and Blankstein, K.R (2003).** 'Self-Critical Perfectionism and Daily Affect: Dispositional and Situational Influences on Stress and Coping.' *Journal of Personality and Social Psychology,* 84 (1) 234-252

**Dweck, C.S (1999).** 'Self-theories: Their role in motivation, personality, and development.' *Philadelphia: Psychology Press.*

**Dweck, C.S and Reppucci, N.D (1973).** 'Learned helplessness and reinforcement responsibility in children.' *Journal of Personality and Social Psychology,* 25 (1) 109-116

**Edwards, C.R, Thompson, A.R, and Blair, A (2007).** 'An 'overwhelming Illness': Women's experiences of learning to live with chronic fatigue syndrome/myalgic encephalomyelitis.' *Journal of Health Psychology,* 12 203-214

**Egan, S.J, Piek, J.P, Dyck, J, and Rees, C.S (2007).** 'The role of dichotomous thinking and rigidity in perfectionism.' *Behaviour Research and Therapy,* 45 1813-1822

**Eiser, J.R, Van der Pligt, J, Raw, M, and Sutton S.R (1985).** 'Trying to Stop Smoking: Effects of Perceived Addiction, Attributions for Failure, and Expectancy of success.' *Journal of Behavioral Medicine,* 8 (4) 321-341

**Emmons, R.A and McCullough, M.E (2003).** 'Counting Blessings Versus Burdens: An Experimental Investigation of Gratitude and Subjective Well-Being in Daily Life.' *Journal of Personality and Social Psychology,* 84 (2) 377-389

**Eysenck (1992).** *Anxiety: the cognitive perspective.* London: Lawrence Erlbaum Associates

**Fenigstein, A (1984).** 'Self-consciousness and the overperception of self as a target.' *Journal of Personality and Social Psychology,* 47 (4) 860-870

**Fenigstein, A and Vanable, P.A (1992).** 'Paranoia and self-consciousness.' *Journal of Personality and Social Psychology,* 62 (1) 129-138

**Ferguson, T.J, Stegge, H, Miller, E.R, and Olsen, M (1999).** 'Guilt, shame, and symptoms in children.' *Developmental Psychology,* 35 (2) 347-357

**Fisak, B and Grills-Taquechel, A.E (2007).** 'Parental Modeling, Reinforcement, and Information Transfer: Risk Factors in the Development of Child Anxiety?' *Clinical Child and Family Psychology,* 10 (3) 213-231

**Fredrickson, B.L (1998).** 'What good are positive emotions?' *Review of General Psychology,* 2 (3) 300-319

**Fredrickson, B.L, Mancuso, R.A, Branigan, C, and Tugade, M.M (2000).** 'The Undoing Effect of Positive Emotions.' *Motivation and Emotion,* 24 (4) 23-258

**Freeman, D and Garety, P (2006).** 'Helping patients with paranoid and suspicious thoughts: a cognitive-behavioural approach.' *Advances in Psychiatric Treatment* Vol. 12, 404-415

**Freeman, D, Garety, P.A, Bebbington, P.E, Smith, B, Rollinson, R, Fowler, D, Kuipers, E, Ray, K, and Dunn, G (2005)** 'Psychological investigation of the structure of paranoia in a non-clinical population.' *British Journal of Psychiatry,* 186, 427-435

**Gale, C.R, Batty, G.D, and Deary, I.J (2008).** 'Locus of Control at Age 10 Years and Health Outcomes and Behaviors at Age 30 Years: The 1970 British Cohort Study.' *Psychosomatic Medicine,* 70 397-403

**Gebhardt, W.A and Brosschot, J.F (2002).** 'Desirability of Control: Psychometric Properties and Relationships with Locus of Control, Personality, Coping, and Mental and Somatic Complaints in Three Dutch Samples.' *European Journal of Personality,* 16 423-438

**Gil, K.M, Abrams, M.R, Phillips, G, and Keefe, F.J (1989).** 'Sickle cell disease pain: Relation of coping strategies to adjustment.' *Journal of Consulting and Clinical Psychology,* 57 (6) 725-731

**Gilbert, P (2000).** 'The Relationship of Shame, Social anxiety and Depression: The Role and Evaluation of Social Rank.' *Clinical Psychology and Psychotherapy,* 7 174-189

**Gill, A.J, and Oberlander, J (2002).** Taking care of the linguistic features of Extraversion. In *Proceedings of the 24th Annual Conference of the Cognitive Science Society,* Fairfax 363-368

**Goodhart, D.E (1985).** 'Some psychological effects associated with positive and negative thinking about stressful event outcomes: Was Pollyanna right?' *Journal of Personality and Social Psychology,* 48 (1) 216-232

**Hagley and Kelly (2009).** 'A survey of client responses following completion of a course of 'Pure Hynoanalysis', (PHA).' Downloadable from www.iaph.org

**Haynes, R.B, Sackett, D.L, Taylor, D.W, Gibson, E.S, and Johnson, A.L (1978).** 'Increased absenteeism from work after detection and labeling of hypertensive patients' *The New England Journal of Medicine* 299 741-744

**Hebert, T.P (1996).** 'Portraits of resilience: the urban life experience of gifted Latino young men.' *Roeper Review,* 19 (2) 82-90

**Kato, K, Sullivan, P, Evengard, B, and Pedersen, N.L (2006).** 'Premorbid predictors of chronic fatigue.' *Archives of General Psychiatry,* 63 1267-1272

**Lee, D.A, Scragg, P, and Turner, S (2001).** 'The role of shame and guilt in traumatic events: A clinical model of shame-based and guilt-based PTSD.' *British Journal of Medical Psychology,* 74 451-466

**Lengacher, C.A, Bennett, M.P, Gonzalez, L, Gilvary, D, Cox, C.E, Cantor, A, Jacobse, P.B, Yang, C, and Djeu, J (2008).** 'Immune responses to guided imagery during breast cancer treatment.' *Biological Research Nursing,* 9 (3) 205-214

**Leserman, J, Jackson, E.D, Petitto, J.M, Golden, R.N, Silva, S.G, Perkins, D.O, Cai, J, Folds, J.D, and Evans, D.L (1999).** 'Progression to AIDS: The effects of stress, depressive symptoms, and social support.' *Psychosomatic Medicine,* 61 397-406

**Lever, J.P, Pinol, N.L, and Uralde, J.H (2005).** 'Poverty, psychological resources and subjective well-being.' *Social Indicators Research,* 73 375-408

**Lewis, S.C, Dennis, M.S, O'Rourke, S.J, and Sharpe, M (2001).** 'Negative attitudes among short-term stroke survivors predict worse long-term survival.' *Stroke,* 32 1640-1645

**Lieb, R, Wittchen, H.S, Hofler, M, Fuetsch, M, Stein, M.B, and Merikangas, K.R (2000).** 'Parental psychopathology, parenting styles, and the risk of social phobia in offspring.' *Arch Gen Psychiatry,* 57 859-866

**Liu K.P, Chan C.C, Lee T.M, and Hui-Chan, C.W (2004).** 'Mental imagery for promoting relearning for people after stroke: a randomized controlled trial.' *Archives of Physical Medicine and Rehabilitation,* 85 (9) 1403-1408

**Lutgendorf, S.K, Antoni, M.H, Ironson, G, Fletcher, M.A, Penedo, F, Baum, A, Schnelderman, N, and Klimas, N (1995).** 'Physical Symptoms of Chronic Fatigue Syndrome Are Exacerbated By the Stress of Hurricane Andrew.' *Psychosomatic* Medicine, 57 310-323

**Lyubomirsky, S and Tkach, C (2004).** 'The consequences of dysphoric rumination.' *Depressive Rumination: Nature, Theory and Treatment,* 2 21-41

**Maqsud, M and Rouhani, S (1991).** 'Relationships Between Socioeconomic Status, Locus of Control, Self-Concept, and Academic Achievement of Batswana Adolescents.' *Journal of Youth and Adolescence,* 20 (1) 107-114

**Martin, K.A and Hall, C.R (1995).** 'Using mental imagery to enhance intrinsic motivation.' *Journal of Sport & Exercise Psychology,* 17 (1) 54-69

**Martin, R.C, and Dahlen, E.R (2005).** 'Cognitive emotion regulation in the prediction of depression, anxiety, stress, and anger.' *Personality and Individual Differences,* 39 1249-1260

**McMillan, J.H and Reed, D.F (1994).** 'At-risk students and resiliency: Factors contributing to academic success.' *The Clearing House,* 137-140

**McClun and Merrell (1998).** 'Relationship Of Perceived Parenting Styles, Locus Of Control Orientation, And Self-Concept Among Junior High Age Students'

**Mcmurtry, C.M, Mcgrath, P.J, and Chambers, C.T (2006).** 'Reassurance can hurt: Parental behavior and painful medical procedures.' *Journal of Pediatrics,* 148 560-1

**Meaney, Michael, J (2001).** 'Nature, nurture and the disunity of knowledge.' *Annals of The New York Academy of Sciences,* 935 50-61

**Mirowsky, J and Ross, C.E (1983).** 'Paranoia and the structure of powerlessness.' *American Sociological Review,* 48 (2) 228-339

**Mirowsky, J and Ross, C.E (1990).** 'Control or Defense? Depression and the Sense of Control over Good and Bad Outcomes.' *Journal of Health and Social Behavior,* 31 (1) 71-86

**Mold, J.W Hamm, R.M, and Jafri, B (2000).** 'The effect of labelling on perceived ability to recover from acute illnesses and injuries.' *The Journal Of Family Practice,* 49 (5)

**Moss-Morris, R, Spence, M.J, and Hou, R (2010).** 'The pathway from glandular fever to chronic fatigue syndrome: can the cognitive behavioural model provide the map?' *Psychological Medicine,* 21 1-9

**Mueller, S.L and Thomas (2000).** 'Culture and Entrepreneurial Potential: A Nine Country Study of Locus of Control and Innovativeness'. *Journal of Business Venturing,* 16 51-75

**Neale, A.V (1991).** 'Behavioural Contracting as a Tool to Help Patients Achieve Better Health.' *Family Practice,* 8 (4) 336-342

**Nolen-Hoeksema, S (1991).** 'Responses to depression and their effects on the duration of depressive episodes.' *Journal of Abnormal Psychology,* 100 (4) 569-582

**O'Connor, L.E, Berry, J.W, Weiss J, and Gilbert, P (2002).** 'Guilt, fear, submission, and empathy in depression.' *Journal of Affective Disorders,* 71 19-27

**Parry, C and Chesler, M.A (2005).** 'Thematic Evidence of Psychosocial Thriving in Childhood Cancer Survivors.' *Qualitative Health Research,* 15 (8) 1055-1073

**Peden, A.R, Hall, L.A, Rayens, M.K, and Beebe, L (2000).** 'Negative Thinking Mediates the Effect of Self-Esteem on Depressive Symptoms in College Women.' *Nursing Research,* 49 (4) 201-207

**Pennebaker and King (1999).** Linguistic styles: Language use as an individual difference.' *Journal of Personality and Social Psychology,* 77 (6) 1296-312.

**Pennebaker, Mayne, and Francis (1997).** 'Linguistic predictors of adaptive bereavement.' *Journal of Personality and Social Psychology,* 73 (4) 863-871.

**Pennebaker, J.W, Mehl, M.R, and Niederhoffer, K.G (2003).** 'Psychological aspects of natural language use: our words, our selves.' *Annual Review of Psychology,* 54 547-77

**Peterson, C (1978).** 'Locus of Control and Belief in Self-Oriented Superstitions.' *The Journal of Social Psychology,* 105 305-306

**Price, J.H, Desmond, S.M, Krol, R.A, Snyder, F.F, and O'Connell, J.K (1987).** 'Family practice physicians' beliefs, attitudes, and practices regarding obesity.' *Am J Prev Med, 3* 339-45.

**Reed, G.M, Kemeny, M.E, Taylor, S.E, and Visscher, B.R (1999).** 'Negative HIV-specific expectancies and AIDS-related bereavement as predictors of symptom onset in asymptomatic HIV-positive gay men.' *Health Psychology,* 18 (4) 354-63

**Rodin, J, and Langer, E.J, (1977).** 'Long-Term Effects of a Control-Relevant Intervention With the Institutionalized Aged.' *Journal of Personality and Social Psychology,* 35 (12) 897-902

**Rosen, G.M (1987).** 'Self-Help Treatment Books and the Commercialization of Psychotherapy.' *American Psychologist,* 42 (1) 46-52

**Rotter (1966).** 'Generalized expectancies of internal versus external control of reinforcements.' *Psychological Monographs,* 80

**Sanderson, W.C, Rapee, R.M, and Barlow, D.H (1989).** 'The influence of perceived control on panic attacks induced via inhalation of 5.5% CO2-enriched air.' *Archives of General Psychiatry,* 46 (2) 157-162

**Scheier, M.F, and Carver, C.S (1993).** 'On the power of positive thinking: The benefits of being optimistic.' *Current Directions in Psychological Sciences,* 2 26-30

**Seaman, M, and Lewis, S (1995).** 'Powerlessness, health and mortality: a longitudinal study of older men and mature women.' *Social Science and Medicine,* 41 (4) 517-525

**Seligman, M.E.P (1972).** 'Learned Helplessness.' *Annual Review of Medicine,* 23 407-412

**Seligman, M.E.P (1975).** Helplessness: On Depression, Development, and Death. San Francisco: W.H. Freeman

**Seligman, M.E.P, and Maier, S.F (1967).** 'Failure to escape traumatic shock.' *Journal of Experimental Psychology,* 74 1-9

**Shekelle, R.B, Raynor, W.J, Ostfeld, A.M, Garron, D.C, Bieliauskas, L.A, Liu, S.C, Maliza, C, and Paul, O (1981).** 'Psychological Depression and 17-Year Risk of Death from Cancer.' *Psychosomatic Medicine,* 43 (2) 117-125

**Sieswerda, S, Arntz, A, Mertens, I, and Vertommen, S (2006).** 'Hypervigilance in patients with borderline personality disorder: Specificity, automaticity, and predictors.' *Behaviour Research and Therapy,* 45 1011-1024

**Slenker, S.E, Price, J.H, and O'Connell, J.K (1985).** 'Health Locus Of Control Of Joggers And Nonexercisers.' *Perceptual and Motor Skills,* 61 323-328

**Starcevic, V (2005).** 'Fear of Death in Hypochondriasis: Bodily Threat and Its Treatment Implications.' *Journal of Contemporary Psychotherapy,* 35 (3) 227-237

**Sturmer, T, Hasselbach, P, and Amelang, M (2006).** 'Personality, lifestyle, and risk of cardiovascular disease and cancer: follow-up of population based cohort.' *British Medical Journal BMJ,* 332 (7554) 1359-1362

**Sullivan, M.J.L, Thorn, B, Haythornthwaite, J.A, Keefe, F, Martin, M, Bradley, L.A, and Lefebvre, J.C, (2001).** 'Theoretical Perspectives on the Relation between Catastrophizing and Pain.' *The Clinical Journal of Pain,* 17 52-64

**Tangney, J.P, Wagner, P, and Gramzow, R (1992).** 'Proneness to shame, proneness to guilt, and psychopathology.' *Journal of Abnormal Psychology,* 101 (3) 469-478

**Taylor, C.M, Schepers, J.M, and Crous, F (2006).** 'Locus of Control in Relation to Flow.' *SA Journal of Industrial Psychology,* 32 (3) 63-71

**Tobacyk, J (1988).** 'A Revised Paranormal Belief Scale.' unpublished manuscript, Louisiana Tech University, Rushton, LA

**Tschuschke, V, Hertenstein, B, Arnold, R, Bunjes, D, Denzinger, R, and Kaechele, H (2001).** 'Associations between coping and survival time of adult leukemia patients receiving allogeneic bone marrow transplantation: Results of a prospective study.' *Journal of Psychosomatic Research,* 50, 277-285

**Twenge, J.M, Zhang, L, and Im, C (2004).** 'It's Beyond My Control: A Cross-Temporal Meta-Analysis of Increasing Externality in Locus of Control.' 1960-2002. *Personality and social psychology review,* Vol. 8, No. 3, 308-319

**Van de Putte, E.M, Engelbert, R.H.H, Kuis, W, Sinnema, G, Kimpen, J.L.L, and Uiterwaal, CSPM (2005).** 'Chronic fatigue syndrome and health control in adolescents and parents.' *Archives of Disease in Childhood,* 90 1020-1024

**Van Gerwen, L.J, Spinhoven, P, Diekstra, R.F.W, and Van Dyck, R (1997).** 'People Who Seek Help for Fear of Flying: Typology of Flying Phobics.' *Behavior Therapy, 28 237-251*

**Vervoort, T, Eccleston, C, Goubert, L, Buyssea, A, and Crombez, G (2010).** 'Children's catastrophic thinking about their pain predicts pain and disability 6 months later.' *European Journal of Pain,* 14 (1) 90-96

**Vervoort, T, Goubert, L, Eccleston, C, Bijttebier, P, and Crombez, G (2005).** 'Catastrophic Thinking About Pain is Independently Associated with Pain Severity, Disability, and Somatic Complaints in School Children and Children with Chronic Pain.' *Journal of Pediatric Psychology,* 31(7) 674-683

**Walker, L.S, Claar, R.L, and Garber, J. (2002).** 'Social Consequences of Children's Pain: When Do They Encourage Symptom Maintenance?' *Journal of Pediatric Psychology,* 27 (8) 689-698

**Walters, V, and Charles, N (1997).** '"I just cope from day to day": unpredictability and anxiety in the lives of women.' *Social Science and Medicine,* 45 (11) 1729-1739

**Wang, S.S, Brownell, K.D, and Wadden, T.A (2004).** 'The influence of the stigma of obesity on overweight individuals.' *International Journal of Obesity,* 28 1333-133

**Watson, M, Haviland, J.S, Greer, S, Davidson, J, and Bliss, J.M (1999).** 'Influence of psychological response on survival in breast cancer: a population-based cohort study.' *The Lancet,* 354 1331-1336

**Werner (1984).** 'Resilient children.' *Young Children,* 40 (1) 68-72

**Williams, B.R, Bezner, J, Chesbro, S.B, and Leavitt, R (2005).** 'The effect of a behavioural contract on adherence to a walking program in postmenopausal African American women.' *Topics in Geriatric Rehabilitation,* 21 (4) 332-342

**Wiseman, R (2003).** Superstition survey *http://www.richardwiseman.com/resources/superstition_report.pdf*

**Wiseman, R (2009).** 'Happiness is A Pencil.' *59 Seconds,* Macmillan

**Wolf, Sedway, Bulik, Kordy (2007).** 'Linguistic analyses of natural written language: Unobtrusive assessment of cognitive style in eating disorders.' *International Journal of Eating Disorders,* 40 (8) 711-717

**Wood, M.D, Britt, T.W, Thomas, J.L, Klocko, R.P, and Bliese, P.D (2011).** 'Buffering Effects of Benefit Finding in a War Environment.' *Military Psychology,* 23 (2) 202-219

**Yoshino, S, and Mukai, E, (2003).** 'Neuroendocrine-immune system in patients with rheumatoid arthritis.' *Modern Rheumatology,* 13 (3) 193-198

**Young M.E, Norman G.R, and Humphreys K.R (2008).** 'The Role of Medical Language in Changing Public Perceptions of Illness.' *PLoS ONE* 3(12).